IEE TELECOMMUNICATIONS SERIES 42

Series Editors: Professor C. J. Hughes
Professor D. Parsons
Professor G. White

Video coding
an introduction to standard codecs

Other volumes in this series:

Video coding

an introduction to standard codecs

Mohammed Ghanbari

The Institution of Electrical Engineers

Published by: The Institution of Electrical Engineers, London,
United Kingdom

© 1999: The Institution of Electrical Engineers

The Institution of Electrical Engineers,
Michael Faraday House,
Six Hills Way, Stevenage,
Herts. SG1 2AY, United Kingdom

British Library Cataloguing in Publication Data

A CIP catalogue record for this book
is available from the British Library

ISBN 0 85296 762 4

Printed in England by Short Run Press Ltd., Exeter

Contents

Preface

Television is an important part of our life today. In developing countries, where TV sets can outnumber telephones by more than 50:1, its impact can be even greater. Advances in the multimedia industry, the advent of digital TV and other services will only increase its influence in global terms.

There is a considerable and growing will to support these developments through global standards. As an example, the call for videoconferencing proposals in the 1980s, which led to the H.261 audiovisual codec, attracted 15 proposals; in February 1999, 650 research proposals on MPEG-7 were submitted to the MPEG committee meeting in Lancaster, UK.

This book aims to address some of these exciting developments by looking at the *fundamentals* behind them. The intention is to provide material which is useful to a wide range of readers, from researchers in video coding to managers in the multimedia industry.

In writing this book I have made use of invaluable documents prepared by the working parties of the ISO/IEC and ITU. I am also in debt to the work of my former and current research students and assistants. In particular I would like to acknowledge the work by: Pedro Assuancao, Soroush Ghanbari, Ebroul Izquierdo, Fernando Lopes, Antonio Pinheiro, Eva Rosdiana, Vassilis Seferidis, Tamer Shanableh, Eduardo da Silva, Kuan Hui Tan, Kwee Teck Tan, Qi Wang, David Wilson and John Woods, who have directly or indirectly contributed to the realisation of this book.

Finally, I would like to express my deepest gratitude to my mentor Professor Charles Hughes, who with his great vision and tireless effort taught me how to be a competitive researcher. He encouraged me to write this book, and very patiently read every chapter of it and made numerous valuable comments. Charles, thanks for everything.

Mohammed Ghanbari
June 1999

To
Sorour and Shirin

Chapter 1

History of video coding

Digital video compression techniques have played an important role in the world of telecommunication and multimedia systems where bandwidth is still a valuable commodity. Hence, video coding techniques are of prime importance for reducing the amount of information needed for a picture sequence without losing much of its quality, judged by the human viewers. Modern compression techniques involve very complex electronic circuits and the cost of these can only be kept to an acceptable level by high volume production of LSI chips. Standardisation of the video compression techniques is therefore essential.

An analogue videophone system had been tried out in the 1960s, but it required a wide bandwidth and the postcard-size black-and-white pictures produced did not add appreciably to the voice communication. In the 1970s, it was realised that visual speaker identification could substantially improve a multiparty discussion and videoconference services were considered. Interest increased with improvements in picture quality and digital coding. With the available technology in the 1980s, COST211 video codec, based on Differential Pulse Code Modulation (DPCM) was standardised by CCITT, under the H.120 standard. The codec's target bit rate was at 2 Mbit/s for Europe and 1.544 Mbit/s for North America, suitable for their respective first levels of digital hierarchy. However, the image quality, although having very good spatial resolution (due to the nature of DPCM working on pixel-by-pixel bases), had a very poor temporal quality. It was soon realised that in order to improve the image quality, without exceeding the target bit rate, less than one bit should be used to code each pixel. This was only possible if a group of pixels were coded together, such that the bit per pixel is fractional. This led to the design of so-called *block based codecs*.

During the late 1980s study period, of the 15 block based videoconferencing proposals submitted to the ITU-T (formerly CCITT), 14 of them were based on the Discrete Cosine Transform (DCT) and only one on Vector Quantisation (VQ). The subjective quality of video sequences presented to the panel showed hardly any significant differences between the two coding techniques. In parallel to ITU-T's investigation during 1984-1988, the Joint Photographic Experts Group (JPEG) was also interested in compression of static images. They chose the DCT as the main unit of compression, mainly due to the possibility of progressive image transmission. JPEG's decision undoubtedly influenced the ITU-T in favouring DCT over VQ. By now there was worldwide activity in implementing the DCT in chips and on DSPs.

By the late 1980s it was clear that the recommended ITU-T videoconferencing codec would use a combination of interframe DPCM for minimum coding delay and the DCT. The codec showed greatly improved picture quality over H.120. In fact, the image quality for videoconferencing applications was found reasonable at 384 kbit/s or higher and good quality was possible at significantly higher bit rates of around 1 Mbit/s. This effort, although originally directed at video coding at 384 kbit/s, was later extended to systems based on multiples of 64 kbit/s ($p \times$ 64 kbit, where p can take values from 1 to 30). The standard definition was completed in late 1989 and is officially called the H.261 standard (the coding method is often referred to as '$p \times$ 64').

The success of H.261 was a milestone for low bit rate coding of video at reasonable quality. In the early 1990s, the Motion Picture Experts Group (MPEG) started investigating coding techniques for storage of video, such as CD-ROMs. The aim was to develop a video codec capable of compressing highly active video such as movies, on hard discs, with a performance comparable to that of VHS home video cassette recorders (VCRs). In fact, the basic framework of the H.261 standard was used as a starting point in the design of the codec. The first generation of MPEG, called the MPEG-1 standard, was capable of accomplishing this task at 1.5 Mbit/s. Since for storage of video, encoding and decoding delays are not a major constraint, one can trade delay for compression efficiency. For example in the temporal domain a DCT might be used rather than DPCM, or DPCM used but with much improved motion estimation, such that the motion compensation removes temporal correlation. This latter option was adopted within MPEG-1.

It is ironic that in the development of H.261, motion compensation was thought to be optional, since it was believed that after motion compensation little was left to be decorrelated by the DCT. However, later research showed that efficient motion compensation can reduce the bit rate. For example, it is difficult to compensate for the uncovered background, unless one looks ahead at the movement of the objects. This was the main principle in MPEG-1, where the motion in most picture frames is looked at from past and future, and this proved to be very effective.

These days, MPEG-1 decoders/players are becoming commonplace for multimedia on computers. MPEG-1 decoder plug-in hardware boards (e.g. MPEG magic cards) have been around for a few years, and now, software MPEG-1 decoders are available with the release of new operating systems or multimedia extensions for PC and Mac platforms. Since in all standard video codecs, only the decoders have to comply with proper syntax, software based coding has added extra flexibility that might even improve the performance of MPEG-1 in the future.

Although MPEG-1 was optimised for typical applications using non-interlaced video of 25 frames/s (in European format) or 30 frames/s (in North America) at bit rates in the range of 1.2 to 1.5 Mbit/s (for image quality comparable to home

VCRs), it can certainly be used at higher bit rates and resolutions. Early versions of MPEG-1 for interlaced video, such as those used in broadcast, were called MPEG-1+. Broadcasters, who were initially reluctant to use any compression on video, fairly soon adopted a new generation of MPEG, called MPEG-2 for coding of interlaced video at bit rates 4-9 Mbit/s. MPEG-2 is now well on its way to making a significant impact in a range of applications such as digital terrestrial broadcasting, digital satellite TV, digital cable TV, digital versatile disc (DVD) and many others. In November 1998, OnDigital started terrestrial broadcasting of BBC and ITV programmes in MPEG-2 coded digital forms, and almost at the same time several satellite operators such as Sky-Digital launched MPEG-2 coded television pictures direct to homes.

Since in MPEG-2 the number of bi-directionally predicted pictures is at the discretion of the encoder, this number may be chosen for an acceptable coding delay. This technique may then be used for telecommunication systems. For this reason ITU-T has also adopted MPEG-2 under the generic name of H.262 for telecommunications. H262/MPEG-2 apart from coding high resolution and higher bit rate video, also has the interesting property of scalability, such that from a single MPEG-2 bit-stream two or more video images at various spatial, temporal or quality resolutions can be extracted. This scalability is very important for video networking applications. For example in applications such as video on demand, multicasting, etc., the client may wish to receive video of his/her own quality choice, or in networking applications during network congestion less essential parts of the bit-stream can be discarded without significantly impairing the received video pictures.

Following the MPEG-2 standard, coding of High Definition Television (HDTV) was seen to be the next requirement. This became known as MPEG-3. However, the versatility of MPEG-2, being able to code video of any resolution, left no place for MPEG-3, and hence it was abandoned. Although Europe has been slow in deciding whether to use HDTV, it is foreseen that in the USA by the year 2014, the existing transmission of analogue NTSC video will cease, and instead HDTV with MPEG-2 compression will be used in terrestrial broadcasting.

After so much development on MPEG-1 and 2, one might wonder what is next. Certainly we have not yet addressed the question of sending video at very low bit rates, such as of 64 kbit/s or less. This of course depends on the demand for such services. However, there are signs that in the very near future such demands may arise. For example, currently, owing to a new generation of modems allowing bit rates of 56 kbit/s or so over Public Switched Telephone Networks (PSTN), videophones at such low bit rates are needed. In the near future there will be demands for sending video over mobile networks, where the channel capacity is very scarce. To fulfil this goal, MPEG group started working on a very low bit rate video codec, under the name of MPEG-4. Before achieving acceptable image quality at such bit rates, new demands arose. These were mainly caused by the requirements of multimedia, where there was a considerable demand for coding of multiviewpoint scenes, graphics, and synthetic as well as natural scenes. Applications such as virtual studio and interactive video were the main driving forces. Ironically, critics say that since MPEG-4 could not deliver what was promised, the goal post was changed.

Work on very low bit rate systems, due to the requirement of PSTN and mobile applications, was carried out by ITU-T. A new video codec named H.263 has been devised to fulfil the goal of MPEG-4. This codec which is an extension of H.261, but uses lessons learned from MPEG developments, is sophisticated enough to code small dimensioned video pictures at low frame rates within 10-64 kbit/s. Due to a very effective coding strategy used in this codec, the recommendation even defines the application of this codec to very high resolution images such as HDTV, albeit at higher bit rates.

Before leaving the subject on MPEG-4, I should add that today's effort on MPEG-4 is on functionality, since this is what makes MPEG-4 distinct from other coders. In MPEG-4 images are coded as objects, and the generated bit-stream is scalable. This provides the possibility of interacting with video, choosing the parts which are of interest. Moreover, natural images can be mixed with synthetic video, in what is called virtual studio. MPEG-4 defines a new coding method based on models of objects for coding synthetic objects. It also uses the Wavelet transform for coding of still images. This mode is to be compatible with the new method of coding of still images under JPEG-2000. However, MPEG-4, as part of its functionality for coding of natural images, uses a similar technique to H.263; hence it is now equally capable of coding video at very low bit rates. The study phase of MPEG-4 is well advanced and it is expected that the standard will be published in the fairly near future.

Finally, work on MPEG-4 has brought new requirements, in particular in image databases. Currently a working group under MPEG-7 has undertaken to study these requirements. The MPEG-7 standard builds on the other standards, such as MPEG-1, 2 and 4. Its main function is to define a search engine for multimedia databases to look for specific image/video clips, using image characteristics such as colour, texture and information about the shape of objects. These pictures may be coded by either of the standard video codecs, or even in analogue forms.

In this book, we start by reviewing briefly the basics of video, including scanning, formation of colour components and various video formats. Principles of video compression techniques used in the standard codecs are given in chapter 3. These include the three fundamental elements of compression: spatial, temporal and intersymbol redundancy reductions. The discrete cosine transform (DCT), as the core element of all the standard codecs, and its fast implementation is presented. Quantisation of the DCT coefficients for bit rate reduction is given. The most important element of temporal redundancy reduction, namely motion compensation, is discussed in this chapter. Two variable length coding techniques for reduction of the entropy of the symbols, namely Huffman and Arithmetic coding, are described. Special attention is paid on the Arithmetic coding, because of its role and importance in most recent video codecs. The chapter ends with an overview of a generic interframe video codec, which is used in the following chapters to describe various standard codecs.

Coding of still pictures, under the Joint Photographic Experts Group (JPEG), is presented in chapter 4. Lossless and lossy compression versions of JPEG are described. The baseline JPEG and its extension with sequential and progressive modes are described. The chapter also includes a new standard for still image coding, under JPEG-2000. Potential for improving the picture quality under this new codec and its compatibility with the still image coding mode of MPEG-4 is discussed.

Chapter 5 describes the H.261 video codec for teleconferencing applications. Structure of picture blocks and the concept of the macroblock as the basic unit of coding are defined. Selection of the best macroblock type for efficient coding is presented. The chapter examines the efficiency of zigzag scanning of the DCT coefficients for coding. The efficiency of two-dimensional variable length coding of zigzag scanned DCT coefficients is compared with one-dimensional variable length codes.

Chapter 6 explains MPEG-1 video coding technique for storage applications. The concept of group-of-pictures for flexible access to compressed video is explained. Differences between MPEG-1 and H.261, as well as the similarities, are highlighted. These include the nature of motion compensation and various forms of coding of picture types used in this codec. Editing, pause, fast forward and fast reverse picture tricks are discussed.

Chapter 7 is devoted to coding of high quality moving pictures with the MPEG-2 standard. The concept of level and profile with its applications are defined. The two main concepts of interlacing and scalability, which discriminate this codec from MPEG-1, are given. The best prediction for the non-scalable codecs from the fields, frames and/or their combinations are discussed. On the scalability, the four fundamental scalable codecs, Spatial, SNR, Temporal and Data partitioning codecs are analysed, and the quality of some coded pictures with these methods are contrasted against each other.

Chapter 8 discusses the H.263 video coding for very low bit rate applications. The fundamental differences and similarities between this codec and H.261 and MPEG-1/2 are highlighted. Special interest is paid to the importance of motion compensation in this codec. Methods of improving the compression efficiency and the relative compression performance of this codec are compared with the other video codecs. Error correction for transmission of video over mobile networks is discussed. Extension of this codec for short and long term standardisation under the H.263+ and H.263L, respectively, are presented. The chapter looks at transmission of video over packet networks, such as ATM, and reviews the effect of loss concealment on the perceived video quality.

In the last chapter a new method of video coding based on the image content is presented. The concept of image plane which enables users to interact with the individual objects and change their characteristics is introduced. Coding of arbitrary shaped objects with a particular emphasis on coding of their shapes is studied. The shape-adaptive DCT as a natural coding scheme for these objects is analysed.

Coding of synthetic objects with model-based coding and still images with the wavelet transform is introduced. Techniques for efficient coding of wavelet coefficients, exploiting the similarities between the sub-images and creation of trees of zeros are discussed. The chapter ends with a description of a new family of MPEG, named MPEG-7, for content search and video browsing.

Chapter 2

Video basics

Before discussing the fundamentals of video compression, let us look at how video signals are generated. Their characteristics will help us to understand how they can be exploited for bandwidth reduction without actually introducing perceptual distortions. In this regard, we will first look at image formation and colour video. Interlaced/progressive video is explained, and its impact on the signal bandwidth and display units is discussed. Representation of video in digital form and the need for bit rate reductions will be addressed. Finally, the image formats to be coded for various applications will be analysed.

2.1 Analogue video

2.1.1 Scanning

Video signals are normally generated at the output of a camera by scanning a two-dimensional moving scene and converting them into a one-dimensional electric signal. A moving scene is a collection of individual pictures or images, where each scanned picture generates a *frame* of the picture. Scanning starts at the top-left corner of the picture and ends at the bottom-right.

The choice of number of scanned lines per picture is a trade-off between the bandwidth, flicker and resolution. Increasing the number of scanning lines per picture increases the spatial resolution. Similarly, increasing the number of pictures per second will increase the temporal resolution. There is a lower limit to the number of pictures per second, below which flicker becomes perceptible. Hence, flicker-free, high-resolution, video requires larger bandwidth.

If a frame is formed by the single scanning of a picture, it is called *progressive* scanning. Alternatively, two pictures may be scanned at two different times, with the lines interleaved, such that two consecutive lines of a frame belong to alternate fields to form a frame. In this case, each scanned picture is called a *field*, and the scanning is called *interlaced*. Figure 2.1 shows progressive and interlaced frames.

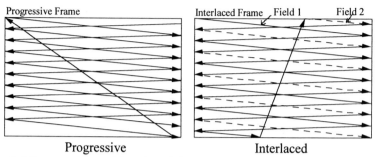

Figure 2.1 Progressive and interlaced frames

The concept behind interlaced scanning is to trade-off vertical-spatial resolution with that of the temporal. For instance, slow-moving objects can be perceived with higher vertical resolution, since there are not many changes between the successive fields. At the same time, the human eye does not perceive flicker since the objects are displayed at field rates. For fast moving objects, although vertical resolution is reduced, the human eye is not sensitive to spatial resolutions at high display rates. Therefore the bandwidth of television signals is halved without significant loss of picture resolution. Usually, in interlaced video, the number of lines per field is half the number of lines per frame, or the number of fields per second is twice the number of frames per second. Hence the number of lines per second remains fixed.

It should be noted that if high spatio-temporal video is required, for example in high definition television (HDTV), then the progressive mode should be used. Although interlaced video is a good trade-off in television, it may not be suitable for computer displays, owing to the closeness of the screen to the viewer and the type of material normally displayed, such as text and graphs. If television pictures were to be used with computers, the result would be an annoying large area flicker, interline flicker, line crawling, etc. To avoid these problems, computer displays use non-interlaced (also called progressive or sequential) displays with refresh rates higher than 50/60 frames per second, typically 72 frames/s.

2.1.2 Colour components

During the scanning, a camera generates three primary colour signals called red, green and blue, the so-called RGB signals. These signals may be further processed for transmission and storage. For compatibility with the black-and-white video and because of the fact that the three colour signals are highly correlated, a new set of signals at different colour space are generated. These are called colour systems, and the three standards are NTSC, PAL and SECAM [1]. We will concentrate on the PAL system as an example, although the basic principles involved in the other systems are very similar.

The colour space in PAL is represented by YUV, where Y represents the Luminance and U and V represent the two colour components. The basis YUV colour space can be generated from gamma-corrected RGB (referred to in equations as R'G'B') components as follows:

$$Y = 0.299R' + 0.587G' + 0.114B'$$
$$U = -0.147R' - 0.289G' + 0.436B' = 0.492\left(B' - Y\right)$$
$$V = 0.615R' - 0.515G' - 0.100B' = 0.877\left(R' - Y\right)$$

(2.1)

In the PAL system the luminance bandwidth is normally 5 MHz, though in PAL system-I, used in the UK, it is 5.5 MHz. The bandwidth of each colour component is only 1.5 MHz, because the human eye is less sensitive to colour resolution. For this reason, in most image processing applications, such as motion estimation, decisions on the type of blocks to be coded or not coded (see chapter 5) are made on the luminance component only. The decision is then extended to the corresponding colour components. Note that for higher quality video, such as High Definition Television (HDTV) the luminance and chrominance components may have the same bandwidth, but nevertheless all the decisions are made on the luminance components. In some applications the chrominance bandwidth may be reduced much further than the ratio of 1.5 MHz/5 MHz.

2.2 Digital video

The process of digitising analogue video involves the three basic operations of filtering, sampling and quantisation. The filtering operation is employed to avoid the aliasing artefacts of the follow-up sampling process. The filtering applied to the luminance can be different from those of chrominance, owing to different bandwidth requirements.

Filtered luminance and chrominance signals are sampled to generate a discrete time signal. The minimum rate at which each component can be sampled is its Nyquist rate and corresponds to twice the signal bandwidth. For a PAL system this is in the range of 10-11 MHz. However, due to the requirement to make the sampling frequency a harmonic of the analogue signal line frequency, the sampling rate for broadcast quality signals has been recommended by CCIR to be 13.5 MHz, under recommendation CCIR-601 [2]. This is close to three times the PAL subcarrier frequency. The chrominance sampling frequency has also been defined to be half the luminance sampling frequency. Finally, sampled signals are quantised to 8-bit resolution, suitable for video broadcasting applications.

It should be noted that colour space recommended by CCIR-601 is very close to the PAL system. The precise luminance and chrominance equations under this recommendation are:

$$Y = 0.257R' + 0.504G' + 0.098B' + 16$$
$$C_b = -0.148R' - 0.291G' + 0.439B' + 128 \qquad (2.2)$$
$$C_r = 0.439R' - 0.368G' - 0.071B' + 128$$

The slight departure from the PAL parameters is due to the requirement that in the digital range, Y should take values in the range of 16 to 235 quantum levels. Also, the normally AC chrominance components of U and V are centred on the grey level 128, and the range is defined from 16 to 240. The reasons for these modifications are:

(i)   to reduce the granular noise of all three signals in later stages of processing, and

(ii)   to make chrominance values positive to ease processing operations (e.g. storage).

Note that despite a unique definition for Y, C_b and C_r, the CCIR-601 standard for European broadcasting is different from that for North America and the Far East. In the former, the number of lines per frame is 625 and the number of frames per second is 25. In the latter these values are 525 and 30 respectively. The number of samples per active line, called *picture elements* (pixels) is 720 for both systems. Note that the total number of pixels per line, including the horizontal blanking, is 13.5 MHz times 64 µs, equal to 864 pixels. Note also that despite the differences in the number of lines and frames rates, the number of pixels generated per second under both CCIR-601/625 and CCIR-601/525 is the same. This is because in digital television we are interested in the active parts of the picture, and the number of active television lines per frame in CCIR-601/625 is 576 and the total number of pixels per second becomes equal to $720 \times 576 \times 25 = 10,368,000$. In CCIR-601/525 the number of active lines is 480, and the total number of pixels per second is $720 \times 480 \times 30 = 10,368,000$.

The total bit rate is then calculated by considering that there are half the luminance pixels for each of the chrominance pixels, and with 8 bits per pixel, the total bit rate becomes $10,368,000 \times 2 \times 8 = 165,888,000$ bits/s. Had we included all the horizontal and vertical blanking, then the total bandwidth would be $13.5 \times 10^6 \times 2 \times 8 = 216$ Mbit/s. Either of these values is much greater than the equivalent analogue bandwidth, hence the video compression to reduce the digital bit rate is very demanding. In the following chapters we will show how such a huge bit rate can be compressed down to less than 10 Mbit/s, without noticeable effect on picture quality.

2.3 Image format

CCIR-601 is based on an image format for broadcast quality. For other applications, images with various degrees of resolutions and dimensions might be preferred. For example, in video conferencing or video telephone, small image sizes with lower resolutions require much less bandwidth than the broadcast video, and at the same time the resultant image quality is quite acceptable for the application. On the other hand, for HDTV, larger image sizes with improved luminance and chrominance resolutions are preferred.

2.3.1 SIF images

In most cases the video sources to be coded by standard video codecs are produced by CCIR-601 digitised video signals direct from the camera. It is then logical to relate picture resolutions and dimensions of various applications to those of CCIR-601. The first set of images related to CCIR-601 are the lower resolution images for storage applications.

   A lower resolution to CCIR-601 would be an image sequence with half the CCIR-601 resolutions in each direction. That is, in each CCIR-601 standard, active parts of the image in the horizontal, vertical and temporal dimensions are halved. For this reason it is called *Source Input Format*, or SIF [3]. The resultant picture is non-interlaced (progressive). The positions of the chrominance samples share the same block boundaries with those of the luminance samples, as shown in Figure 2.2. For every four luminance samples, Y, there will be one pair of chrominance components, C_b and C_r.

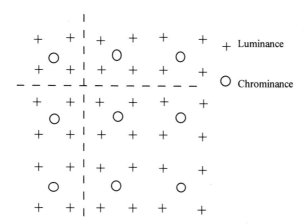

Figure 2.2 Positioning of luminance and chrominance samples (dotted lines indicate macroblock boundaries)

Thus, for the European standard, the SIF picture resolution becomes 360 pixels per line, 288 lines per picture and 25 pictures per second. For North America and the Far East, these values are 360, 240 and 30, respectively.

One way of converting the source video rate (temporal resolution) is to use only odd or even fields. Another method is to take the average values of the two fields. Discarding one field normally introduces aliasing artefacts, but simple averaging blurs the picture. For better SIF picture quality more sophisticated methods of rate conversion are required, which inevitably demand more processing power. The horizontal and vertical resolutions are halved after filtering and subsampling of the video source.

Considering that in CCIR-601 the chrominance bandwidth is half of the luminance, then the number of each chrominance pixel per line is half of the luminance pixels, but their frame rates and the number of lines per frame are equal. This is normally referred to as 4:2:2 image format. Figure 2.3 shows the luminance and chrominance components for the 4:2:2 image format. As the figure shows, in the scanning direction (horizontal) there is a pair of chrominance samples for every alternate luminance sample, but the chrominance components are present in every line. For SIF pictures, there are a pair of chrominance samples for every four luminance pixels as shown in the figure.

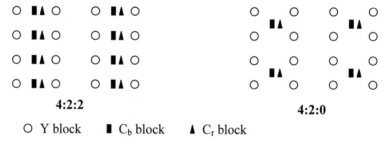

Figure 2.3 Sampling pattern for 4:2:2 (CCIR 601) and 4:2:0 SIF

Thus in SIF, the horizontal and vertical resolutions of luminance will be half of the source resolutions, but for the chrominance, while horizontal resolution is halved, the vertical resolution has to be one-quarter. This is called 4:2:0 format.

The low pass filters used for filtering the source video are different for luminance and chrominance coefficients. The luminance filter coefficient is a 7-tap filter with characteristics

$$[-29 \quad 0 \quad 88 \quad 138 \quad 88 \quad 0 \quad -29]//256 \tag{2.3}$$

Use of a power of two for the devisor allows a simple hardware implementation. For the chrominance the filter characteristic is a four-tap filter of the type

[1   3   3   1]//8   (2.4)

Hence the chrominance samples have to be placed at a horizontal position in the middle of the luminance samples, with a phase shift of half a sample. These filters are not part of the international standard, and other filters may be used. Figure 2.4 illustrates the subsampling and low pass filtering of the CCIR-601 format video into SIF format.

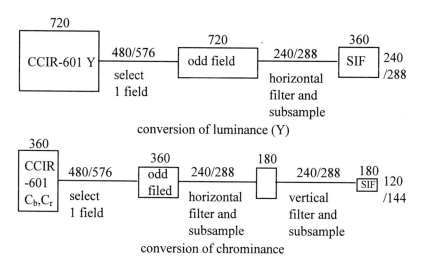

Figure 2.4 Conversion of CCIR-601 to SIF

Note that the number of luminance pixels per line of CCIR-601 is 720. Hence the horizontal resolutions of SIF luminance and chrominance should be 360 and 180 respectively. Since in the standard codecs the coding unit is based on macroblocks of 16×16 pixels, 360 is not divisible by 16. Therefore from each of the leftmost and rightmost sides of SIF, four pixels are removed.

The preprocessing into SIF format is not normative. Other preprocessing steps and other resolutions may be used. The picture size need not even be a multiple of 16. In this case a video coder adds padding pixels to the right or bottom edges of the picture. For example, a horizontal resolution of 360 pixels could be coded by adding eight pixels to the right edge of each horizontal row, bringing the total to 368. Now 23 macroblocks would be coded in each row. The decoder would discard the extra padding pixels after decoding, giving the final decoded resolution of 360 pixels.

The sampling format of 4:2:0 should not be confused with that of the 4:1:1 format used in some digital VCRs. In this format chrominance has the same vertical resolution as luminance, but horizontal resolution is one-quarter. This can be represented with a sampling pattern shown in Figure 2.5. Note that 4:1:1 has the same number of pixels as 4:2:0!

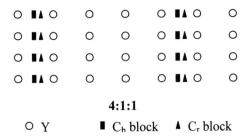

4:1:1

O Y   ▪ C_h block   ▲ C_r block

Figure 2.5 Sampling pattern of 4:1:1 image format

2.3.2 Conversion from SIF to CCIR-601 format

An SIF is converted to its corresponding CCIR-601 format by spatial up-sampling as shown in Figure 2.6. A linear phase Finite Impulse Response (FIR) is applied after the insertion of zeros between samples [3]. A filter that can be used for up-sampling the luminance is a 7-tap FIR filter with the impulse response of

$$[-12 \quad 0 \quad 140 \quad 256 \quad 140 \quad 0 \quad -12]//256 \tag{2.5}$$

At the end of the lines some special techniques such as replicating the last pixel must be used. Note that the DC response of this filter has a gain of 2. This is due to the inserted alternate zeros in the up-sampled samples, such that the up-sampled values retain their maximum nominal value of 255.

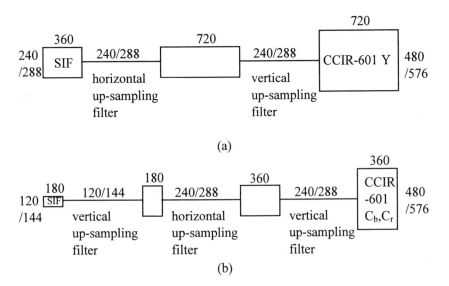

Figure 2.6 Up-sampling and filtering of: (a) luminance and (b) chrominance signals from SIF to CCIR-601 format

According to CCIR recommendation 601, the chrominance samples need to be co-sited with the luminance samples 1, 3, 5,.... In order to achieve the proper location, the up-sampling filter should have an even number of taps, as given by

$$[1 \quad 3 \quad 3 \quad 1]//4 \tag{2.6}$$

Note again, the filter has a gain of 2.

The SIF may be reconstructed by inserting four black pixels to each end of the horizontal luminance line in the decoded bitmap, and two grey pixels (value of 128) to each of the horizontal chrominance lines. The luminance SIF may then be up-sampled horizontally and vertically. The chrominance SIF should be up-sampled once horizontally and twice vertically, as shown in Figure 2.6(b).

2.3.3   CIF image format

For a worldwide videoconferencing, a video codec has to cope with the CCIR-601 of both European (625 line, 50 Hz) and North America and Far East (525 line, 60 Hz) video formats. Hence CCIR-601 video sources from these two different formats had to be converted to a common format. The picture resolutions also needed to be reduced, to be able to code them at lower bit rates.

Considering that in CCIR-601 the number of pixels per line in both 625/50 and 525/60 standards is 720 pixels per line, then half of this value, 360 pixels/line, was chosen as the horizontal resolution. For the vertical and temporal resolutions, a value intermediate between the two standards was chosen such that the combined vertical × temporal resolutions were one-quarter of that of CCIR-601. The 625/50 system has the greater vertical resolution. Since the active picture area is 576 lines, half of this value is 288 lines. On the other hand, the 525/60 system has the greater temporal resolution, so that the half rate is 30 Hz. The combination of 288 lines and 30 Hz gives the required vertical × temporal resolution. This is illustrated in Figure 2.7.

Such an intermediate selection of vertical resolution from one standard and temporal from the other leads to the adopted name *Common Intermediate Format* (CIF). Therefore a CIF picture has a luminance with 360 pixels per lines, 288 lines per picture and 30 (precisely 29.97) pictures per second [4]. The colour components are at half the spatial resolution of luminance, with 180 pixels per line and 144 lines per picture. Temporal resolutions of colour components are the same as for the luminance at 29.97 Hz.

In CIF format, like SIF, pictures are progressive (non-interlaced), and the positions of the chrominance samples share the same block boundaries with that of the luminance samples, as shown in Figure 2.2. Also like SIF, the image format is also 4:2:0 and similar down-conversion and up-conversion filters to those shown in Figures 2.4 and 2.6 can also be applied to CIF images. Note the difference between SIF-625 and CIF and SIF-525 and CIF. In the former the only difference is in the number of pictures per second, while in the latter they differ in the number of lines per picture.

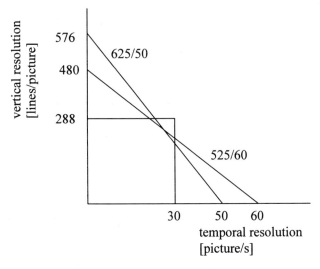

Figure 2.7 Spatio-temporal relation in CIF format

2.3.4 Sub-QCIF, QSIF, QCIF

For certain applications such as video over mobile networks or video telephony it is possible to reduce the frame rate. Known reduced frame rates for CIF and SIF-525 are 15, 10 and 7.5 frames/s. These rates for SIF-625 are 12.5 and 8.3 frames/s. To balance the spatio-temporal resolutions, the spatial resolutions of the images are normally reduced, nominally by halving in each direction. These are called *Quarter-SIF* (QSIF) and *Quarter-CIF* (QCIF) for SIF and CIF formats respectively. Conversion of SIF or CIF to QSIF and QCIF (or vice versa) can be carried out with a similar method of converting CCIR-601 to SIF and CIF, respectively, using the same filter banks shown in Figures 2.4 and 2.6. Lower frame rate QSIF and QCIF images are normally used for very low bit rate video.

Certain applications, such as video over mobile networks, even demand smaller image sizes. Sub-QCIF is the smallest standard image size, with the horizontal and vertical picture resolutions of 128 pixels by 96 pixels, respectively. The frame rate can be very low (e.g. 5 frames/s) to suit the channel rate. The image format in this case is 4:2:0, and hence the chrominance resolution is half the luminance resolution in each direction.

2.3.5   HDTV

Currently there is no European standard for HDTV. The North American and Far Eastern HDTV has a nominal resolution of twice the 525 line CCIR-601 format. Hence the filter banks of Figures 2.4 and 2.6 can also be used for the image size conversion. Also, since in HDTV higher chrominance bandwidth is desired, they are made equal to the luminance. Hence there will be a pair of chrominance pixels for every luminance pixel, and the image format is called 4:4:4. In most cases HDTV is progressive, to improve vertical resolution.

It is common practice to define image format in terms of relations between 8×8 pixel blocks with a macroblock of 16×16 pixels. The concept of macroblock and block will be explained in chapter 5. Figure 2.8 shows how blocks of luminance and chrominance in various 4:2:0, 4:2:2 and 4:4:4 image formats are defined.

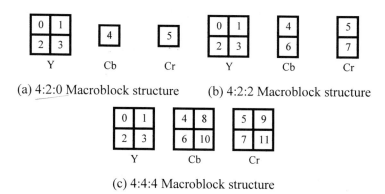

(a) 4:2:0 Macroblock structure   (b) 4:2:2 Macroblock structure

(c) 4:4:4 Macroblock structure

Figure 2.8 Macroblock structures in 4:2:0, 4:2:2 and 4:4:4 image formats

For a more detail representation of image formats, specially discriminating 4:2:0 from 4:1:1, one can relate the horizontal and vertical resolutions of the chrominance components to those of luminance as shown in Table 2.1. Note, the luminance resolution is the same as the number of pixels in each scanning direction.

Table 2.1 Percentage of each chrominance component resolution with respect to luminance in the horizontal and vertical directions

Image format	Horizontal [%]	Vertical [%]
4:4:4	100	100
4:2:2	50	100
4:2:0	50	50
4:1:1	25	100

2.3.6 *Conversion from film*

Sometimes sources available for compression consist of film material, which have a nominal frame rate of 24 pictures per second. This rate can be converted to 30 pictures per second by the pulldown technique [3]. In this mode digitised pictures are shown alternately for 3 and 2 television field times, generating 60 fields per second. This alteration may not be exact, since the actual frame rate in the 525/60 system is 29.97 frames per second. Editing and splicing of compressed video after the conversion might also have changed the pulldown timing. A sophisticated encoder might detect the duplicated fields, average them to reduce digitisation noise and code the result at the original 24 pictures per second rate. This should give a significant improvement in quality over coding at 30 pictures per second. This is because first of all, coding at 24 pictures per second, the bit rate budget per frame is larger than that for 30 pictures per second. Secondly, direct coding of 30 pictures per second destroys the 3:2 pulldown timing and gives a jerky appearance to the final decoded video.

2.3.7 *Temporal resampling*

Since the picture rates are limited to those commonly used in the television industry, the same techniques may be applied. For example, conversion from 24 pictures per second to 60 fields can be achieved by the technique of 3:2 pulldown. Video coded at 25 pictures per second can be converted to 50 fields per second by displaying the original decoded lines in the odd CCIR-601 fields, and the interpolated lines in the even fields. Video coded at 29.97 or 30 pictures per second may be converted to a field rate twice as large as using the same method.

2.4 Picture quality assessment

Conversion of digital pictures from one format to another, as well as their compression for bit rate reduction, introduces some distortions. It is of great importance to know whether the introduced distortion is acceptable to the viewers. Traditionally this has been done by subjective assessments, where the degraded pictures are shown to a group of subjects, and their views on the perceived quality of distortions are sought.

Over the years, many subjective assessment methodologies have been developed and validated. Among them are: the *double stimulus impairment scale* (DSIS), where the subjects are asked to rate the impairment of the processed picture with respect to the reference un-impaired picture; and the *double stimulus continuous quality scale* (DSCQS), where the order of the presentation of the reference and processed pictures is unknown to the subjects. The subjects will then give a score for each picture, and their difference is an indication of the quality. The *single stimulus continuous quality evaluation* (SSCQE), is normally used for video quality evaluation, where the time varying picture quality of the processed video without the reference is evaluated by the subjects [5].

Although these methodologies give reliable indications of the perceived image quality, they are unfortunately time-consuming and expensive. An alternative is the objective measurement, which employs mathematical models simulating the human observers. Objective measurements are usually much faster and cheaper than subjective assessments. The simplest objective measurement is the ratio of the peak-to-peak signal to the root mean squared processing noise. This is referred to the *peak-to-peak signal-to-noise ratio* (PSNR) and defined as

$$PSNR = 10\log_{10}\left[\frac{255^2}{\frac{1}{N}\sum_i\sum_j\left(Y_{ref}(i,j) - Y_{prc}(i,j)\right)^2}\right] \qquad (2.7)$$

where $Y_{ref}(i,j)$ and $Y_{prc}(i,j)$ are the pixel values of the reference and processed images respectively, and N is the total number of pixels in the image. In this equation, the peak signal with an 8-bit resolution is 255, and the noise is the square of the pixel-to-pixel difference (error) between the reference image and the image under study. Although it has been claimed that in some cases PSNR's accuracy is doubtful, its relative simplicity makes it a very popular choice. If accuracy is a main concern, then some more sophisticated perceptual error models than simple pixel differences might be used [6].

References

[1] Netravali A.N. and Haskell B.G. 'Digital pictures, representation and compression and standards', Second edition, Plenum Press, New York, (1995).

[2] CCIR Rec601 'Digital methods of transmitting television information', Recommendation 601, Encoding parameters of digital television for studios.

[3] MPEG-1: 'Coding of moving pictures and associated audio for digital storage media at up to about 1.5 Mbit/s', *ISO/IEC 11172-2: Video* (November 1991).

[4] Okubo S. 'Video codec standardisation in CCITT study group XV', *Signal Processing: Image Communication*, pp. 45-54, (1989).

[5] Recommendation ITU-R BT.500 (Revised), 'Methodology for the subjective assessment of the quality of television pictures'.

[6] Tan K.T, Ghanbari M. and Pearson D.E. 'An objective measurement tool for MPEG video quality', *Signal Processing*, 7, pp. 279-294, (1998).

Chapter 3

Principles of video compression

The statistical analysis of video signals indicates that there is a strong correlation both between successive picture frames and within the picture elements themselves. Theoretically decorrelation of these signals can lead to bandwidth compression without significantly affecting image resolution. Moreover, the insensitivity of the human visual system to loss of certain spatio-temporal visual information can be exploited for further reduction. Hence, subjectively lossy compression techniques can be used to reduce video bit rates while maintaining an acceptable image quality.

For coding still images, only the spatial correlation is exploited. Such a coding technique is called *Intraframe* coding and is the basis for JPEG coding. If temporal correlation is exploited as well, then it is called *Interframe* coding. Interframe predictive coding is the main coding principle that is used in all standard video codecs, such as H.261, H.263, MPEG-1, 2 and 4. It is based on three fundamental redundancy reduction principles:

1. Spatial redundancy reduction: to reduce spatial redundancy among the pixels within a picture (similarity of pixels, within the frames), by employing some data compressors, such as transform coding.

2. Temporal redundancy reduction: to remove similarities between the successive pictures, by coding their differences.

3. Entropy coding: to reduce the redundancy between the compressed data symbols, using variable length coding techniques.

A detailed description of these redundancy reduction techniques is given in the following sections.

3.1 Spatial redundancy reduction

3.1.1 Predictive coding

In the early days of image compression, both signal processing tools and storage devices were scarce resources. At the time, a simple method for redundancy reduction was to predict the value of pixels based on the values previously coded, and code the prediction error. This method is called *Differential Pulse Code Modulation* (DPCM). Figure 3.1 shows a block diagram of a DPCM codec, where the differences between the incoming pixels from the predictions in the predictor are quantised and coded for transmission. At the decoder the received error-signal is added to the prediction to reconstruct the signal. If the quantiser is not used it is called *loss-less* coding, and the compression relies on the entropy coder, which will be explained later.

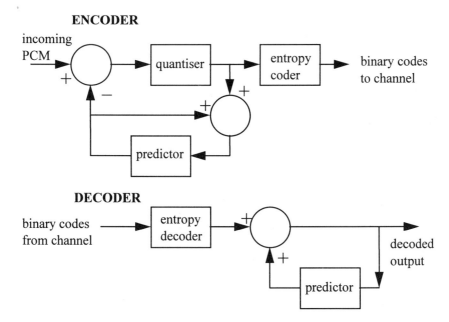

Figure 3.1 Block diagram of a DPCM codec

Best predictions are those from the neighbouring pixels, either from the same frame or pixels from the previous frame, or their combinations. The former is called *Intraframe predictive coding* and the latter is *Interframe predictive coding*. Their combination is called *Hybrid predictive coding*.

It should be noted that, no matter what prediction is used, every pixel is predictively coded. The minimum number of bits that can be assigned to each prediction error is 1 bit. Hence this type of coding is not suitable for low bit rate video coding. Lower bit rates can be achieved if a group of pixels are coded together, such that the average bit per pixel can be less than 1 bit. Block transform coding is most suitable for this purpose. Despite this, DPCM is still used in video compression. For example interframe DPCM has lower coding latency than interframe block coding. Also, DPCM might be used in coding of motion vectors, or block addresses. If motion vectors in a moving object move in the same direction, coding of their differences will reduce the motion vector information. Of course, the coding would be loss-less.

3.1.2   Transform coding

Transform domain coding is mainly used to remove the spatial redundancies in images by mapping the pixels into a transform domain prior to data reduction. The strength of transform coding in achieving data compression is that the image energy of most natural scenes is mainly concentrated in the low frequency region, and hence into a few transform coefficients. These coefficients can then be quantised with the aim of discarding insignificant coefficients, without significantly affecting the reconstructed image quality. This quantisation process is however lossy in that the original values cannot be retained.

The basis vectors of the *Discrete Cosine Transform* (DCT) are the universal choice for the transformation matrix. The reason for this is that it has smoothly varying basis vectors that resemble the intensity variations of most natural images, such that image energy is matched to a few coefficients. For this reason its rate-distortion performance closely follows that of the Karhunen-Loève transform, which is known to be optimal [1]. Equally important is the availability of efficient fast DCT transformation algorithms that can be used, especially in software based image coding applications [2].

Since in natural image sequences, pixels are correlated in the horizontal, vertical directions as well as in the temporal direction of the image sequence, a natural choice for DCT is a three-dimensional one. However, any transformation in the temporal domain requires storage of several picture frames, introducing a long delay, which restricts application of transform coding in telecommunications. Hence transformation is confined to two dimensions.

A two-dimensional DCT is a separable process that is implemented using two one-dimensional DCTs: one in the horizontal direction followed by one in the vertical. For a block of $M \times N$ pixels, the forward one-dimensional transform of N pixels is given by

$$F(u) = \frac{1}{\sqrt{N}} C(u) \sum_{x=0}^{N-1} f(x) \cos\left(\frac{\pi(2x+1)u}{2N}\right), \quad u = 0,1,\ldots,N-1 \qquad (3.1)$$

where
$$C(u) = \frac{1}{\sqrt{2}} \text{ for } u = 0$$
$$C(u) = 1 \text{ otherwise}$$

$f(x)$ represents the intensity of the xth pixel, and $F(u)$ represents the N one-dimensional transform coefficients. The inverse one-dimensional transform is thus defined as

$$f(x) = \frac{1}{\sqrt{N}} \sum_{u=0}^{N-1} C(u)F(u)\cos\left(\frac{\pi(2x+1)u}{2N}\right) \quad x = 0,1,\dots, N-1 \tag{3.2}$$

Note that the $1/\sqrt{N}$ normalisation factor is used to make transformation orthonormal. That is, the energy in both pixel and transform domains is to be equal. In the standard codecs the normalisation factor in the DCT domain is defined as 1/2. This gives the DCT coefficients in the range of −2047 to +2047. The normalisation factor in the pixel domain is then adjusted accordingly (e.g. it becomes $2/N$).

To derive the final two-dimensional transform coefficients, N sets of one-dimensional transforms of length M are taken over the one-dimensional transform coefficients of similar frequency in the vertical direction:

$$F(u,v) = \frac{1}{\sqrt{M}} C(v) \sum_{y=0}^{M-1} F(u,y)\cos\left(\frac{\pi(2y+1)}{2M}\right) \quad v = 0,1,\dots, M-1 \tag{3.3}$$

where $C(v)$ is defined similarily to $C(u)$.

Thus a block of MN pixels are transformed into MN coefficients. The $F(0,0)$ coefficient represents the DC value of the block. Coefficient $F(0,1)$, which is the DC value of all the first one-dimensional AC coefficients, represents the first AC coefficient in the horizontal direction of the block. Similarly, $F(1,0)$, which is the first AC coefficient of all one-dimensional DC values, represents the first AC coefficient in the vertical direction, and so on.

In practice $M=N=8$, such that a two-dimensional transform of $8 \times 8 = 64$ pixels results in 64 transform coefficients. The choice of such a block size is a compromise between the compression efficiency and the blocking artefacts of coarsely quantised coefficients. While larger block sizes have good compression efficiency, the blocking artefacts are subjectively very annoying. At the early stage of standardisation of video codecs, the block sizes were made optional at 4×4, 8×8 and 16×16. Now the block size in standard codecs is 8×8.

3.1.3   Fast DCT transform

To calculate transform coefficients, every one-dimensional forward or inverse transformation requires eight multiplications and seven additions. This process is repeated for 64 coefficients, both in the horizontal and vertical directions. Since software based video compression is highly desirable, methods of reducing such a huge computational burden are highly desirable.

The fact that DCT is a type of discrete Fourier transform, with the advantage of all-real coefficients, then one can use a fast transform, similar to the fast Fourier transform, to calculate transform coefficients with complexity proportional to $N \log_2 N$, rather than N^2. Figure 3.2 shows a butterfly representation of the fast DCT [2]. Intermediate nodes share some of the computational burden, hence reducing the overall complexity. In the figure, p[0]-p[7] are the inputs to the forward DCT and b[0]-b[7] are the transform coefficients. The inputs can be either the eight pixels for the source image, or eight transform coefficients of the first stage of the one-dimensional transform. Similarly, for inverse transformation, b[0]-b[7] are the inputs to the IDCT, and p[0]-p[7] are the outputs. A 'C' language programme for fast forward DCT is given in Appendix A. In this program, some modifications to the butterfly matrices are made to trade off the number of additions for multiplications, since multiplications are more computationally intensive than additions. A similar program can be written for the inverse transform.

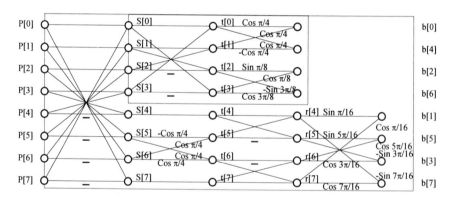

Figure 3.2 A fast DCT flow chart

3.2   Quantisation of DCT coefficients

The domain transformation of the pixels does not actually yield any compression. A block of 64 pixels is transformed into 64 coefficients. Due to the orthonormality of transformation, the energy in both the pixel and the transform domains are equal, hence no compression is achieved. However transformation causes the significant part of the image energy to be concentrated at the lower frequency components, with the majority of the coefficients having little energy. It is the quantisation and variable length coding of the DCT coefficients that lead to bit rate reduction. Moreover by exploiting the human eye's characteristics, which are less sensitive to picture distortions at higher frequencies, one can apply even coarser quantisation at these frequencies, to give greater compression. Coarser quantisation step sizes force more coefficients to zero and as a result, more compression is gained, but of course the picture quality deteriorates accordingly.

The class of quantiser that has been used in all standard video codecs is based around the so called *uniform threshold quantiser* (UTQ). It has equal step sizes with reconstruction values pegged to the centriod of the steps. This is illustrated in Figure 3.3.

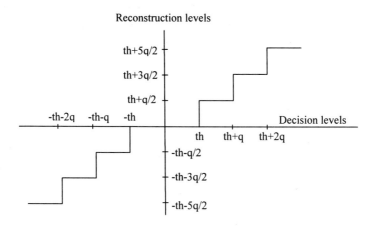

Figure 3.3 Quantisation characteristics

The two key parameters that define a UTQ are the threshold value, *th*, and the step size, *q*. The centroid value is typically defined mid-way between quantisation intervals. Note that, although AC transform coefficients have non-uniform characteristics, and hence can be better quantised with non-uniform quantiser step sizes (the DC coefficient has a fairly uniform distribution), bit rate control would be easier if they were quantised linearly. Hence, a key property of UTQ is that the step sizes can be easily adapted to facilitate rate control.

A further two sub-classes of UTQ can be identified within the standard codecs, namely those with and without a *dead zone*. They are illustrated in Figure 3.4 and will be hereafter abbreviated as UTQ-DZ and UTQ respectively. The term dead zone commonly refers to the central region of the quantiser, whereby the coefficients are quantised to zero.

Typically, UTQ is used for quantising intraframe DC, $F(0,0)$, coefficients, while UTQ-DZ is used for the AC and the DC coefficients of interframe prediction error. This is intended primarily to cause more non-significant AC coefficients to become zero, so increasing the compression. In UTQ, coefficients $F(u,v)$ are quantised by their division to the quantiser step size, q, with rounding towards the nearest integer.

$$I(u,v) = \frac{F(u,v) \pm q}{2q} \qquad (3.4)$$

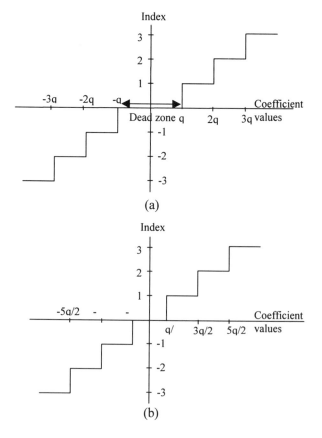

Figure 3.4 *Uniform quantisers (a) with and (b) without dead zone*

Such a ratio, $I(u,v)$, is called the *quantisation index*. It is the quantisation index that is sent to the decoder, since it has a much smaller entropy than the quantised coefficient. At the decoder, the reconstructed coefficients, $F^q(u,v)$, after inverse quantisation are given by

$$F^q(u,v) = I(u,v) \times 2q \tag{3.5}$$

Quantisation indices employing UTQ-DZ are obtained by using integer division which will truncate the resultant towards zero:

$$I(u,v) = \frac{F(u,v)}{2q} \tag{3.6}$$

In the inverse quantisation, depending on the polarity of the index, an addition or subtraction of half the quantisation step is required to deliver the centroid representation:

$$F^q(u,v) = \{2I(u,v) \pm 1\} \times q \tag{3.7}$$

3.3   Temporal redundancy reduction

By using the differences between successive images, temporal redundancy is reduced. This is called *interframe* coding. For static parts of the image sequence, temporal differences will be close to zero, and hence are not coded. Those parts which change between the frames, either due to illumination variation or to motion of the objects, result in significant image error which needs to be coded. Image changes due to motion can be significantly reduced if the motion of the object can be estimated, and the difference is taken on the motion compensated image. Figure 3.5 shows the interframe error between successive frames of the "Claire" test image sequence and its motion compensated counterpart. It is clear that motion compensation can substantially reduce the interframe error.

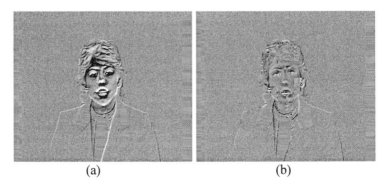

(a)   (b)

Figure 3.5 (a) Interframe and (b) motion compensated interframe pictures

3.3.1 Motion estimation

To carry out motion compensation, the motion of the moving objects has to be estimated first. This is called *motion estimation*. The commonly used motion estimation technique in all the standard video codecs is the *Block Matching Algorithm* (BMA). In a typical BMA, a frame is divided into blocks of $M \times N$ pixels or, more usually, square blocks of N^2 pixels [3]. Then, for a maximum motion displacement of w pixels per frame, the current block of pixels is matched against a corresponding block at the same co-ordinates but in the previous frame, within the square window of width $N + 2w$ (Figure 3.6).

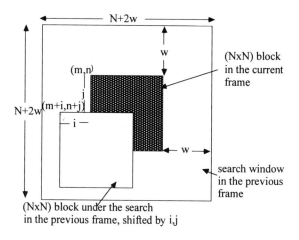

Figure 3.6 The current and previous frames in a search window

The best match on the basis of a matching criterion yields the displacement.

Various measures such as the crosscorrelation function (CCF), mean squared error (MSE) and mean absolute error (MAE) can be used in the matching criterion [4–6]. For the best match, in the CCF the correlation has to be maximised, whereas in the latter two the distortion must be minimised. In practical coders both MSE and MAE are used, since it is believed that CCF would not give good motion tracking, especially when the displacement is not large [6]. The matching functions of the type MSE and MAE are defined as:

for MSE:

$$M(i, j) = \frac{1}{N^2} \sum_{m=1}^{N} \sum_{n=1}^{N} \left(f(m,n) - g(m+i, n+j) \right)^2, \quad -w \le i, j \le w \qquad (3.8)$$

and for MAE:

$$M(i, j) = \frac{1}{N^2} \sum_{m=1}^{N} \sum_{n=1}^{N} \left| f(m,n) - g(m+i, n+j) \right|, \quad -w \le i, j \le w \qquad (3.9)$$

where $f(m,n)$ represents the current block of N^2 pixels at co-ordinates (m,n) and $g(m+i, n+j)$ represents the corresponding block in the previous frame at new co-ordinates $(m+i, n+j)$.

To locate the best match by full search, $(2w+1)^2$ evaluations of the matching criterion are required. To reduce processing cost, MAE is preferred to MSE, and hence is used in all the video codecs. However, for each block of N^2 pixels we still need to carry out $(2w+1)^2$ tests, each with almost $2N^2$ additions and subtractions. This is still far from being suitable for implementation of BMA in software based codecs. In fact studies by Downton [7] have shown that in the H.261 and MPEG-1 codecs, motion estimation comprises almost 60-70% of the codec complexity. Hence fast motion estimation techniques are highly desirable.

3.3.2 Fast motion estimation

In the past two decades a number of fast search methods for motion estimation have been introduced to reduce the computational complexity of BMA. The basic principle of these methods is that the number of search points can be reduced, by selectively checking only a small number of specific points, assuming that the distortion measure monotonically decreases towards the best matched point. Jain and Jain [6] were the first to use a two-dimensional logarithmic (TDL) search method to track the direction of a minimum mean-squared error distortion measure. In their method, the distortion for the five initial positions, one at the centre of the co-ordinate and four at co-ordinates $(\pm w/2, \pm w/2)$ of the search window, are computed first. In the next step, three more positions with the same step size in the direction of the previous minimum position are searched. The step size is then halved and the above procedure is continued until the step size becomes unity. Finally all the nine positions are searched. With this method, for $w=5$ pixels/frame, 21 positions are searched as opposed to 121 positions required in the full search method.

Koga *et al.* [8] use a three-step search (TSS) method to compute motion displacements up to 6 pixels/frame. In their method all eight positions surrounding the co-ordinate with a step size of $w/2$ are searched first. At each minimum position the search step size is halved and the next eight new positions are searched. This method, for $w=6$ pixels/frame, searches 25 positions to locate the best match. The technique is the recommended method for the test of software based H.261 [9] for videophone applications.

In Kappagantula and Rao's [4] modified motion estimation algorithm (MMEA), prior to halving the step sizes, two more positions are also searched. With this method for $w = 7$ pixels/frame, only 19 MAE computations are required. In Srinivasan and Rao's [10] conjugate direction search (CDS) method, at every iteration of the direction search, two conjugate directions with a step size of one pixel, centred at the minimum position, are searched. Thus, for $w = 5$ pixels/frame, there will be only 13 searches at most.

Another method of fast BMA is the cross-search algorithm (CSA) [11]. In this method, the basic idea is still a logarithmic step search, which has also been exploited in [4,6,8], but with some differences which lead to fewer computational search points. The main difference is that, at each iteration there are four search locations, which are the end points of a cross ($\times$) rather than (+). Also, at the final stage, the search points can be either the end points of ($\times$) or (+) crosses, as shown in Figure 3.7. For a maximum motion displacement of w pixels/frame, the total number of computations becomes $5 + 4 \log_2 w$.

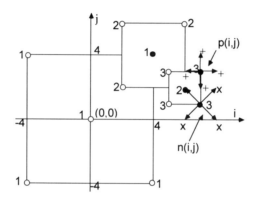

Figure 3.7. An example of the CSA search for w=8 pixels/frame

Puri *et al.* [12] have introduced the Orthogonal Search Algorithm (OSA), in which, with a logarithmic step size, at each iteration four new locations are searched. This is the fastest method of all known fast MBAs. In this method, at every step, two positions are searched alternately in the vertical and horizontal directions. The total number of test points is $1 + 4 \log_2 w$.

Table 3.1 shows the computational complexity of various fast search methods, for a range of motion speed from 4 to 16 pixels/frame. The motion compensation efficiency of these algorithms for a motion speed of $w=8$ pixels/frame for two test image sequences are tabulated in Table 3.2.

Table 3.1 Computational complexity

Algorithm	Maximum number of search points	w		
		4	8	16
FSM	$(2w+1)^2$	81	289	1089
TDL	$2 + 7 \log_2 w$	16	23	30
TSS	$1 + 8 \log_2 w$	17	25	33
MMEA	$1 + 6 \log_2 w$	13	19	25
CDS	$3 + 2w$	11	19	35
OSA	$1 + 4 \log_2 w$	9	13	17
CSA	$5 + 4 \log_2 w$	13	17	21

Table 3.2 Compensation efficiency

Algorithm	Split Screen		Trevor White	
	Entropy (bits/pel)	Standard deviation	Entropy (bits/pel)	Standard deviation
FSM	4.57	7.39	4.41	6.07
TDL	4.74	8.23	4.60	6.92
TSS	4.74	8.19	4.58	6.86
MMEA	4.81	8.56	4.69	7.46
CDS	4.84	8.86	4.74	7.54
OSA	4.85	8.81	4.72	7.51
CSA	4.82	8.65	4.68	7.42

It can be seen that while fast search methods reduce the computational complexity of the full search method (FSM) significantly, their motion estimation accuracy (compensation efficiency) has not been degraded noticeably.

3.3.3   Hierarchical motion estimation

The assumption of monotonic variation of image intensity, employed in the fast BMAs often causes false estimations, especially for larger picture displacements. These methods perform well for slow moving objects, such as those in video conferencing. However, for higher motion speeds, due to the intrinsic selective nature of these methods, they often converge to a local minimum of distortion.

One method of alleviating this problem is to subsample the image to smaller sizes, such that the motion speed is reduced by the sampling ratio. The process is done on a multilevel image pyramid, known as the *Hierarchical Block Matching Algorithm* (HBMA) [13]. In this technique, pyramids of the image frames are reconstructed, by successive two-dimensional filtering and sub-sampling of the current and past image frames. Figure 3.8 shows a three-level pyramid, where for simplicity, each level of the upper level of the pyramid is taken as the average of four adjacent pixels of one level below. Effectively this is a form of low pass filtering.

Conventional block matching with a block size of 16 pixels, either full search or any fast method, is first applied to the highest level of the pyramid (level 2 in Figure 3.8). This motion vector is then doubled in size, and further refinement within one pixel search is carried out in the following level. The process is repeated to the lowest level. Therefore with an n-level pyramid the maximum motion speed of w at the highest level is reduced to $w/2^{n-1}$.

For example a maximum motion speed of 32 pixels/frame with a three-level pyramid is reduced to 8 pixels/frame, which is quite manageable by any fast search method. Note also this method can also be regarded as another type of fast search, with a performance very close to the full search, irrespective of the motion speed, but the computational complexity can be very close to the fast logarithmic methods.

As an example, for a maximum motion speed of 32 pixels/frame, which is very common in high definition video or most TV sports programmes, while the non-hierarchical full search BMA requires $(2 \times 32 + 1)^2 = 4225$ operations, a 4-level hierarchy, where the motion speed at the top level is $32/2^{4-1} = 4$ pixels/frame, only requires $(2 \times 4 + 1)^2 + 3 \times 9 = 108$ operations. Here 81 operations are carried out at the top level, and at each lower level nine new positions are searched.

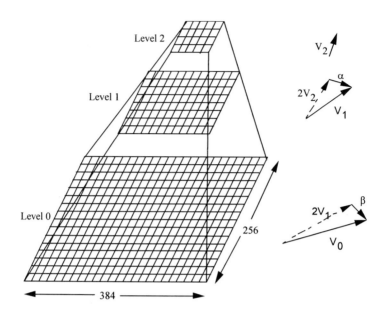

Figure 3.8 A three-level image pyramid

3.4   Variable length coding

For further bit rate reduction, the transform coefficients and the co-ordinates of the motion vectors are variable length coded (VLC). In VLC, short code words are assigned to the highly probable values and long code words to the less probable ones. The lengths of the codes should vary inversely with the probability of occurrences of the various symbols in VLC. The bit rate required to code these symbols is defined as the logarithm of probability, p, at base 2 (bits), i.e. $\log_2 p$. Hence, the entropy of the symbols which is the minimum average bits required to code the symbols can be calculated as

$$H(x) = -\sum_{i=1}^{n} p_i \log_2 p_i \qquad (3.10)$$

There are two types of VLC which are employed in the standard video codecs. They are the *Huffman* coding and *Arithmetic* coding. It is noted that Huffman coding is a practical VLC code, but its compression can never reach as low as the entropy due to the constraint that the assigned symbols must have an integral number of bits. However, the arithmetic coding can approach the entropy since the symbols are not coded individually [14]. Huffman coding is employed in all standard codecs to encode the quantised DCT coefficients as well as motion vectors. Arithmetic coding is used, for example, in JPEG, H.263 and shape and still image coding of MPEG-4 [15–17], where extra compression is demanded.

3.4.1 Huffman coding

Huffman coding is the most commonly known variable length coding method based on probability statistics. Huffman coding assigns an output code to each symbol with the output codes being as short as 1 bit, or considerably longer than the input symbols, depending on their probability. The optimal number of bits to be used for each symbol is $-\log_2 p$, where p is the probability of a given symbol.

However, since the assigned code words have to consist of an integral number of bits, this makes Huffman coding sub-optimum. For example, if the probability of a symbol is 0.33, the optimum number of bits to code that symbol is around 1.6 bits, but the Huffman coding scheme has to assign either 1 or 2 bits to the code. In either case, on average it will lead to more bits compared to its entropy. As the probability of a symbol becomes very high, Huffman coding becomes very non-optimal. For example, for a symbol with a probability of 0.9, the optimal code size should be 0.15 bits, but Huffman coding assigns a minimum value of 1 bit code to the symbol, which is six times larger than necessary. Hence, it can be seen that resources are wasted.

To generate the Huffman code for symbols with a known probability of occurrence, the following steps are carried out:

- Rank all the symbols in the order of their probability of occurrence.
- Successively merge every two symbols with the least probability to form a new composite symbol, and rerank order them. This will generate a tree, where each node is the probability of all nodes beneath it.
- Trace a path to each leaf, noting the direction at each node.

Figure 3.9 shows an example of Huffman coding of seven symbols, A–G. Their probabilities in descending order are shown in the third column. In the next column the two smallest probabilities are added and the combined probability is included in the new order. The procedure continues to the last column, where a single probability of 1 is reached. Starting from the last column, for every branch of probability a "0" is assigned on the top and "1" in the bottom, shown in bold digits in the figure. The corresponding codeword (shown in the first column) is read off by following the sequence from right to left. While with fixed word length each sample is represented by 3 bits, they are represented in VLC from 2 bits to 4.

Code   Symbol   Prob

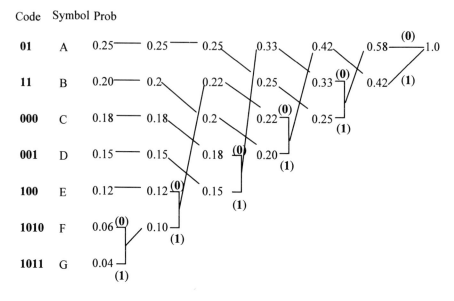

01	A
11	B
000	C
001	D
100	E
1010	F
1011	G

Figure 3.9 An example of Huffman code for seven symbols

The average bit per symbol is then
$$0.25 \times 2 + 0.20 \times 2 + 0.18 \times 3 + 0.15 \times 3 + 0.12 \times 3 + 0.06 \times 4 + 0.04 \times 4 = 2.65 \text{ bits}$$
which is very close to the entropy given by
$$-\left(\begin{array}{l}0.25\log_2 0.25 + 0.2\log_2 0.2 + 0.18\log_2 0.18 + 0.15\log_2 0.15 + 0.12\log_2 0.12\\ +0.06\log_2 0.06 + 0.04\log_2 0.04\end{array}\right)$$
$$= 2.62 \text{ bits}$$

It should be noted that for a large number of symbols, such as the values of DCT coefficients, such a method can lead to a long string of bits for the very rarely occurring values, and is impractical. In such cases normally a group of symbols are represented by their aggregate probabilities, and the combined probabilities are Huffman coded, the so called *modified Huffman* code. This method is used in JPEG. Another method, which is used in H.261 and MPEG, is to use two-dimensional Huffman, or three-dimensional Huffman in H.263 [9,16].

3.4.2 *Arithmetic coding*

Huffman coding can be optimum if the symbol probability is an integer power of 1/2, which is usually not the case. Arithmetic coding is a data compression technique that encodes data by creating a code string which represents a fractional value on the number line between 0 and 1 [14]. It encourages clear separation between the model for representing data and the encoding of information with respect to that model. Another advantage of arithmetic coding is that it dispenses with the restriction that each symbol must translate into an integral number of bits, thereby coding more efficiently. It actually achieves the theoretical entropy bound to compression efficiency for any source. In other words, arithmetic coding is a practical way of implementing entropy coding.

There are two types of modelling used in arithmetic coding: *fixed* model and *adaptive* model. Modelling is a way of calculating, in any given context, the distribution of probabilities for the next symbol to be coded. It must be possible for the decoder to produce exactly the same probability distribution in the same context. It is to note that probabilities in the model are represented as integer frequency counts. Unlike the Huffman-type, arithmetic coding accommodates adaptive models easily and is computationally efficient. The reason why data compression requires adaptive coding is that the input data source may change during encoding, due to motion and texture.

In the fixed model, both encoder and decoder know the assigned probability to each symbol. These probabilities can be determined by measuring frequencies in representative samples to be coded and the symbol frequencies remain fixed. Fixed models are effective when the characteristics of the data source are close to the model and have little fluctuation.

In the adaptive model, the assigned probabilities may change as each symbol is coded, based on the symbol frequencies seen so far. Each symbol is treated as an individual unit and hence there is no need for a representative sample of text. Initially all the counts might be the same, but they update, as each symbol is seen, to approximate the observed frequencies. The model updates the inherent distribution so the prediction of the next symbol should be close to the real distribution mean, making the path from the symbol to the root shorter.

Due to the important role of arithmetic coding in the advanced video coding techniques, in the following sections a more detailed description of this coding technique is given.

3.4.2.1 Principles of arithmetic coding

The fundamental idea of arithmetic coding is to use a scale in which the coding intervals of real numbers between 0 and 1 are represented. This is in fact the cumulative probability density function of all the symbols which add up to 1. The interval needed to represent the message becomes smaller as the message becomes longer, and the number of bits needed to specify that interval is increased. According to the symbol probabilities generated by the model, the size of the interval is reduced by successive symbols of the message. The more likely symbols reduce the range less than the less likely ones and hence they contribute fewer bits to the message.

To explain how arithmetic coding works, a fixed model arithmetic code is used in the example for easy illustration. Suppose the alphabet is {**a**, **e**, **i**, **o**, **u**, **!**} and the fixed model is used with the probabilities shown in Table 3.3.

Table 3.3 Example; fixed model for alphabet {a,e,i,o,u,!}

Symbol	Probability	Range
a	0.2	[0.0,0.2)
e	0.3	[0.2,0.5)
i	0.1	[0.5,0.6)
o	0.2	[0.6,0.8)
u	0.1	[0.8,0.9)
!	0.1	[0.9,1.0)

Once the symbol probability is known, each individual symbol needs to be assigned a portion of the [0, 1) range that corresponds to its probability of appearance in the cumulative density function. Note also that the character with a range of [lower, upper) "owns" everything from lower up to, but not including, the upper value. So, the alphabet 'u' with probability 0.1, defined in the cumulative range of [0.8, 0.9), can take any value from 0.8 to 0.8999....

The most significant portion of an arithmetic coded message is the first symbol to be encoded. Using the example that a message **eaii!** is to be coded, the first symbol to be coded is 'e'. Hence, the final coded message has to be a number greater than or equal to 0.2 and less than 0.5. After the first character is encoded, we know that the lower number and the upper number now bound our range for the output. Each new symbol to be encoded will further restrict the possible range of the output number during the rest of the encoding process.

The next character to be encoded, 'a', is in the range of 0–0.2 in the new interval. Since it is not the first number to be encoded, so it belongs to the range corresponding to 0–0.2, but in the new sub-range of [0.2, 0.5). This means that the number is now restricted to the range of [0.2, 0.26), since the previous range was 0.3 units long and one-fifth of that is 0.06. The next symbol to be encoded, 'i', is in the range of [0.5, 0.6), that corresponds to 0.5 - 0.6 in the new sub-range of [0.2, 0.26) and gives the smaller range [0.23, 0.236). Applying this rule for coding of successive characters, Table 3.4 shows the successive build up of the range of the message coded so far.

Table 3.4 Representation of arithmetic coding process

	New character	Range
Initially:		[0, 1)
After seeing a symbol:	e	[0.2, 0.5)
	a	[0.2, 0.26)
	i	[0.23, 0.236)
	i	[0.233, 0.2336)
	!	[0.23354, 0.2336)

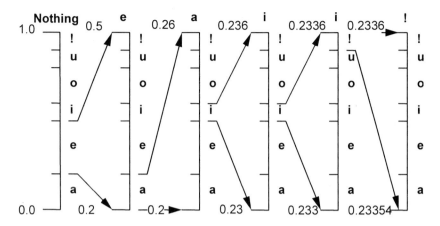

*Figure 3.10 Representation of arithmetic coding process with the interval scaled up at each stage for the message **eaii!***

Figure 3.10 shows another representation of the encoding process.

The range is expanded to fill the whole range at every stage and marked with a scale that gives the endpoints as a number. The final range, [0.23354, 0.2336) represents the message **eaii!**. This means that if we transmit any number in the range of $0.23354 \le x < 0.2336$, that number represents the whole message of **eaii!**.

Given this encoding scheme, it is relatively easy to see how during the decoding the individual elements of the **eaii!** message are decoded. To verify this, suppose a number $x=0.23355$ in the range of $0.23354 \le x < 0.2336$ is transmitted. The decoder, using the same probability intervals as the encoder, performs a similar procedure. Starting with the initial interval [0, 1), only the interval [0.2, 0.5) of '**e**' envelops the transmitted code of 0.23355. So the first symbol can only be '**e**'. Similar to the encoding process, the symbol intervals are then scaled to the new interval [0.2, 0.5) and compared again to the transmitted value of 0.23355. Only the interval [0.2, 0.26) of this range envelops this value, so the second symbol can only be '**a**'. Proceeding like this, the decoder can identify the whole elements of the message. Table 3.5 shows the whole decoding process of the message '**eaii!**'.

At the end of each message, the decoder needs to know when to stop decoding. To resolve the ambiguity, each message has to end with a special symbol known to both encoder and decoder. In the above example, character '**!**' was used to terminate the coding and decoding process. When the decoder sees this symbol, it stops decoding.

Table 3.5 Representation of decoding process of arithmetic coding

Encoded number	Output symbol	Range
0.23354	e	[0.2, 0.5)
0.233	a	[0.0, 0.2)
0.23	i	[0.5, 0.6)
0.23	i	[0.5, 0.6)
0.2	!	[0.9, 1.0)
0		

3.4.2.2 Binary arithmetic coding

In the preceding section we saw that, as the number of symbols in the message increases, the range of the message becomes smaller. If we continue coding more symbols then the final range may even become smaller than the precision of any computer, to define such a range. To resolve this problem we can work with binary arithmetic coding.

In Figure 3.10 we saw that after each stage of coding, if we expand the range to its full range of [0, 1), the apparent range is increased. However, still the values of the lower and upper numbers are small. Therefore, if the initial range of [0, 1) is replaced by a larger range of [0, MAX_VAL), where MAX_VAL is the largest integer number that a computer can handle, then the precision problem is resolved. If we use 16-bit integer numbers, then $MAX\_VAL = 2^{16}-1$. Hence rather than defining the cumulative probability in the range of [0,1), we define their cumulative frequencies scaled up within the range of [0, $2^{16}-1$).

At the start, the coding interval [lower, upper) is initialised to the whole scale [0, MAX_VAL]. The model's frequencies, representing the probability of each symbol in this range, are also set to their initial values in the range. To encode a new symbol element e_k assuming that symbols $e_1...e_{k-1}$ have already being coded, we project the model scale to interval resulting from the sequence of events. The new interval [*lower'*, *upper'*) for the sequence $e_1...e_k$ is calculated from the old interval [*lower*, *upper*) of the sequence $e_1...e_{k-1}$ as follows:

$$lower' = lower + width * low / maxfreq$$
$$width' = width * symb\_width / maxfreq$$
$$upper' = lower' + width'$$
$$= lower + width * (low + symb\_width) / maxfreq$$
$$= lower + width * up / maxfreq$$

with :
$$width = upper - lower \ (old \ interval)$$
$$width' = upper' - lower' \ (new \ interval)$$
$$symb\_width = up - low \ (model's \ frequency)$$

At this stage of the coding process, we do not need to keep the previous interval [*lower, upper*) in the memory, so we allocate the new values [*lower', upper'*). We then compare the new interval with the scale [0, *MAX_VAL*) to determine whether there is any bit for transmission down the channel. These bits are due to the redundancy in the binary representation of lower and upper values. For example, if values of both lower and upper are less than half the [0, *MAX_VAL*) range, then their most significant number in binary form is 0. Similarly if both belong to the upper half range, their most significant number is 1. Hence we can make a general rule:

- if lower and upper levels belong to the first half of the scale, the most significant bit for both will be 0.
- if lower and upper belong to the second half of the scale, their most significant bit will be 1.
- otherwise, when lower and upper belong to the different halves of the scale their most significant bits will be different (0 and 1).

Thus for the cases where lower and upper values have the same most significant bit, we send this bit down the channel and calculate the new interval as follows:

- Sending a 0 corresponds to removal of the second half of the scale and keeping its first half only. The new scale is expanded by a factor 2 to obtain its representation in the whole scale of [0, *MAX_VAL*) again, as shown in Figure 3.11.

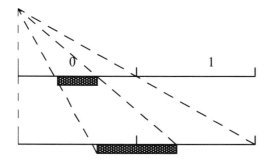

If *lower* and *upper* belong to the **first** half of the scale, their higher bits will both be" **0**"

Figure 3.11 Both lower and upper values in the first half

- Sending a 1 corresponds to the shift of the second half of the scale to its first half. That is subtracting half of the scale value and multiplying the result by a factor 2 to obtain its representation in the whole scale again, as shown in Figure 3.12.

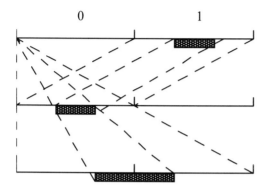

If *lower* and *upper* belong to the **second** half of the scale, their higher bits will both be" **1**"

Figure 3.12 Both lower and upper values in the second half

If the interval always remains in either half of the scale after a bit has been sent, the operation is repeated as many times as necessary to obtain an interval occupying both halves of the scale. The complete procedure is called the *interval testing loop*.

Now we go back to the case where both of the lower and upper values are not in either of the half intervals. Here we identify two cases: first the lower value is in the second quarter of the scale and the upper value is in the third quarter. Hence the range of frequency is less than 0.5. In this case, in the binary representation, the two most significant bits are different, 01 for lower and 10 for the upper, but we can deduce some information from them. That is, in both cases, the second bit is the complementary bit to the first. Hence if we can find out the second bit, the previous bit is its complement. Therefore, if the second bit is 1, then the previous value should be 0, and hence we are in the second quarter, meaning the lower value. Similar conclusions can be drawn for the upper value.

Thus we need to divide the interval within the scale of $[0, MAX\_VAL)$ into four segments instead of two. Then the scaling and shifting for this case will be done only on the portion of the scale containing second and third quarters, as shown in Figure 3.13

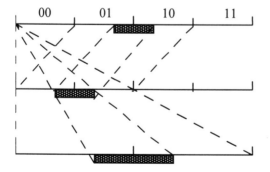

If *lower* and *upper* belong to the **second & third** quarter of the scale, an "**unknown**" bit is sent to a waiting buffer for later transmission, and the interval shifted by quarter

Figure 3.13 Lower and upper levels in the second and third quarter respectively

Thus the general rule for this case is that:

- if the interval belongs to the second and third quarters of the scale: an "unknown" bit "**?**" is sent to a waiting buffer for later definition and the interval transformed as shown in Figure 3.13.

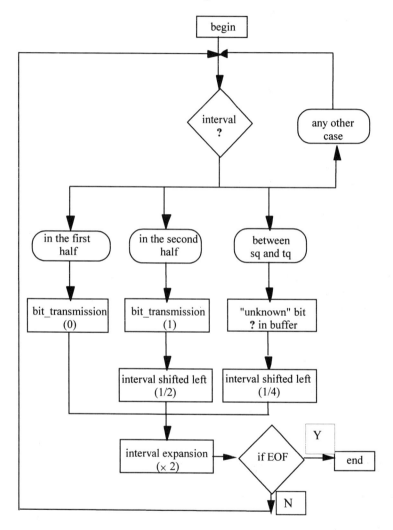

Figure 3.14 A flow chart for binary arithmetic coding

Finally,
- if the interval belongs to more than two different quarters of the scale (the interval occupies parts of three or four different quarters), there is no need

to transform the coding interval. The process exits from this loop and goes to the next step in the execution of the program. This means that if the probability in that interval is greater than 0.5, no bits are transmitted. This is the most important part of arithmetic coding which leads to low bit rate.

A flow chart of the *interval testing loop* is shown in Figure 3.14 and a detailed example of coding a message is given in Figure 3.15. For every symbol to be coded we invoke the flow chart of Figure 3.14, except where the symbol is the end of file symbol, where the programme stops. After each testing loop, the model can be updated (frequencies modified if the adaptive option has been chosen).

A "C" program of binary arithmetic coding is given below.

```c
#define q1 16384
#define q2 32768
#define q3 49152
#define top  65535

static long low, high, opposite_bits, length;
void encode_a_symbol (int index, int cumul_freq[])
{
   length = high - low +1;
   high =low -1 + (length * cumul_freq[index]) / cumul_freq[0];
   low += (length * cumul_freq[index+1])/ cumul_freq[0];
   for( ; ; ){
     if(high <q2){
        send out a bit " 0" to PSC_FIFO;
        while (opposite_bits > 0) {
           send out a bit " 1" to PSC_FIFO;
           opposite_bits--;
        }
     }
     else if (low >= q2) {
        send out a bit " 1" to PSC_FIFO;
        while (opposite_bits > 0) {
        send out a bit " 0" to PSC_FIFO;
        opposite_bits--;
     }
     low -= q2;
           high -= q2;
   }
   else if (low >= q1 && high < q3) {
      opposite_bits += 1;
      low -= q1;
      high -= q1;
   }
   else break;
   low *= 2;
   high = 2 * high + 1;
   }
}
```

The values of low and high are initialised to 0 and top, respectively. PSC_FIFO is a first-in-first-out (FIFO) for buffering the output bits from the arithmetic encoder. The model is specified through cumul_freq[], and the symbol is specified using its index in the model.

3.4.2.3 An example of binary arithmetic coding

Because of the complexity of the arithmetic algorithm, a simple example is given below. To simplify the operations further, we use a fixed model with four symbols **a**, **b**, **c** and **d**, where their fixed probabilities and cumulative probabilities are given in Table 3.6, and the message sequence of events to be encoded is **bbacd**.

Considering what we saw earlier, we start by initialising the whole range to [0, 1). In sending **b**, which has a range of [0.3 , 0.8), since the lower = 0.3 is in the second quarter and the upper = 0.8 in the fourth quarter (occupying more than two quarters) nothing is sent, and no scaling is required, as shown in Table 3.7.

Table 3.6 Probability and cumulative probability of four symbols as an example

Symbol	pdf	cdf
a	0.3	[0.0 , 0.3)
b	0.5	[0.3 , 0.8)
c	0.1	[0.8 , 0.9)
d	0.1	[0.9 , 1.0)

To send the next **b**, i.e. **bb**, since the previous width = 0.8 − 0.3 = 0.5, the new interval becomes [0.3 + 0.3 × 0.5 , 0.3 + 0.8 × 0.5) = [0.45 , 0.7). This time lower = 0.45 is in the second quarter but upper = 0.7 is in the third quarter, so the unknown bit "**?**" is sent to the buffer, such that its value is to be determined later.

Note that since range [0.45, 0.7) covers second and third quarters, according to Figure 3.13, we have to shift both of them by a quarter (0.25) and then magnify by a factor of 2, i.e. the new interval is [(0.45−0.25) × 2, (0.7−0.25) × 2) = [0.4, 0.9) which has a width of 0.5. To code the next symbol **a**, the range becomes [0.4+0 × 0.5, 0.4+0.3 × 0.5) = [0.4, 0.55). Again since lower and upper are at the second and third quarters, the unknown "**?**" is stored. According to Figure 3.13 both quarters are shifted by 0.25 and magnified by 2, [0+(0.4−0.25) × 2, (0.55−0.25) × 2) = [0.3, 0.6).

Again [0.3 , 0.6) is in the second and third interval so another "**?**" is stored. If we shift and magnify again [(0.3−0.25) × 2, (0.6−0.25) × 2) = [0.1, 0.7), which now lies in the first and third quarters, so nothing is sent and not scaled. Now if we code **c**, i.e. **bbac**, the interval becomes [0.1+0.8 × 0.6, 0.1+0.9 × 0.6) = [0.58, 0.64).

Now since [0.58, 0.64) is in the second half so we send **1**. We now go back and convert all **"?"** to **000** complementary to **1**. Thus we have sent **1000** so far. Note that bits belonging to **"?"** are transmitted after finding a "1" or "0". Similarly the subsequent symbols are coded and the final generated bit sequence becomes **1000010001**. Table 3.7 shows this example in a tabular representation. A graphical representation is given in Figure 3.15.

*Table 3.7 Generated binary bits of coding **bbacd** message*

encoding	coding interval	width	bit
initialisation:	[0 , 1)	1	
after b:	[0.3 , 0.8)	0.5	
after bb:	[0.45 , 0.7)	0.25	
after interval test	[0.4 , 0.9)	0.5	?
after bba:	[0.40 , 0.55)	0.15	
after interval test	[0.3 , 0.6)	0.3	?
after interval test	[0.1 , 0.7)	0.6	?
after bbac:	[0.58 , 0.64)	0.06	
after interval test	[0.16 , 0.28)	0.12	**1000**
after interval test	[0.32 , 0.56)	0.24	**0**
after interval test	[0.14 , 0.62)	0.48	?
after bbacd:	[0.572 , 0.620)	0.048	
after interval test	[0.144 , 0.240)	0.096	**10**
after interval test	[0.288 , 0.480)	0.192	**0**
after interval test	[0.576 , 0.960)	0.384	**0**
after interval test	[0.152 , 0.920)	0.768	**1**

3.4.2.4 Adaptive arithmetic coding

In adaptive arithmetic coding, the assigned probability to the symbols changes as each symbol is coded [18]. For binary (integer) coding, this is accomplished by assigning a frequency of 1 to each symbol at the start of the coding (initialisation). As a symbol is coded, the frequency of that symbol is incremented by one. Hence the frequencies of symbols are adapted to their number of appearances so far. The decoder follows a similar procedure. At every stage of coding, a test is done to see if the cumulative frequency (sum of the frequencies of all symbols) exceeds the *MAX_VAL*. If this is the case, all frequencies are halved (minimum 1), and encoding continues. For a better adaptation, the frequencies of the symbols may be initialised to a pre-defined distribution that matches the overall statistics of the symbols better. For better results, the frequencies are updated from only N most recently coded symbols. It has been shown that this method of adaptation with a limited past history can reduce the bit rate by more than 30% below the first order entropy of the symbols [19]. The reason for this is that, if some rare events that normally have high entropy could occur in clusters, then within the only N most recent events, they now become the more frequent events, and hence require lower bit rates.

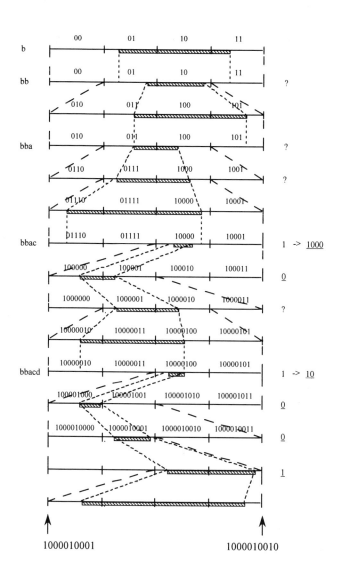

Figure 3.15 Derivation of the binary bits for the given example

3.5   A generic interframe video codec

Figure 3.16 shows a generic interframe encoder which is used in all the standard video codecs, such as H.261, H.263, MPEG-1, MPEG-2 and MPEG-4 [20,16,21,22,17]. In the following sections each element of this codec is described in a general sense. The specific aspects of these codecs will be addressed in more detail in the relevant chapters.

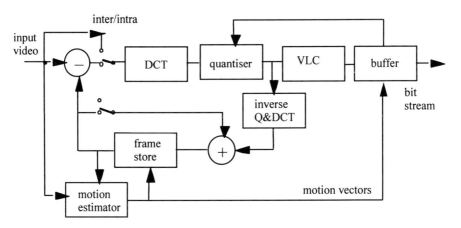

Figure 3.16 A generic interframe predictive coder

3.5.1   Interframe loop

In interframe predictive coding, the difference between pixels in the current frame and their prediction values from the previous frame are coded and transmitted. At the receiver after decoding the error signal of each pixel, it is added to a similar prediction value to reconstruct the picture. The better the predictor, the smaller the error signal, and hence the transmission bit rate. If the scene is still, a good prediction for the current pixel is the same pixel in the previous frame. However, when there is a motion, assuming that movement in the picture is only a shift of object position, then a pixel in the previous frame, displaced by a motion vector, is used.

3.5.2   Motion estimator

Assigning a motion vector to each pixel is very costly. Instead, a group of pixels are motion compensated, such that the motion vector overhead per pixel can be very small. In standard codecs a block of 16×16 pixels, known as a *Macroblock* (MB) (to be differentiated from 8×8 DCT blocks), are motion estimated and compensated. It should be noted that motion estimation is only carried out on the luminance parts of the pictures. A scaled version of the same motion vector is used for compensation of chrominance blocks, depending on the picture format.

3.5.3 Inter/intra switch

Every MB is either interframe or intraframe coded, called *Inter/intra* MBs. The decision on the type of MB depends on the coding technique, which will be explained in greater detail in the relevant chapters. For example, in JPEG, all MBs are intraframe coded, as JPEG is mainly used for coding of still pictures.

3.5.4 DCT

Every MB is divided into 8×8 luminance and chrominance pixel blocks. Each block is then transformed via the DCT. There are four luminance blocks in each MB, but the number of chrominance blocks depends on the colour resolutions (image format).

3.5.5 Quantiser

As mentioned in Section 3.2, there are two types of quantisers. One with a dead zone for the AC coefficients and the DC coefficient of Inter-MB. The other without the dead zone is used for the DC coefficient of Intra-MB. The range of quantised coefficients can be from −2047 to +2047. With a dead zone quantiser, if the modulus (absolute value) of a coefficient is less than the quantiser step size q it is set to zero, otherwise it is quantised according to equation 3.6, to generate quantiser indices. The quantisation indices have values between 1 and 31.

3.5.6 Variable length coding

The quantiser indices are variable length coded, according to the type of VLC used. Motion vectors, as well as the address of coded macroblocks, are also VLC coded.

3.5.7 IQ and IDCT

To generate a prediction for interframe coding, the quantised DCT coefficients are first inverse quantised and inverse DCT coded. These are added to their previous picture values (after a frame delay by the frame store), to generate a replica of decoded picture. The picture is then used as a prediction for coding of the next picture in the sequence.

3.5.8 Buffer

The generated bit rate by an interframe coder is variable. This is because the bit rate is primarily a function of picture activity (motion of objects and their details). Therefore, to transmit coded video into fixed rate channels (e.g. 2 Mbit/s links), they have to be regulated. Storing the coded data in a buffer and then emptying the buffer at the channel rate does this. However, if the picture activity is such that the buffer may overflow (violent motion) then a feedback from the buffer to the quantiser can regulate the bit rate. Here as the buffer occupancy increases, the feedback forces the quantiser step size to be increased to reduce the bit rate. Similarly, if the picture activity is less (coding mainly slow motion parts of frames), then the quantiser step size is reduced to improve the picture quality. This method of coding is called constant bit rate (CBR). For variable bit rate (VBR) coding, the feedback and the smoothing buffer are no longer needed. The quantiser step size in this case is fixed.

References

[1]   Jain A.K. 'Fundamentals of digital image processing', Prentice Hall, (1989).

[2]   Chen W., Smith C. and Fralick S. 'A fast computational algorithm for the discrete cosine transform', *IEEE Trans. Commun.*, **COM-25**, pp. 1004-1009, (1979).

[3]   Ishiguro T. and Iinuma K. 'Television bandwidth compression transmission by motion-compensated interframe coding', *IEEE Commun. Mag.* **10**, pp. 24-30, (1982).

[4]   Kappagantula S. and Rao K.R. 'Motion compensated predictive coding', in *Proc. Inter. Tech. Symposium, SPIE,* San Diago, CA, (August 1983).

[5]   Bergmann H.C. 'Displacement estimation based on the correlation of image segments', *IRE Conference on the Electronic Image Processing,* York, U.K. (July 1982).

[6]   Jain J.R. and Jain A.K. 'Displacement measurement and its application in interframe image coding', *IEEE Trans. Commun.*, **COM-29**, pp. 1799-1808, (December 1981).

[7]   Downton A.C. 'Speed-up trend analysis for H.261 and model-based image coding algorithms and parallel-pipeline model', *Signal Processing, Image Commun.*, **7: (4-6)**, pp. 489-502, (1995).

[8]   Koga T., Iinuma K., Hirano A., Iijima Y. and Ishiguro T. 'Motion compensated interframe coding for video conferencing', in *Proc. National Telecommun. Conf.,* pp G5.3.1 - G5.3.5., New Orleans, LA, November 29-

December 3,(1981).

[9]   CCITT Working Party XV/4, 'Description of reference model 8 (RM8)', Specialists Group on Coding for Visual Telephony, Doc. 525, (June 1989).

[10] Srinivasan R. and Rao K.R. 'Predictive coding based on efficient motion estimation', *IEEE Inter. Conf. on Commun.*, pp. 521-526, Amsterdam, (May 14-17, 1984).

[11] Ghanbari M. 'The cross search algorithm for motion estimation', *IEEE Trans. Commun.*, **38:7**, pp. 950-953, (July 1990).

[12] Puri A., Hang H.M. and Schilling D.L. 'An efficient block-matching algorithm for motion compensated coding', in *Proc. IEEE ICASSP*'87, pp. 25.4.1 - 25.4.4, (1987).

[13] Bierling M. 'Displacement estimation by hierarchical block matching', *Proc. SPIE, vol. 1001, Visual Communications and Image Processing*, pp. 942-951, (1988).

[14] Langdon G.G. 'An introduction to arithmetic coding', *IBM Journal, Res. Develop.*, **28:2**, pp. 135-149, (1984).

[15] Pennebaker W.B. and Mitchell J.L. 'JPEG: still image compression standard', Van Nostrand Reinhold, New York, (1993).

[16] H.263: 'Draft ITU-T Recommendation H.263, Video coding for low bit rate communication', (September 1997).

[17] MPEG-4: 'Testing and evaluation procedures document', ISO/IEC JTC1/SC29/WG11, N999 (July 1995).

[18] Witten I.H., Neal R.M. and Cleary J.G. 'Arithmetic coding for data compression', *Communications of the ACM*, **30:6**, pp. 520-540, (1987).

[19] Ghanbari M. 'Arithmetic coding with limited past history', *Electronics Letters*, **27:13**, pp. 1157-1159, (June 1991).

[20] H.261: 'ITU-T Recommendation H.261, video codec for audiovisual services at p×64 kbit/s', Geneva, (1990).

[21] MPEG-1: 'Coding of moving pictures and associated audio for digital storage media at up to about 1.5 Mbit/s', *ISO/IEC 1117-2: video* (November 1991).

[22] MPEG-2: 'Generic coding of moving pictures and associated audio information', *ISO/IEC 13818-2 Video*, Draft International Standard (November 1994).

Chapter 4

Coding of still pictures (JPEG)

The JPEG standard for coding of digital images, designed by the Joint Photographic Experts Group, is in fact a product of a collaborative effort between ITU-T and ISO (International Standards Organisation) [1]. It aims to support a wide variety of applications for compression of continuous-tone images and is the most frequently used means of compressing still images. It can code full colour images, achieving an average compression ratio of 15:1 for subjectively transparent quality [2]. Its design meets special constraints, which make the standard very flexible. For example, the JPEG encoder is parametrisable, so that the desired compression/quality trade-offs can be determined based on the application or the wishes of the user [3]. Other examples of applications that JPEG algorithm supports include Adobe's PostScript language for printing systems, the Raster Content portion of the ISO Office Document Architecture and Interchange format, the future ITU-T colour facsimile standard and European ETSI videotext standard [1].

JPEG can also be used in coding of video, on the basis that video is a succession of still images. In this case the process is called *Motion JPEG*. Currently, Motion JPEG has found numerous applications. The most notable one is video coding for transmission over packet networks with unspecified bandwidth or bit rates (UBR). A good example of UBR networks is the Internet, where, due to unpredictability of the network load, congestion may last for a significant amount of time. Since in Motion JPEG, each frame is independently coded, it is an ideal encoder of video for such a hostile environment.

Another application of Motion JPEG is video compression for recording on magnetic tapes, where again the independent coding of pictures increases the flexibility of the encoder for recording requirements, such as editing, pause, fast forward, fast rewind, etc. Also such an encoder can be very resilient to loss of information, since the channel error will not propagate through the image sequence. However, since the coding of I-pictures in the MPEG-2 standard is similar to Motion JPEG, normally video compression for recording purposes is carried out with the I-picture part of the MPEG-2 encoder. The I-pictures are those which are encoded without reference to previous or subsequent pictures. This will be explained in chapter 6.

4.1   Lossless compression

The JPEG standard specifies two classes of encoding and decoding namely *lossless* and *lossy* compression. Lossless compression is based on a simple predictive DPCM method using neighbouring pixel values while DCT is employed for the lossy mode.

Figure 4.1 shows the main elements of a lossless JPEG image encoder.

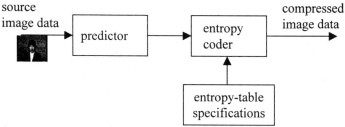

Figure 4.1 Lossless encoder

The digitised source image data in the forms of either RGB or YC_bC_r is fed to the predictor. The image can take any format from 4:4:4 down to 4:1:0, with any size and amplitude precision (e.g. 8 bit/pixel). The predictor is of the simple DPCM type (see Figure 3.1 of chapter 3), where every individual pixel of each colour component is differentially coded. The prediction for an input pixel x is made from combinations of up to three neighbouring pixels at positions a, b and c from the same picture of the same colour component, as shown in Figure 4.2.

c	b	
a	x	

Figure 4.2 Three-sample prediction neighbourhood

The prediction is then subtracted from the actual value of the pixel at position x, and the difference is losslessly entropy coded by either Huffman or arithmetic coding. The entropy-table specifications unit determines the characteristics of the variable length codes of either entropy coding method.

The encoding process might be slightly modified by reducing the precision of input image samples by one or more bits prior to lossless coding. For lossless processes, sample precision is specified to be between 2 and 16 bits. This achieves higher compression than normal lossless coding, but has lower compression than DCT based lossy coding for the same bit rate and image quality. Note that this is in fact a type of lossy compression, since reduction in the precision of input pixels by b bits is equivalent to the quantisation of the difference samples by a quantiser step size of 2^b.

4.2   Lossy compression

In addition to the lossless compression, the JPEG standard defines three lossy compression modes. These are called *baseline sequential* mode, *progressive* mode and *hierarchical* mode. These modes are all based on the Discrete Cosine Transform (DCT) to achieve a substantial compression while producing a reconstructed image with high visual fidelity. The main difference between these modes is the way in which the DCT coefficients are transmitted.

The simplest DCT-based coding is referred to as the *baseline sequential* process. It provides the capability that is sufficient for many applications. The other DCT-based processes which extend the baseline sequential process to a broader range of applications are referred to as *Extended* DCT-based processes. In any extended DCT-based decoding processes, the baseline decoding is required to be present in order to provide a default decoding capability.

4.2.1   Baseline sequential mode compression

The baseline sequential mode compression is usually called baseline coding for short. In this mode, an image is partitioned into 8×8 non-overlapping pixel blocks from left to right and top to bottom. Each block is DCT coded, and all the 64-transform coefficients are quantised to the desired quality. The quantised coefficients are immediately entropy coded and output as part of the compressed image data, thereby minimising coefficient storage requirements.

Figure 4.3 illustrates the JPEG's baseline compression algorithm. Each 8-bit sample is level shifted by subtracting 128 before being DCT coded. The 64 DCT coefficients are then uniformly quantised according to the step size given in the application-specific quantisation matrix. The use of a quantisation matrix allows different weighting to be applied according to the sensitivity of the human visual system to a coefficient of the frequency.

Two examples of quantisation tables are given in Tables 4.1 and 4.2. [4]. These tables are based on psychovisual thresholding and are derived empirically using luminance and chrominance with a 2:1 horizontal subsampling. These tables may not be suitable for any particular application, but they give good results for most images with an 8-bit precision.

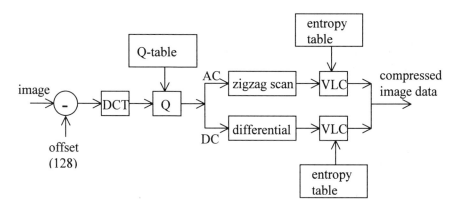

Figure 4.3 Block diagram of a baseline JPEG encoder

Table 4.1 Luminance Q-table	*Table 4.2 Chrominance Q-table*

16	11	10	16	24	40	51	61
12	12	14	19	26	58	60	55
14	13	16	24	40	57	69	56
14	17	22	29	51	87	80	62
18	22	37	56	68	109	103	77
24	35	55	64	81	104	113	92
49	64	78	87	103	121	120	101
72	92	95	98	112	100	103	99

17	18	24	47	99	99	99	99
18	21	26	66	99	99	99	99
24	26	56	99	99	99	99	99
47	66	99	99	99	99	99	99
99	99	99	99	99	99	99	99
99	99	99	99	99	99	99	99
99	99	99	99	99	99	99	99
99	99	99	99	99	99	99	99

If the elements of the quantisation tables of luminance and chrominance are represented by $Q(u,v)$, then a quantised DCT coefficient with the horizontal and the vertical spatial frequencies of u and v, $F^q(u,v)$, is given by

$$F^q(u,v) = \left\lfloor \frac{F(u,v)}{Q(u,v)} \right\rfloor \tag{4.1}$$

where $F(u,v)$ is the transform coefficient value prior to quantisation, and $\lfloor . \rfloor$ means rounding the division to the nearest integer. At the decoder the quantised coefficients are inverse quantised by

$$F^Q(u,v) = F^q(u,v) \times Q(u,v) \tag{4.2}$$

to reconstruct the quantised coefficients.

A quality factor *q_JPEG* is normally used to control the elements of the quantisation matrix $Q(u,v)$ [5]. The range of *q_JPEG* percentage value is between 1% and 100%. The JPEG quantisation matrices of Tables 4.1 and 4.2 are used for *q_JPEG* = 50, for the luminance and chrominance respectively. For other quality factors, the elements of the quantisation matrix, $Q(u,v)$, are multiplied by the compression factor α, defined as [5]:

$$\alpha = \frac{50}{q\_JPEG} \qquad \text{if } 1 \le q\_JPEG \le 50$$

$$\alpha = 2 - \frac{2 \times q\_JPEG}{100} \qquad \text{if } 50 \le q\_JPEG \le 99 \tag{4.3}$$

subject to the condition that the minimum value of the modified quantisation matrix elements, $\alpha\, Q(u,v)$, is 1. For a 100 per cent quality, *q_JPEG* = 100, that is lossless compression; all the elements of $\alpha\, Q(u,v)$ are set to 1.

After quantisation, the DC (commonly referred to as (0,0) coefficient) and the 63 AC coefficients are coded separately as shown in Figure 4.3. The DC coefficients are DPCM coded with prediction of the DC coefficient from the previous block, as shown in Figure 4.4, i.e. DIFF = $DC_i - DC_{i-1}$. This separate treatment from the AC coefficients is to exploit the correlation between the DC values of adjacent blocks and to code them more efficiently as they typically contain the largest portion of the image energy. The 63 AC coefficients starting from coefficient AC(1,0) are *Run-Length* coded following a *zigzag* scan as shown in Figure 4.4.

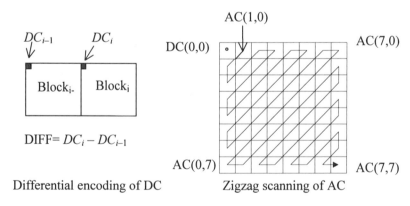

Differential encoding of DC   Zigzag scanning of AC

Figure 4.4 Preparing of the DCT coefficients for entropy coding

The adoption of a zigzag scanning pattern is to facilitate entropy coding by encountering the most likely non-zero coefficients first. This is due to the fact that, for most natural scenes, the image energy is mainly concentrated in a few low frequency transform coefficients.

4.2.2 Run-length coding

The entropy coding of the baseline encoder is accomplished in two stages. The first stage is the translation of the quantised DCT coefficients into an intermediate set of *symbols*. In the second stage, variable length codes are assigned to each symbol. For the JPEG standard a symbol is structured in two parts; a variable length code (VLC) for the first part, normally referred to as *symbol-1*, followed by a binary representation of the amplitude for the second part, *symbol-2*.

4.2.2.1 Coding of DC coefficients

Instead of assigning individual variable length code-words (e.g. Huffman code) to each DIFF, the DIFF values are categorised based on the magnitude range called CAT. The CAT is then variable length coded. Table 4.3 shows the categories for the range of amplitudes in the baseline JPEG. Since the DCT coefficient values are in the range –2047 to 2047, then there are 11 categories for non-zero coefficients. Category zero is not used for symbols; it is used for defining the end-of-block (EOB) code.

Table 4.3 The category (CAT) of the baseline encoder

CAT	Range
0	-
1	–1, 1
2	–3,–2, 2,3
3	–7,...–4, 4,...7
4	–15,...–8, 8,...15
5	–31,...–16, 16,...31
6	–63,...–32, 32,...63
7	–127,...–64, 64,...127
8	–255,...–128, 128,...255
9	–511,...–256, 256,...511
10	–1023,...–512, 512,...1023
11	–2047,...–1024, 1024,...2047

The CAT after being VLC coded is appended with additional bits to specify the actual DIFF values (amplitude) within the category. Here CAT is symbol-1 and the appended bits represent symbol-2.

When the DIFF is positive the appended bits are just the lower order bits of the DIFF. When it is negative, the appended bits become the lower order bits of DIFF-

1. The lower order bits start from the point where the most significant bit of the appended bit sequence is one for positive differences and zero for negative differences. For example: for DIFF=6=0000...00110, the appended bits start from 1, hence it would be 110. This is because DIFF is positive and the most significant bit of the appended bits should be 1. Also, since 6 is in the range of 4 to 7 (Table 4.3) the vale of CAT is 3. From Table-DC of Appendix B, the code-word for CAT=3 is 100. Thus the overall code-word for DIFF=6 is **100110**, where 100 is the VLC code of CAT (symbol-1) and 110 is the appended code word (symbol-2).

For a negative DIFF, such as DIFF= −3, first of all −3 is in the range of −3 to −2, thus from Table 4.3, CAT=2, and its VLC code from Table-DC of Appendix B is 011. However, to find the appended bits, DIFF−1 = −4 =1111...100, where the lower order bits are 00. Note the most significant bit of the appended bits is 0. Thus the code-word becomes **01100**.

4.2.2.2 Coding of AC coefficients

For each non-zero AC coefficient in zigzag scan order, symbol-1 is described as a two-dimensional *event* of (RUN, CAT), sometimes called RUN/SIZE. For the baseline encoder, CAT is the category for the amplitude of a non-zero coefficient in the zigzag order, and RUN is the number of zeros preceding this non-zero coefficient. The maximum length of run is limited to 15. Encoding of runs greater than 15 is done by a special symbol (15, 0), which is a runlength of 15 zero coefficients followed by a coefficient of zero amplitude. Hence it can be interpreted as the extension symbol with 16 zero coefficients. There can be up to 3 consecutive (15, 0) symbols before the terminating symbol-1 followed by a single symbol-2. For example a (RUN=34, CAT=5) pair would result in three symbols *a*, *b*, and *c*, with *a*=(15, 0), *b*=(15, 0) and *c*=(2, 5).

An *end-of-block* (EOB) is designated to indicate that the rest of the coefficients of the block in the zigzag scanning order are quantised to zero. The EOB symbol is represented by (RUN=0, CAT=0).

The AC code table for symbol-1 consists of one Huffman code-word (maximum length 16 bits, not including additional bits) for each possible composite event. Table-AC of Appendix B shows the code-words for all possible combinations of RUN and CAT of symbol-1 [4]. The format of the additional bits (symbol-2) is the same as in the coding of DIFF in DC coefficients. For the kth AC coefficient in the zigzag scan order, $ZZ(k)$, the additional bits are either the lower-order bits of $ZZ(k)$ when $ZZ(k)$ is positive, or the lower-order bits of $ZZ(k)$-1, when $ZZ(k)$ is negative. In order to clarify this, let us look at a simple example.

Example: The quantised DCT coefficients of a luminance block are shown in Figure 4.5. If the DC coefficient in the previous luminance block was 29, find the code-words for coding of the DC and AC coefficients.

31	18	0	0	0	0	0	0
-21	-13	0	0	0	0	0	0
0	5	0	0	0	0	0	0
0	0	0	0	0	0	0	0
0	0	0	0	0	0	0	0
0	0	0	0	0	0	0	0
0	0	0	0	0	0	0	0
0	0	0	0	0	0	0	0

Figure 4.5 Quantised DCT coefficients of a luminance block

Code-word for the DC coefficient:
DIFF = 31 − 29 = 2. From Table 4.3, CAT = 2 and according to Table-DC of Appendix B, the Huffman code for this value of CAT is 011. To find the appended bits, since DIFF = 2 >0, then 2=000…00$\underline{10}$. Thus the appended bits are 10. Hence the overall code-word for coding the DC coefficient is 01110.

Code-words for the AC coefficients:
Scanning starts from the first non-zero AC coefficient that has a value of 18. From Table 4.3, the CAT value for 18 is 5, and since there is no zero-value AC coefficient before it, then RUN=0. Hence symbol-1 is (0, 5). From Table-AC of Appendix B, the code-word for (0, 5) is 11010. The symbol-2 is the lower-order bits of ZZ(k) = 18 = 000…0$\underline{10010}$, which is 10010. Thus the first AC code-word is 1101010010.

The next non-zero AC coefficient in the zigzag scan order is −21. Since it has no zero coefficient before it and it is in the range of −31 to −16, then it has a RUN=0, and CAT=5. Thus symbol-1 of this coefficient is (0, 5), which again from Table-AC of Appendix B, has a code-word of 11010. For symbol-2, since − 21 < 0, then ZZ(k) −1 = −21 −1 = −22 = 111…11$\underline{01010}$, and symbol-2 becomes 01010 (note the appended bits start from where the most significant bit is 0). Thus the overall code-word for the second non-zero AC coefficient is 1101001010.

The third non-zero AC coefficient in the scan is −13, which has one zero coefficient before it. Then RUN=1 and, from its range, CAT is 4. From Table-AC of Appendix B, the code-word for (RUN=1, CAT=4) is 111110110. To find symbol-2, ZZ(k) −1 = −13 −1 = −14 = 111…11$\underline{0010}$. Thus symbol-2 = 0010, and the whole code-word becomes 1111101100010.

The fourth and the final non-zero AC coefficient is 5 (CAT = 3), which is preceded by three zeros (RUN = 3). Thus symbol-1 is (3, 3), which, from Table-AC of Appendix B, has a code-word of 111111110101. For symbol-2, since ZZ(k) = 5 = 000…00$\underline{101}$, then the lower-order bits are 101, and the whole code-word becomes 111111110101101.

Since 5 is the last non-zero AC coefficient, then the encoding terminates here and the end-of-block (EOB) code is transmitted which is defined as (0, 0) symbol with no appended bits. From the Table-AC of Appendix B, its code-word is 1010.

4.2.2.3 Entropy coding

For coding of the magnitude categories or runlength events, the JPEG standard specifies two alternative entropy coding methods, namely Huffman coding and arithmetic coding. Huffman coding procedures use Huffman tables, and the type of table is determined by the *entropy table specifications*, shown in Figure 4.3. Arithmetic coding methods use arithmetic coding conditioning tables, which may also be determined by the entropy table specification. There can be up to four different Huffman and Arithmetic coding tables for each DC and AC coefficient. No default values for Huffman tables are specified, so the applications may choose tables appropriate for their own environment. Default tables are defined for the arithmetic coding conditioning. The baseline sequential coding uses Huffman coding, while the extended DCT-based and lossless processes may use either Huffman or arithmetic coding (see Table 4.4, p. 62).

In arithmetic coding of AC coefficients, the length of zero-run is no longer limited to 15; it can go up to the end of the block (e.g. 62). Also, arithmetic coding may be made adaptive to increase the coding efficiency. Adaptive means that the probability estimates for each context are developed based on a prior coding decision for that context. The adaptive binary arithmetic coder may use a statistical model to improve encoding efficiency. The statistics model defines the contexts which are used to select the conditional probability estimates used in the encoding and decoding procedures.

4.2.3   Extended DCT-based process

The baseline encoder only supports basic coding tools, which are sufficient for most image compression applications. These include input image with 8-bit/pixel precision, Huffman coding of the runlength, and sequential transmission. If other modes, or any input image precision are required, and in particular if arithmetic coding is employed to achieve higher compression, then the term 'extended DCT-based process' is applied to the encoder. Table 4.4 summarises all the JPEG supported coding modes.

Figure 4.6 illustrates the reconstruction of a decoded image in a sequential mode (baseline or extended). As mentioned, as soon as a block of pixels is coded, its 64 coefficients are quantised, coded and transmitted. The receiver after decoding the coefficients, inverse quantisation and inverse transformation, sequentially adds them to the reconstructed image. Depending on the channel rate, it might take some time to reconstruct the whole image. In Figure 4.6, reconstructed images at 25%, 50%, 75% and 100% of image are shown.

In the progressive mode, the quantised coefficients are stored in the local buffer and transmitted later. There are two procedures by which the quantised coefficients in the buffer may be partially encoded within a scan. Firstly, for the highest image quality (lowest quantisation step size) only a specified *band* of coefficients from the zigzag scanned sequence need to be coded. This procedure is called *spectral selection*, since each band typically contains coefficients which occupy a lower or higher part of the frequency spectrum for the 8×8 block. Secondly, the coefficients within the current band need not be encoded to their full accuracy within each scan (coarser quantisation). On a coefficient's first encoding, a specified number of the most significant bits are encoded first. In subsequent scans, the less significant bits are then encoded. This procedure is called *successive approximation*. Either procedure may be used separately, or they may be mixed in flexible combinations.

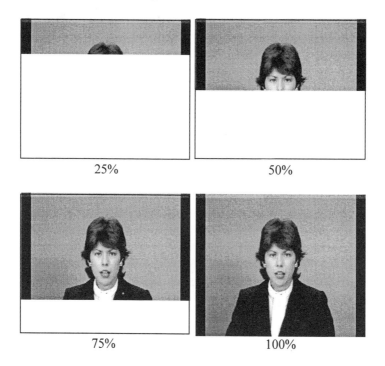

25% 50%

75% 100%

Figure 4.6 Reconstructed images in sequential mode

Figure 4.7 shows the reconstructed image quality with the first method. In this figure, the first image is reconstructed from the DC coefficient only, with its full-quantised precision. The second image is made up of DC (coefficient 0) plus the AC coefficients 1 and 8, according to the zigzag scan order. That is, after receiving the two new AC coefficients, a new image is reconstructed from these coefficients and the previously received DC coefficients. The third image is made up of coefficients 0, 1, 8, 16, 9, 2, 3, 10, 17 and 24. In the last image, all the significant coefficients (up to EOB) are included.

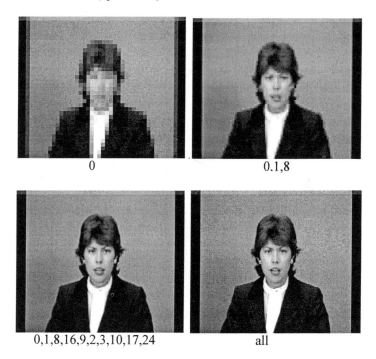

Figure 4.7 Image reconstruction in progressive mode

4.2.4　Hierarchical mode

In the hierarchical mode, an image is coded as a sequence of layers in a pyramid. Each lower size image provides prediction for the next upper layer. Except for the top level of the pyramid, for each luminance and colour component at the lower levels, the difference between the source components and the reference-reconstructed image is coded. The coding of the differences may be done using only DCT-based processes, only lossless processes, or DCT-based processes with a final lossless process for each component.

Downsampling and upsampling filters, similar to those of Figures 2.4 and 2.6 of chapter 2, may be used to provide a pyramid of spatial resolution, as shown in Figure 4.8. The hierarchical coder including the downsampling and upsampling filters is shown in Figure 4.9. In this figure, the image is low pass filtered and subsampled by 4:1, in both directions, to give a reduced image size 1/16. The baseline encoder then encodes the reduced image. The decoded image at the receiver may be interpolated by 1:4 to give the full-size image for display. At the encoder, another baseline encoder encodes the difference between the subsampled input image by 2:1 and the 1:2 upsampled decoded image. By repeating this process, the image is progressively coded, and at the decoder it is progressively built up. The bit rate at each level depends on the quantisation step size at that level. Finally, for lossless reversibility of the coded image, the difference between the input image and the latest decoded image is lossless entropy coded (no quantisation).

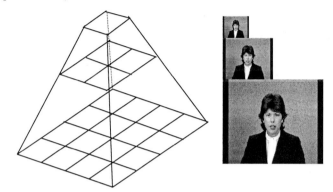

Figure 4.8 Hierarchical multiresolution encoding

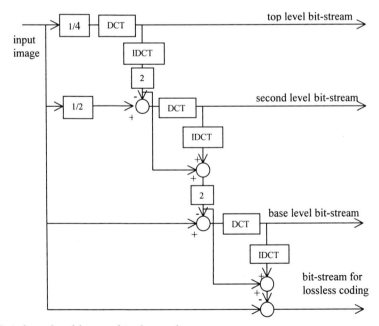

Figure 4.9 A three-level hierarchical encoder

As we see the hierarchical mode offers a progressive representation similar to the progressive DCT-based mode, but it is useful in environments which have multi-resolution requirements. The hierarchical mode also offers the capability of progressive transmission to a final lossless stage, as shown in Figure 4.9.

Table 4.4 Summary: Essential characteristics of coding process

Baseline process (required for all DCT-based decoders)
• DCT-based process
• Source image: 8-bit samples within each component
• Sequential
• Huffman coding: 2 AC and 2 DC tables
• Decoders shall process scans with 1, 2, 3 and 4 components
• Interleaved and non-interleaved scans

Extended DCT-based processes
• DCT-based process
• Source image: 8-bit or 12-bit samples
• Sequential or progressive
• Huffman or Arithmetic coding: 4 AC and 4 DC tables
• Decoder shall process scans with 1, 2, 3 and 4 components
• Interleaved and non-interleaved scans

Lossless process
• Predictive process (not DCT-based)
• Source image; N-bit samples ($2 \leq N \leq 16$)
• Sequential
• Huffman or Arithmetic coding: 4 tables
• Decoders shall process scans with 1, 2, 3 and 4 components
• Interleaved and non-interleaved scans

Hierarchical processes
• Multiple layers (non-differential and differential)
• Uses extended DCT-based or lossless processes
• Decoders shall process scans with 1, 2, 3 and 4 components
• Interleaved and non-interleaved scans

4.2.5   Extra features

In coding of colour pictures, encoding is called *non-interleaved* if all blocks of a colour component are coded before beginning to code the next component. Encoding is *interleaved* if the encoder compresses a block of 8×8 pixels from each component in turn, considering the image format. For example, with the 4:4:4 format, one block from each luminance and two chrominance components are coded. In the 4:2:0 format, the encoder codes four luminance blocks before coding one block from each of C_b and C_r.

The encoder is also flexible to allow different blocks within a single component to be compressed using different quantisation tables resulting in a variation in the reconstructed image quality, based on their perceived relative importance. This method of coding is called *Region-of-interest* coding. Also, the standard can allow different regions within a single image block to be compressed at different rates.

4.3   JPEG-2000

This standard is intended to advance standardised image coding systems to serve applications into the next millennium. It will provide a set of features vital to many high-end and emerging imaging applications by taking advantage of new modern technologies. Specifically, this new standard will address areas where current standards fail to produce the best quality or performance including the following JPEG [6]. It will also provide capabilities to markets that currently do not use compression. Features of the new standard include:

Low bit rate compression performance: Current standards, such as ISO 10918-1 (JPEG), offer excellent rate-distortion performance in mid and high bit rates. However, at low bit rates (e.g. below 0.25 bit per pixel for highly detailed grey-level images) the distortion, especially when judged subjectively, becomes unacceptable.

Lossless and lossy compression: There is no current standard that can provide superior lossless compression and lossy compression in a single code-stream.

Large images: Currently, the JPEG image compression algorithm does not allow for images larger then 64K by 64K pixels without tiling.

Single decompression architecture: The current JPEG standard has 44 modes, many of which are application specific and not used by the majority of the JPEG decoders. Greater interchange between applications can be achieved if a single common decompression architecture encompasses these features.

Transmission in noisy environments: The current JPEG standard has provision for restart intervals, but image quality suffers dramatically when bit errors are encountered.

Computer generated imagery: The current standard was optimized for natural imagery and does not perform well on computer generated imagery.

Compound documents: Currently, JPEG is seldom used in the compression of compound documents because of its poor performance when applied to bi-level (text) imagery.

4.3.1   Criteria for next generation compression

The JPEG-2000 aims to fill a gap in the rate-distortion spectrum (low bit rate) of current still image compression standards and provide a set of features vital to many high-end and emerging image applications. Superior low bit rate performance is the primary goal, and it is desirable to include as many of the other following features as possible.

Superior low bit rate performance: This standard should offer performance superior to the current standards at low bit rates (e.g. below 0.25 bit per pixel for highly detailed grey-scale images). This significantly improved low bit rate performance should be achieved *without sacrificing performance on the rest of the rate-distortion spectrum*. Examples of applications that need this feature include network image transmission and remote sensing. This is the highest priority feature.

Continuous-tone and bi-level compression: It is desired to have a standard coding system that is capable of compressing both continuous-tone and bi-level images [7]. If feasible, the standard should strive to achieve this with similar system resources. The system should compress and decompress images with various dynamic ranges (e.g. 1 bit to 16 bit) for each colour component. Examples of applications that can use this feature include compound documents with images and text, medical images with annotation overlays, graphic and computer generated images with binary and near to binary regions, alpha and transparency planes, and facsimile.

Lossless and lossy compression: It is desired to provide lossless compression naturally in the course of progressive decoding (i.e. difference image encoding, or any other technique, which allows for the lossless reconstruction to be valid). Examples of applications that can use this feature include medical images where loss is not always tolerable, image archival pictures where the highest quality is vital for preservation but not necessary for display, network systems that supply devices with different capabilities and resources, and prepress imagery.

Progressive transmission by pixel accuracy and resolution: Progressive transmission that allows images to be reconstructed with increasing pixel accuracy or spatial resolution is essential for many applications. This feature allows the reconstruction of images with different resolutions and pixel accuracy, as needed or desired, for different target devices. Examples of applications include the World Wide Web, image archival applications, printers, etc. The image architecture provides for the efficient delivery of image data in many applications such as client/server applications (World Wide Web).

Fixed-rate, fixed-size, limited workspace memory: Fixed-rate (fixed local rate) means that the number of bits for a given number of consecutive pixels equals (or is less than) a certain value. This allows the decoder to run in real time through channels with limited bandwidth. Examples are remote imaging, motion coding, etc. Fixed-size (fixed global rate) means that the total size of the code-stream for a complete image equals a certain value. This allows hardware with a limited memory space to hold the complete code-stream regardless of the image. Examples include scanners, printers, etc.

Random code-stream access and processing: Often there are parts of an image that are more important than others. This feature allows user defined *Regions-Of-Interest* (ROI) in the image to be randomly accessed and/or decompressed with less distortion than the rest of the image. Tiling of the image is a common and acceptable technical approach for this feature. Also, random code-stream processing could allow operations such as rotation, translation, filtering, feature extraction, scaling, etc.

Robustness to bit errors: It is desirable to consider robustness to bit errors while designing the code-stream. One application where this is important is wireless communication channels. Portions of the code-stream may be more important than others in determining decoded image quality. Proper design of the code-stream can aid subsequent error correction systems in alleviating catastrophic decoding failures. Usage of error confinement, error concealment, restart capabilities, or source-channel coding schemes can help minimize the effects of bit errors.

Open architecture: It is desirable to allow open architecture to optimise the system for different image types and applications. The development of a highly flexible coding tool or adoption of a syntactic description language, which should allow the dissemination and integration of new compression tools, may achieve this. Work being done in MPEG-4 on the development of a Syntactic Description Language (SDL) may be of use [8]. It is desired to allow the user to select tools appropriate to their application and provide for future growth. With this feature, the decoder is only required to implement the core tool set and a parser that understands the code-stream. If necessary, unknown tools are requested by the decoder and sent from the source.

Sequential build-up capability (real time coding): The standard should be capable of compressing and decompressing images with a single sequential pass. It should also be capable of processing an image using component interleaved order or non-interleaved order. During compression and decompression, the standard should use the context limited to a reasonable number of lines. However, there is no requirement of optimal compression performance during the sequential build-up operation.

Backward compatibility with JPEG: It is desirable to provide for backward compatibility (or easy transcoding) with the current JPEG standards.

Content-based description: Finding an image in a large database of images is an important problem in image processing. For example, a doctor might request only images from a set that are recognised to show a certain type of tumor. This could have major applicability to the medical, law enforcement and environmental communities, and for image archival applications. There is reason to believe that a content-based description of images might be available as a part of the compression system. Regardless of the techniques used, JPEG-2000 should strive to provide the opportunity for solutions to this problem. General methods for content based description are dealt with by MPEG-7 [9] (chapter 9).

Protective image security: Protection of a digital image can be achieved by means of methods such as: watermarking, labelling, stamping, fingerprinting, encryption, scrambling, etc. Watermarking and fingerprinting are invisible marks set inside the image content to pass a protection message to the user. Labelling is already implemented in some imaging formats such as SPIFF, and must be easy to transfer back and forth to the JPEG-2000 image file. Stamping is a mark set on top of a displayed image that can only be removed by a specific process. Encryption and scrambling can be applied on the whole image file or limited to part of it (header, directory, image data) to avoid unauthorised use of the image.

Interface with MPEG-4: The ongoing standardisation process in MPEG-4, is the development of a content based coding scheme in which coding tools are chosen from a repertoire so as to address in an optimal way a wide range of functionality [8]. It is desirable that the coding tool (or tools) developed for the compression of still images in JPEG-2000 are provided with an appropriate interfaces allowing the interchange and the integration of such tools into the framework of a syntax oriented coding scheme such as MPEG-4. In particular IPR information should be maintained in both insertion and extraction of still pictures to/from moving images.

Side channel spatial information (transparency): Side channel spatial information, such as alpha planes and transparency planes, are useful for transmitting information for processing the image for display, print, or editing, etc. An example of this is the transparency plane used in World Wide Web applications.

Object-based functionality:

Object-based composition: The current standard was designed to encode/decode rectangular framed images, which made it difficult to represent specific regions within the image. Multiple objects with arbitrary shape (or transparency) information will enable users to compose different still images with as much flexibility. This part will be discussed in more detail in chapter 9, MPEG-4.

Object-based information embedding: The side information (e.g. description of object) attached to each object will enable the new standard to provide a more efficient method of digital image indexing and retrieval.

It is hoped that by the year 2002 most if not all of the above targets can be fulfilled.

4.3.2   *Methods of compression*

Recognising the needs of the industry and the fact that not all algorithms are suited for all kinds of images, JPEG-2000 includes two types of image compression: a DCT-based coder and a wavelet-based coder. The DCT-based coder is the new baseline JPEG algorithm and is required for backward compatibility with the existing JPEG. The standard should also be able to directly decode the current JPEG compressed image or transcode it in a fast and efficient way. The wavelet mode permits coding of the still images with a high coding efficiency as well as spatial and SNR scalability at fine granularity [10]. Since scalability and wavelet coding have already been employed in the other coding methods, such as MPEG-2 and MPEG-4 respectively, they will be dealt with in a greater depth in these chapters.

References

[1]   ISO 10918-1 (JPEG), 'Digital compression and coding of continuous-tone still images', (1991).

[2]   Furht B. 'A survey of multimedia compression techniques and standards. Part I: JPEG standard', *Real-time Imaging*, pp. 1-49, (1995).

[3]   Wallace G.K. 'The JPEG still picture compression standard', *Communications of the ACM*, **34:4**, pp. 30-44, (1991).

[4]   Pennebaker W.B. and Mitchell J.L. 'JPEG: Still image compression standard', *Van Nostrand Reinhold*, New York, (1993).

[5]   The independent JPEG Group, 'The sixth public release of the Independent JPEG Group's free JPEG software', *C source code of JPEG Encoder release 6b,* (March 1998) [ftp://ftp.uu.net/graphics/jpeg/jpegsrc_v6b_tar.gz].

[6]   JPEG-2000: 'JPEG-2000 requirements and profiles version 4.0', ISO/IEC JTC1/SC29/WG1 N1105R, (December 1998).

[7]   Wang Q. and Ghanbari M. 'Graphics segmentation based coding of multimedia images', *Electronics Letters*, **31:6** , pp. 542-544, (1995).

[8]   MPEG-4: 'Draft of MPEG-4 Requirements', ISO/IEC JTC1/SC29/WG11 MPEG 96/0669, Munich, (January 1996).

[9]   MPEG-7: 'Context and objectives', ISO/IEC JTC1/SC29/WG11, N2460, (October 1998) Atlantic City, USA.

[10] MPEG-2: 'Generic coding of moving pictures and associated audio information: Video', ISO/IEC 13818-2: Draft international standard, (November 1994).

Chapter 5

Coding for video conferencing (H.261)

The H.261 standard defines the video coding and decoding methods for digital transmission over ISDN at rates of $p \times 64$ kbit/s, where p is in the range of 1–30 [1]. The video bit rates will lie between approximately 64 kbit/s and 1920 kbit/s. The recommendation is aimed at meeting projected customer demands for videophone, videoconferencing and other audio-visual services. It was ratified in December 1990.

The coding structure of H.261 is very similar to that of the generic codec of chapter 3 (Figure 3.16). That is, it is an interframe DCT-based coding technique. Interframe prediction is first carried out in the pixel domain. The prediction error is then transformed into the frequency domain, where the quantisation for bandwidth reduction takes place. Motion compensation can be included in the prediction stage, although it is optional. Thus the coding technique removes temporal redundancy by interframe prediction and spatial redundancy by transform coding. Techniques have been devised to make the codec more efficient, and at the same time suitable for telecommunications.

It should be noted that any recommendation only specifies what is expected for a decoder; it does not give information on how to design it. Even less information is given about the encoder. Therefore the design of the encoder and the decoder is at the discretion of the manufacturer, provided they comply with the syntax bit-stream. Since the aim of this book is the introduction to the fundamentals of video coding standards, rather than giving instructions on the details of a specific codec, we concentrate on the Reference Model codec. The reference model is a software-based codec, which is devised to be used in laboratories to study the core elements as a basis for the design of flexible hardware specifications.

During the development of H.261, from May 1988 to May 1989, the reference model underwent eight refinement cycles. The last version, known as *reference model eight* (RM8) [2], is in fact the basis of the current H.261. However, the two may not be exactly identical (though very similar), and the manufacturers may decide on a different approach for better optimisation of their codecs. Herein we interchangeably use RM8 for H.261. Before describing this codec, we will first look at the picture format, and spatio-temporal resolutions of the images to be coded with H.261.

5.1 Video format and structure

Figure 5.1 shows a block diagram of an H.261 based audio-visual system, where a *preprocessor* converts the CCIR-601 video (video at the output of a camera) to a new format. The coding parameters of the compressed video signal are multiplexed and then combined with the audio, data and end-to-end signalling for transmission. The transmission buffer controls the bit rate, either by changing the quantiser step size at the encoder, or in more severe cases by requesting reduction in frame rate, to be carried out at the preprocessor.

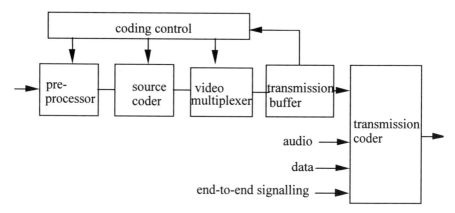

Figure 5.1 A block diagram of an H.261 audio-visual encoder

The H.261 standard also allows up to three pictures to be interpolated between transmitted pictures, so reducing the frame rate to 15, 10 and 7.5 respectively. The use of Quarter-CIF, or QCIF, resolution will reduce the sample rate even further to suit low bit rate channels.

In CIF and QCIF, DCT bocks are grouped into macroblocks of four luminance and two corresponding C_b and C_r chrominance blocks. The macroblocks are in turn grouped into layers termed *Groups of Blocks* (GOB). A CIF frame has 12 GOBs and QCIF has three, as illustrated in Figure 5.2.

The objectives of structuring an image into macroblocks and layers are as follows:

- similar inter/intra coding mode for luminance and chrominance blocks at the same area
- the use of one motion vector for both luminance and chrominance blocks

- efficient coding of the large number of 8×8 DCT blocks that will be expected to be without coded information in interframe coding. This is implemented via the inclusion of VLC codes for *coded block pattern* (CBP) and macroblock addressing [1]
- to allow synchronisation to be re-established when bits are corrupted by the insertion of start codes in the GOB headers. Note that since DCT coefficients are VLC coded, then any error during the transmission renders the remaining VLC coded data undecodable. Hence with a GOB structure, only a portion of the picture is degraded
- to carry side information appropriate for GOB, macroblock or higher layers. This includes picture format, temporal references, macroblock type, quantiser index, etc.

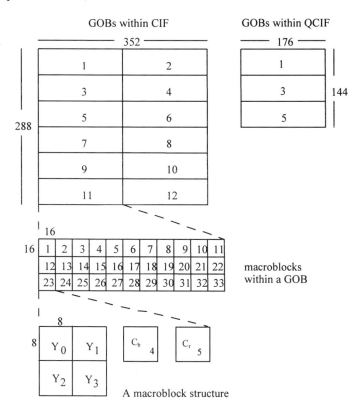

Figure 5.2 Block, macroblock and GOB structure of CIF and QCIF formatted pictures

5.2 Video source coding algorithm

The video coding algorithm is shown in Figure 5.3, which is similar to the generic interframe coder of Figure 3.16 in chapter 3. The main elements are the prediction including motion compensation, transform coding, quantisation, VLC and rate-control. The prediction error (inter-mode) or the input picture (intra-mode) is subdivided into 16×16 macroblock pixels, which may or may not be transmitted. Macroblocks that are to be transmitted are divided into 8×8 pixel blocks, which are transform coded (DCT), quantised and VLC coded for transmission. As we discussed in Section 5.1 of this chapter, the atomic coding unit in all standard video codecs is a macroblock. Hence in describing the codec, we will explain how each macroblock is coded.

In Figure 5.3, the function of each coding element and the messages carried by each flag are:

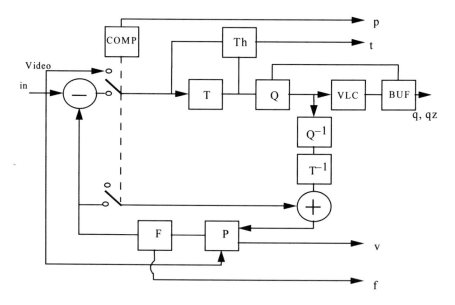

Figure 5.3 A block diagram of H.261 video encoder

COMP   A comprator for deciding inter/intra coding mode for a MB
Th   Threshold, to extend the quantisation range
T   Transform coding blocks of 8×8 pixels
T^{-1} Inverse transform
Q   Quantisation of DCT coefficients
Q^{-1} Inverse quantisation
P   Picture memory with motion compensated variable delay
F   Loop filter

p   Flag for inter/intra
t   Flag for transmitted or not
q   Quantisation index for transform coefficients
qz   Quantiser indication
v   Motion vector information
f   Switching on/off of the loop filter

Details of the functions of each block are described in the following sections.

5.2.1 Prediction

The prediction is inter-picture, which may include motion compensation, since motion compensation in H.261 is optional. The decoder accepts one motion vector per macroblock. Both horizontal and vertical components of these motion vectors have integer values not exceeding ± 15 pixels/frame. Motion estimation is only based on the luminance pixels and the vector is used for motion compensation of all four luminance blocks in the macroblock. Halving the component values of the macroblock motion vector and truncating them towards zero derives the motion vector for each of the two chrominance blocks. Motion vectors are restricted such that all pixels referenced by them are within the coded picture area.

For the transmission of motion vectors, their differences are variable length coded. The differential technique is based on one-dimensional prediction, that is the difference between the successive motion vectors in a row of GOBs. For the first macroblock in the GOB, the initial vector is set to zero.

5.2.2 MC/NO_MC decision

Not all the macroblocks in a picture are motion compensated. The decision whether a macroblock should be motion compensated or not depends on whether motion compensated prediction can substantially reduce the prediction error. Figure 5.4 shows the region (shaded) where motion compensation is preferred. In this figure the absolute values of frame difference, *fd*, and those of motion compensated frame difference, *mfd*, normalised to $16 \times 16 = 256$ pixels inside the macroblock are compared.

From the figure we see that if motion compensated error is slightly, but not significantly, less than the non-motion compensated error, we prefer to use non-motion compensation. This is because motion compensation entails a motion vector overhead (even if it might be zero); hence, if the difference between MC and NO-MC error cannot justify the extra bits, there is no advantage in using motion compensation.

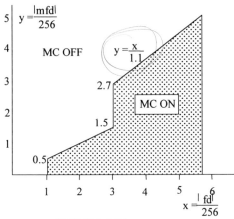

Figure 5.4 Characteristics of MC/NO-MC

5.2.3 Inter/intra decision

Sometimes it might be advantageous to intraframe code a macroblock, rather than interframe coding it. There are at least two reasons for intraframe coding:

1. Scene cuts or, in the event of violent motion, interframe prediction error may not be less than that of the intraframe. Hence intraframe pictures might be coded at lower bit rates.

2. Intraframe coded pictures have a better error resilience to channel errors. Note that, in interframe coding, at the decoder the received data are added to the previous frame to reconstruct the coded picture. In the event of channel error, the error propagates into the subsequent frames. If that part of the picture is not updated, the error can persist for a long time.

Similar to the MC/NO-MC decision, one can make a similar decision for coding a macroblock in inter or intra mode. In this case the variance of intraframe MB is compared with the variance of inter (motion compensated or not). The smallest is chosen. Figure 5.5 shows the characteristics of the function for inter/intra decision. Here for large variances no preference between the two modes is given, but for smaller variances, interframe is preferred. The reason is that, in intra mode, the DC coefficients of the blocks have to be quantised with a quantiser without a dead zone and with 8-bit resolutions. This increases the bit rate compared to that of the interframe mode, and hence interframe is preferred.

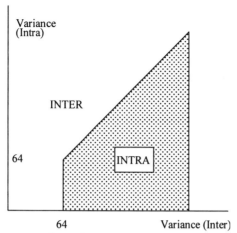

Figure 5.5 Characteristics of inter/intra

5.2.4 Forced updating

As mentioned, intraframe coded MB increases the resilience of H.261 codec to channel errors. In case in inter/intra macroblock decision, no intra mode is chosen, some of the macroblocks in a frame are forced to be intra coded. The specification recommends that a macroblock should be updated at least once every 132 frames. This means that for *common intermediate format* (CIF) pictures with 396 macroblocks per frame, on the average 3 MBs of every frame, are intraframe coded. This has an important impact on the quality of pictures due to errors. For example, in CIF pictures at 10 Hz, the effect of channel errors may corrupt up to 132 frames, and be visible for almost 13 s.

5.3 Other types of macroblocks

In H.261 there are as many as eight different types of macroblocks:

1. *Inter coded*: interframe coded macroblocks with no motion vector or with a zero motion vector.

2. *MC coded*: motion compensated MB, where the MC-error is significant and needs to be DCT coded.

3. *MC not coded*: these are motion compensated error MBs, where the motion compensated error is insignificant. Hence there is no need to be DCT coded.

4. *Intra*: intraframe coded macroblocks.

5. *Not-coded*: if all the six blocks in a macroblock, without motion compensation have an insignificant energy they are not coded. These MBs are sometimes called "Skipped", "Not-coded" or "Fixed" MBs. These types of MBs normally occur at the static parts of the image sequence. Fixed MBs are therefore not transmitted and at the decoder they are copied from the previous frame.

Since the quantiser step sizes are determined at the beginning of each GOB or row of GOBs, they have to be transmitted to the receiver. Hence the first MBs have to be identified. Therefore we can have some new macroblock types, which are:

6. *Inter coded + Q*

7. *MC coded + Q*

8. *Intra + Q*

To summarise the type of macroblock selection, we can draw a flow chart indicating how each one of the 396 MBs in a picture is coded. Decisions on the types of coding follow Figure 5.6 from left to right.

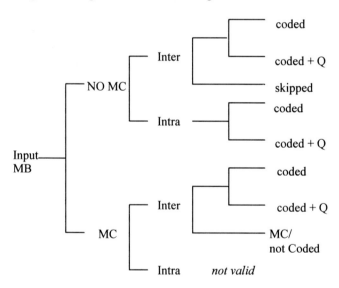

Figure 5.6 Decision tree for macroblock type

5.3.1 Addressing of macroblocks

If all the quantised components in one of the six blocks in a MB are zero, the *block* is declared as not coded. When all six blocks are not coded, the MB is declared *not coded* (fixed MB or skipped MB). In other cases the MBs are declared *coded*, and are variable length coded. The shortest code is assigned to inter code MB and the longest to intra+Q, as they are the most frequent and most rare MB types respectively.

Since a MB has six blocks, four luminance and two chrominance, then there will be $2^6 = 64$ different combinations of the coded/non-coded blocks. Except the one with all six blocks not coded (fixed MB), the remaining 63 are identified within 63 different patterns. The pattern information consists of a set of 63 *coded block patterns* (CBP) indicating coded/non-coded blocks within a macroblock. With a coding order of Y_0, Y_1, Y_2, Y_3, C_b and C_r, the block pattern information or pattern number is defined as

$$Pattern\_Number = 32Y_0 + 16Y_1 + 8Y_2 + 4Y_3 + 2C_b + C_r \qquad (5.1)$$

where in the equation the coded and non-coded blocks are assigned "1" and "0" respectively. Each pattern number is then VLC coded. It should be noted that if a macroblock is intra coded (or intra+Q), its pattern information is not transmitted. This is because, in intraframe coded MB, all blocks have significant energy and will be definitely coded. In other words, there will not be any non-coded blocks in an intra coded macroblock. Figure 5.7 illustrates two examples of the coded block pattern, where some of the luminance or chrominance blocks are not coded.

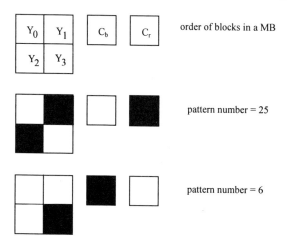

Figure 5.7 Examples of bit pattern for indicating the coded/not-coded blocks in a MB (black coded, white not coded)

Once the type of a macroblock is identified and it is VLC coded, its position inside the GOB should also be determined. Considering that H.261 is a videoconferencing codec, normally used for coding head-and-shoulders pictures, it is more likely that coded macroblocks are in the foreground of the picture. Hence they are normally clustered in regions. Therefore the overhead information for addressing of the positions of the coded MB is minimised if they are relatively addressed to each other. The relative addresses are represented by runlengths, which are the number of fixed MBs to the next coded MB. Figure 5.8 shows an example of addressing the coded MBs within a GOB. Numbers represent the relative addressing value of the number of fixed macroblocks preceding a non-fixed MB. The GOB start code indicates the beginning of the GOB. These relative addressing numbers are finally VLC coded.

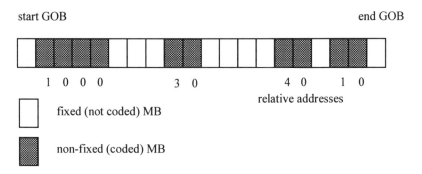

Figure 5.8 Relative addressing of coded MB

5.4 Quantisation and coding

Every one of the six blocks of a selected MB is transform coded with a two-dimensional DCT. The DCT coefficients of each block are then quantised and coded. In Section 3.2 of chapter 3 we described two types of quantisers. The one without a dead zone which is used for quantising the DC coefficient of intra-MB. For the H.261 standard, this quantiser uses a fixed step size of 8. The second type is with a dead zone for coding AC coefficients and the DC coefficient of interframe coded MB (MC or NO-MC).

For the latter case, a threshold, *th*, may be added to the quantiser scale, such that the dead zone is increased, causing more zero coefficients for efficient compression. Figure 5.9 shows this quantiser, where a threshold, *th*, is added to every step size. The value of the threshold is sent to the receiver as side information (see Figure 5.3). Ratios of the quantised coefficients to the quantiser step size, called *indices*, are to be coded.

5.4.1 Two-dimensional variable length coding

For transmission of the quantisation indices, a special order is defined which increases the efficiency of capturing the non-zero components. Starting from the

DC coefficient on the top-left corner of an 8×8 coefficient matrix, the values are scanned in a *zigzag* sequence as shown in Figure 5.10.

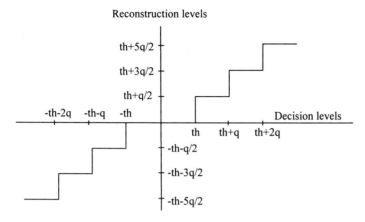

Figure 5.9 A uniform quantiser with threshold

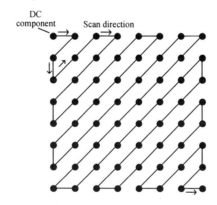

Figure 5.10. Zigzag scanning of 8×8 transform coefficients

The justification for this is that in natural images the main energy of the transform coefficients is concentrated in the lower frequencies (top left corner). Hence the coefficients which normally have the larger values are scanned first. Scanning of the indices terminates when the last non-zero coefficient has been reached.

To increase the coding efficiency a two-dimensional variable length code (2D-VLC) has been adopted. The 2D-VLC is performed in two stages. In the first stage, an *event* is produced for every non-zero index. The event is a combination of the index magnitude (*index*) and the number of zeros preceding that index (*run*).

To see how a two-dimensional index and run generation makes 2D-VLC coding very efficient, the following example is based on a coder having a quantiser step size of $q =16$ with equal threshold levels $th=q$. Let us assume a pixel block is DCT coded with coefficient values as shown partly in Figure 5.11.

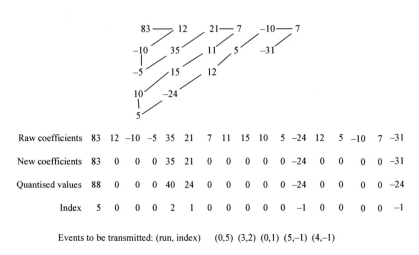

Raw coefficients	83	12	–10	–5	35	21	7	11	15	10	5	–24	12	5	–10	7	–31
New coefficients	83	0	0	0	35	21	0	0	0	0	0	–24	0	0	0	0	–31
Quantised values	88	0	0	0	40	24	0	0	0	0	0	–24	0	0	0	0	–24
Index	5	0	0	0	2	1	0	0	0	0	0	–1	0	0	0	0	–1

Events to be transmitted: (run, index)   (0,5) (3,2) (0,1) (5,–1) (4,–1)

Figure 5.11 Zigzag scanning and run-index generation

After zigzag scanning, coefficients are quantised. For a dead zone of $th = 16$, coefficient values less than this threshold are set to zero. Larger values are quantised according to the quantisation characteristics (see Figure 5.9). Here we see that rather than 1D-VLC coding of 17 individual coefficients we need to code only five two-dimensional events, which require substantially fewer bits.

In this 2D-VLC, since the range of index (possible values of indices) can vary from –127 to +127, and the range of run (number of zeros preceding an index) may vary from 0 to 63, then there will be $2 \times 128 \times 64 = 16384$ possible events. Design of a Huffman code for this large number of symbols is impractical. Some code-words might be as long as 200 bits! Here we use what might be called a modified Huffman code. In this code, all the symbols with small probabilities are grouped together and are identified with an *ESCAPE* symbol. The *ESCAPE* symbol has a probability equal to the sum of all it represents. Now the most commonly occurring events and the *ESCAPE* symbol are encoded with variable length codes (Huffman code) in the usual way. Events with low probabilities are identified with a fixed length *run* and *index*, appended to the *ESCAPE* code. The *EOB* code is also one of the symbols to be variable length coded.

In H.261, *ESCAPE* is 6 bits long (i.e. "000001"), thus rare events with 6 bits *run* (0-63) and 8 bits *index* (–127 to +127) require 20 bits [1]. The *EOB* code is represented with a 2-bit word. The DC/INTRA index is linearly quantised with a step size of 8 and no dead zone. The resulting value is coded with an 8-bit resolution.

Figure 5.12 shows an example of a 2D-VLC table for positive values of indices, derived from statistics of coding the "Claire" test image sequence.

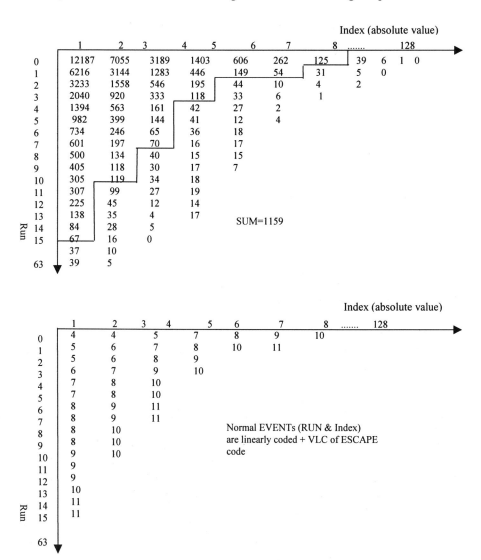

Figure 5.12 An example of run and index frequency and the resulting 2D-VLC table

As we see, most frequent events are registered at low *index* and low *run* values. The sum of the rare events, which represents the frequency of the *ESCAPE*, is even less than some frequent events. The corresponding 2D-VLC table is also shown next to the frequency table. Also in this example the *Sum* has the same frequency as the event (*run*=4, *index*=1). They are expected to have the same word length. Other *events* can be defined as *ESCAPE* + Normal *run* + Normal *index*, with:

ESCAPE code = 6 bits,
Normal *run* = 6 bits (1 out of 64 possible values)
Normal *index* = 8 bits (1 out of 128 values) plus the sign bit
Total bits for the modified Huffman coded *events* = 6+6+8=20.

5.5 Loop filter

At low bit rates the quantiser step size is normally large. Larger step sizes can force many DCT coefficients to zero. If only the DC and a few AC coefficients remain, then the reconstructed picture appears *blocky*. When the positions of blocky areas vary from one frame to another, it appears as a high frequency noise, commonly referred to *mosquito* noise. The blockiness degradations at the slant edges of the image appear as *staircase* noise. Figure 5.13 illustrates single shots of a CIF size "Claire" test image sequence and its coded version at 256 kbit/s. The sequence is in colour, with 352 pixels by 288 lines at 30 Hz, but only the luminance is shown. The colour components have a quarter resolution of luminance (176 pixels by 144 lines). As can be seen at this bit rate the coded image quality is very good with no visible distortions.

Original   256 kbit/s

Figure 5.13 Picture of "Claire", original and H.261coded at 256 kbit/s

At lower bit rates, artefacts begin to appear. This is shown in Figure 5.14, where there are more severe distortions at 64 kbit/s than at 128 kbit/s. When the sequence is displayed at its normal rate (30 Hz), the positions of the distortions move at different directions over the picture, and the appearance of *mosquito noise* is quite visible.

Coarse quantisation of the coefficients which results in the loss of high frequency components implies that compression can be modelled as a low pass filtering process [3, 4]. These artefacts are to some extent reduced by using the loop filter (see position of the *loop filter* in Figure 5.3). The low pass filter removes the high frequency and block boundary distortions. The same pictures with the use of a loop filter are shown in Figure 5.15.

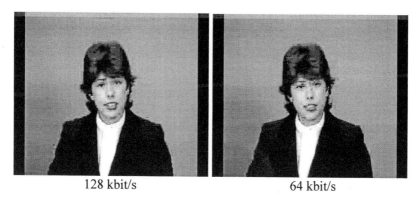

| 128 kbit/s | 64 kbit/s |

Figure 5.14 H.261 coded at 128 and 64 kbit/s

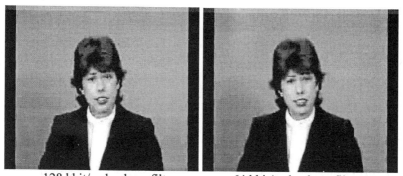

| 128 kbit/s plus loop filter | 64 kbit/s plus loop filter |

Figure 5.15 Coded pictures with loop filter "on"

Loop filtering is introduced after the motion compensator to improve the prediction. It should be noted that the loop filter has a picture blurring effect. It should be activated only for blocks with motion, otherwise non-moving parts of the pictures are repeatedly filtered in the following frames, blurring the picture. Since it is motion based, then loop filtering is thus carried out on a macroblock basis and it has an impulse response given by

$$h(x,y) = \frac{1}{16} \begin{bmatrix} 1 & 2 & 1 \\ 2 & 4 & 2 \\ 1 & 2 & 1 \end{bmatrix} \tag{5.2}$$

for pixels well inside the picture. For pixels at the image border, or corners, another function may be used. Figure 5.16 shows an example of the filter response in these areas.

9	3							
3	1							
			1	2	1			
			2	**4**	2			
			1	2	1			
			1	2	1			
			3	**6**	3			

Figure 5.16 Loop filter impulse response in various parts of the image

The loop filter is only defined for H.261 (no other video codecs use it) and is activated for all 6 DCT blocks of a macroblock. The filtering should be applied for coding rates less than 6 × 64 kbit/s = 386 kbit/s and switched off otherwise. At higher bit rates the filter does not improve the subjective quality of the picture [3]. MPEG-1 does not specify the requirement of a loop filter, because pictures coded with MPEG-1 are at much higher bit rates than 386 kbit/s.

5.6 Rate control

The bit rate resulting from the DCT-based coding algorithm fluctuates according to the nature of the video sequence. Variations in the speed of moving objects, their size and texture are the main cause for bit rate variation. The objective of a rate controller is to achieve a constant bit rate for transmission over a circuit switched network. A transmission buffer is usually needed to smooth out the bit rate fluctuations, which are inherent in the interframe coding scheme.

The usual method for bit rate control is to monitor the buffer occupancy and vary the quantiser step size according to the buffer fullness [3,5]. In Reference

Model 8 (RM8) the quantiser step size is calculated as a linear function of the buffer content and expressed by;

$$q = 2 \left\lfloor \frac{BufferContent}{200p} \right\rfloor + 2 \tag{5.3}$$

where p is the multiplier used in specifying the bit rates as in $p \times 64$ kbit/s, and $\lfloor . \rfloor$ stands for integer division with truncation towards zero.

The buffer control system usually has two additional operating states to prevent buffer underflow or buffer overflow from occurring. If the buffer content reaches the trigger point for overflow-state, current and subsequent coded data are not sent to allow the buffer to be emptied. Only trivial side information pertaining to the coded GOB or frame is transmitted.

On the other extreme, bit stuffing is invoked when buffer underflow is threatened. It is essential that buffer underflow is avoided so that the decoder can maintain synchronisation.

In practice, to allow maximum freedom of the H.261 standard codec structure, a *hypothetical reference decoder* (HRD) buffer is defined. All encoders are required to be compliant with this buffer. The hypothetical reference decoder is best explained with reference to Figure 5.17.

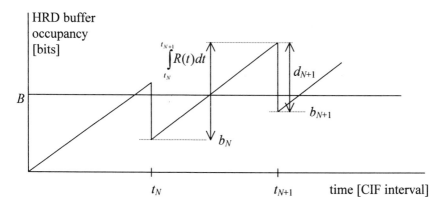

Figure 5.17 Hypothetical reference buffer occupancy

The hypothetical buffer is initially empty. It is examined at CIF intervals ($1/29.97 \cong 33$ ms), and if at least one complete coded picture is in the buffer, then all the data from the earliest picture are instantly removed (e.g. at t_N in Figure 5.17) [6]. Immediately after removing the above data, the buffer occupancy should be less than B, with $B = 4R_{max}/29.97$ and R_{max} being the maximum video bit rate to be used in the connection. To meet this requirement, the number of bits for $(N+1)$th coded picture, d_{N+1} must satisfy

$$d_{N+1} > b_N + \int_{t_N}^{t_{N+1}} R(t)dt - B \tag{5.4}$$

where b_N is the buffer occupancy just after time t_N, t_N is the time at which the Nth coded picture is removed from the hypothetical reference decoder buffer and $R(t)$ is the video bit rate at time t. Note that the time interval $(t_{N+1} - t_N)$ is an integer number of CIF picture periods (1/29.97, 2/29.97, 3/29.97, ...).

This specification constrains all encoders to restrict the picture start lead jitters to four CIF picture period's worth of channel bits. This prevents decoder buffer overflow at the decoder in a correctly designed H.261 codec. Jitters in the opposite direction (phase lag) are not constrained by the H.261 recommendation. Phase lag corresponds to buffer underflow at the decoder, which is simply dealt with by making the decoder wait for sufficient bits to have arrived to continue decoding.

A major deficiency with the RM8/H.261 model rate controls is that bits might be unfairly distributed across the image. For example, in the active parts of the picture sequences, such as in the middle of the head-and-shoulders pictures, the buffer tends to fill up very quickly, and hence the quantiser step size rises rapidly. This causes the rest of the picture to be coded coarsely. One of the key issues in H.261, as well as any video codec, is the way the quantiser step size or the rate control is managed. In the past decade numerous manufacturers have produced H.261 codecs, but they may not perform equally. Because of the need for interoperability, the general structure of H.261 must be based on coding elements as shown in Figure 5.3. Therefore the only part which makes one codec better than the others is the rate control mechanism. This part is kept secret by the manufacturers and is subject to further research.

References

[1]   H.261: 'Recommendation H.261, video codec for audiovisual services at p×64 kbit/s', Geneva, (1990).

[2]   CCITT SG XV WP/1/Q4, 'Specialist group on coding for visual telephony', Description of reference Model 8 (RM8), (1989).

[3]   Plompen R.H.J.M. 'Motion video coding for visual telephony', Proefschrift, (1989).

[4]   Ngan K.N. 'Two-dimensional transform domain decimation technique', *IEEE Int. Conf. Acoust. Speech and Signal Processing, ICASP'96*, pp. 1001-1004, (April 1986).

[5]   Chen C.T. and Wong A. 'A self-governing rate buffer control strategy for pseudoconsant bit rate video coding', *IEEE Trans. On Commun.*, **2:1**, (January 1993).

[6]   Carr M.D., 'Video codec hardware to realise a new world standard', *British Telecom. Journal*, **8:3**, pp. 28-35, (June 1990).

Chapter 6

Coding of moving pictures for digital storage media
(MPEG-1)

MPEG-1 is the first generation of video codecs proposed by the Motion Picture Experts Group as a standard to provide video coding for digital storage media (DSM), such as CD, DAT, Winchester discs and optical drives [1]. This development was in response to industry needs for an efficient way of storing visual information on storage media other than the conventional analogue video cassette recorders (VCR). At the time CD-ROMs had the capability to deliver data at approximately 1.2 Mbit/s, and the MPEG standard aimed to conform roughly with this target. Although in most applications the MPEG-1 video bit rate is in the range of 1 to 1.5 Mbit/s, the international standard does not limit the bit rate, and higher bit rates might be used for other applications.

It was also envisaged that the stored data be within both 625 and 525 line television systems and to provide flexibility for use with workstations and personal computers. For this reason, the MPEG-1 standard is based on progressively scanned images and does not recognise interlacing. Interlaced sources have to be converted to a non-interlaced format before coding. After decoding, the decoded image may be converted back to provide an interlaced format for display.

Since coding for digital storage can be regarded as a competitor to VCRs, then MPEG-1 video quality at the rate of 1 to 1.5 Mbit/s is expected to be comparable to VCRs. Also, it should provide the viewing conditions associated with VCRs such as forward play, freeze picture, fast forward, fast reverse, slow forward and random access. The ability of the decoder to provide these modes depends to some extent on the nature of digital storage media. However, it should be borne in mind that efficient coding and flexibility in operation are not compatible. Provision of the added functionality of random access necessitates regular intraframe pictures in the coded sequence. Those frames that do not exploit temporal redundancy in the video have poor compression, and as a result the overall bit rate is increased.

Both H.261 [2] and MPEG-1 [1] are standards defined for relatively low bit rate coding of low spatial resolution pictures. Like H.261, MPEG-1 utilises DCT for lossy coding of its intraframe and interframe prediction errors. The MPEG-1 video coding algorithm is largely an extension of H.261, and many of the features are common. Their bit-streams are, however, incompatible, although their encoding units are very similar.

The MPEG-1 standard, like H.261, does not specify the design of the decoder, and even less information is given about the encoder. What is expected from MPEG-1, like H.261, is to produce a bit-stream that is decodable. Manufacturers are free to choose any algorithms they wish, and to optimise them for better efficiency and functionality. Therefore in this chapter we again look at the fundamentals of MPEG-1 coding, rather than details of the implementation.

6.1   Systems coding outline

The MPEG-1 standard gives the syntax description of how audio, video and data are combined into a single data stream. This sequence is formally termed as the ISO 11172 stream [3]. The structure of this ISO 11172 stream is illustrated in Figure 6.1. It consists of a compression layer and a systems layer. In this book we study only the video part of the compression layer, but the systems layer is important for the proper delivery of the coded bit-stream to the video decoder, and hence we briefly describe it.

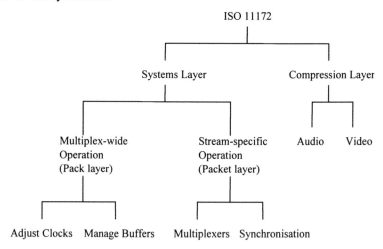

Figure 6.1 Structure of an ISO 11172 stream

The MPEG-1 systems standard defines a packet structure for multiplexing coded audio and video into one stream and keeping it synchronised. The systems layer is organised into two sublayers known as the *pack* and *packet* layers. A pack consists of a pack header that gives the *systems clock reference* (SCR) and the bit rate of the multiplexed stream followed by one or more packets. Each packet has its own header that conveys essential information about the elementary data that it carries. The aim of the systems layer is to support the combination of video and audio elementary streams. The basic functions are as follows:

- synchronised presentation of decoded streams
- construction of the multiplexed stream
- initialisation of buffering for playback start-up
- continuous buffer management
- time identification.

In the systems layer, elements of direct interest to the video encoding and decoding processes are mainly those of the stream-specific operations, namely multiplexing and synchronisation.

6.1.1 Multiplexing elementary streams

The multiplexing of elementary audio, video and data is performed at the packet level. Each packet thus contains only one elementary data type. The systems layer syntax allows up to 32 audio, 16 video and two data streams to be multiplexed together. If more than two data streams are needed, substreams may be defined.

6.1.2 Synchronisation

Multiple elementary streams are synchronised by means of *Presentation Time Stamps* (PTS) in the ISO 11172 bit-stream. End-to-end synchronisation is achieved when the encoders record time-stamps during capture of raw data. The receivers will then make use of these PTS in each associated decoded stream to schedule their presentations. Playback synchronisation is pegged onto a master time base, which may be extracted from one of the elementary streams, the *Digital Storage Media* (DSM), channel or some external source. This prototypical synchronisation arrangement is illustrated in Figure 6.2. The occurrences of PTS and other information such as *Systems Clock Reference* (SCR) and systems headers will also be essential for facilitating random access of the MPEG-1 bit-stream. This set of access codes should therefore be located near to the part of the elementary stream where decoding can begin. In the case of video, this site will be near the head of an intraframe.

To ensure guaranteed decoder buffer behaviour, MPEG-1 systems layer employs a *Systems Target Decoder* (STD) and *Decoding Time Stamp* (DTS). The DTS differs from PTS only in the case of video pictures that require additional reordering delay during the decoding process.

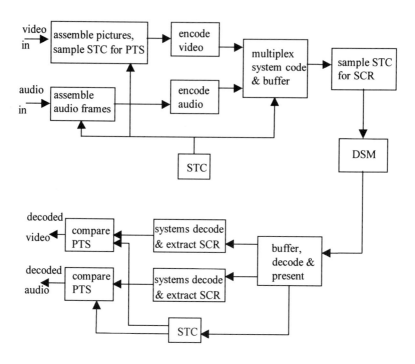

Figure 6.2 MPEG-1's prototypical encoder and decoder illustrating end-to-end synchronisation (STC: Systems Time Clock, SCR: Systems Clock Reference, PTS: Presentation Time Stamp, DSM: Digital Storage Media)

6.2 Preprocessing

The source material for video coding may exist in a variety of forms such as computer files or live video in CCIR-601 format [4]. If CCIR-601 is the source, since MPEG-1 is for coding of video at VCR resolutions, then SIF format is normally used. These source pictures must be processed prior to coding. In chapter 2 we explained how CCIR-601 video was converted to SIF format. If the source is film, we also discussed the conversion methodology in that chapter. However, if computer source files do not have the SIF format, they have to be converted too. In MPEG-1, another preprocessing is required to reorder the input pictures for coding. This is called *picture re-ordering.*

6.2.1 Picture re-ordering

Because of the conflicting requirements of random access and highly efficient coding, the MPEG suggested that not all pictures of a video sequence should be coded in the same way. They identified four types of picture in a video sequence. The first type is called *I-pictures*, which are coded without reference to the previous picture. They provide access points to the coded sequence for decoding. These pictures are intraframe coded as for JPEG, with a moderate compression. The second type is the *P-pictures*, which are *predictively* coded with reference to the previous I- or P-coded pictures. They themselves are used as a reference (anchor) for coding of the future pictures. Coding of these pictures is very similar to H.261. The third type is called *B-pictures*, or *bidirectionally* coded pictures, which may use past, future or combinations of both pictures in their predictions. This increases the motion compensation efficiency, since occlusion parts of moving objects may be better compensated from the future frame. B-pictures are never used for predictions. This part, which is unique to MPEG, has two important implications:

(i)   If B-pictures are not used for predictions of future frames, then they can be coded with the highest possible compression without any side-effects. This is because, if one picture is coarsely coded and is used as a prediction, the coding distortions are transferred to the next frame. This frame then needs more bits to clear the previous distortions, and the overall bit rate may increase rather than decrease.

(ii)   In applications such as transmission of video over packet networks, B-pictures may be discarded (e.g. due to buffer overflow) without affecting the next decoded pictures [5]. Note that if any part of the H.261 pictures, or I- and P-pictures in MPEG, are corrupted during the transmission, the effect will propagate until they are refreshed [6].

Figure 6.3 illustrates the relationship between these three types of picture. Since B-pictures use I- and P-pictures as predictions, then they have to be coded later. This requires re-ordering the incoming picture order, which is carried out at the preprocessor.

The fourth picture type is the *D-pictures*. They are intraframe coded, where only the DC coefficients are retained. Hence the picture quality is poor and normally used for applications like fast forward. D-pictures are not part of the GOP, hence they are not present in a sequence containing any other picture types.

6.3 Video structure

6.3.1   Group of pictures (GOP)

Since in the H.261 standard, successive frames are similarly coded, a picture is the top level of the coding hierarchy. In MPEG-1 due to the existence of several picture types, a *Group of Pictures*, called GOP, is the highest level of the hierarchy. A GOP is a series of one or more pictures to assist random access into the picture sequence. The first coded picture in the group is an I-picture. It is followed by an arrangement for P- and B-pictures, as shown in Figure 6.3.

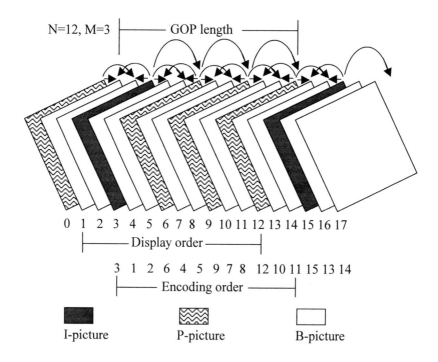

Figure 6.3 An example of MPEG-1 GOP

The GOP length is normally defined as the distance between I-pictures, which is represented by parameter N in the standard codecs. The distance between the anchor I/P to P pictures is represented by M. In the above figure $N=12$ and $M=3$. The group of pictures may be of any length, but it should be at least one I-picture in each GOP. Applications requiring random access, fast forward play or fast and normal reverse play may use short GOPs. GOP may also start at scene cuts or other cases where motion compensation is not effective. The number of consecutive B-pictures is variable. Neither a P- nor a B-picture needs to be present. For most applications, GOP in the SIF-625/50 format has $N=12$ and $M=3$. In SIF-525/60, the values are 15 and 3 respectively.

The encoding or transmission order of pictures differs from the display or incoming picture order. In the figure B-pictures 1 and 2 are encoded after P-picture 0 and I-picture 3 are encoded. Also in this figure B-pictures 13 and 14 are a part of the next GOP. While their display order is 0,1,2,...,11, their encoding order is 3,1,2,6,4,5.... This re-ordering introduces delays amounting to several frames at the encoder (equal to the number of B-pictures between the anchor I- and P-pictures). The same amount of delay is introduced at the decoder, in putting the transmission/decoding sequence back to its original. This format inevitably limits the application of MPEG-1 for telecommunications.

6.3.2 Picture

All the three main picture types, I-, P- and B-, have the same SIF size with 4:2:0 format. In SIF-625 the luminance part of each picture has 360 pixels, 288 lines and 25 Hz, and those of each chrominance are 180 pixels, 144 lines and 25 Hz. In SIF-525, these values for luminance are 360 pixels, 240 lines and 30 Hz, and for the chrominance are 180, 120 and 30 respectively. For 4:2:0 format images, the luminance and chrominance samples are positioned as shown in Figure 2.3 of chapter 2.

6.3.3 Slice

Each picture is divided into a group of macroblocks, called *slices*. In H.261 such a group was called GOB. The reason for defining a slice is the same as that for defining a GOB, namely resetting the variable length code to prevent channel error propagation into the picture. Slices can have different sizes within a picture, and the division in one picture need not be the same as division in any other picture.

The slices can begin and end at any macroblock in a picture, but with some constraints. The first slice must begin at the top left of the picture (the first macroblock) and the end of the last slice must be the bottom right macroblock (the last macroblock) of the picture, as shown in Figure 6.4. Therefore the minimum number of slices per picture is one, and the maximum number is equal to the number of macroblocks (e.g. 396 in SIF-625).

Each slice starts with a *slice start code*, and is followed by a code that defines its position and a code that sets the quantisation step size. Note that in H.261 the quantisation step sizes were set at each GOB or row of GOBs, but in MPEG-1 they can be set at any macroblock (see below). Therefore, in MPEG-1 the main reason for defining slices is not to reset a new quantiser, but to prevent the effects of channel error propagation. If the coded data are corrupted, and the decoder detects it, then it can search for the new slice, and the decoding starts from that point. Part of the picture slice from the start of the error to the next slice can then be degraded. Therefore in a noisy environment it is desirable to have as many slices as possible. On the other hand each slice has a large overhead, called slice-start-code (minimum of 32 bits). This creates a large overhead in the total bit rate. For example, if we use the slice structure of Figure 6.4, where there is one slice for each row of MBs, then for SIF-625 video there are 18 slices per picture, and with 25 Hz video, the slice overhead can be $32 \times 18 \times 25 = 14400$ bit/s.

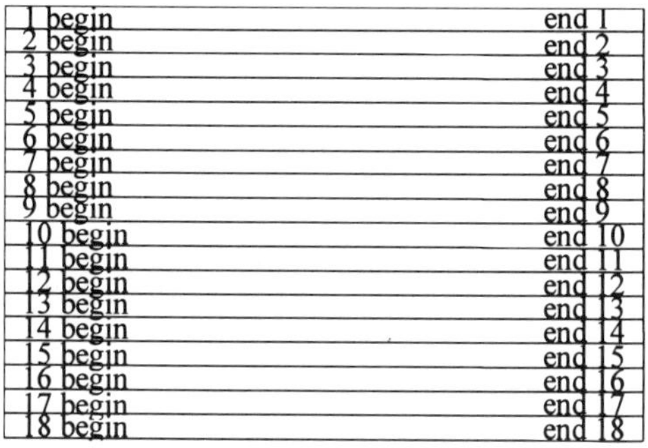

Figure 6.4 An example of slice structure for SIF-625 pictures

To optimise the slice structure, that is, to give a good immunity from channel errors and at the same time to minimise the slice overhead, one might use short slices for macroblocks with significant energy (such as Intra-MB), and long slices for less significant ones (e.g. macroblocks in B-pictures). Figure 6.5 shows a slice structure, where in some parts the slice length extends beyond several rows of macroblocks, and in some cases is less than one row.

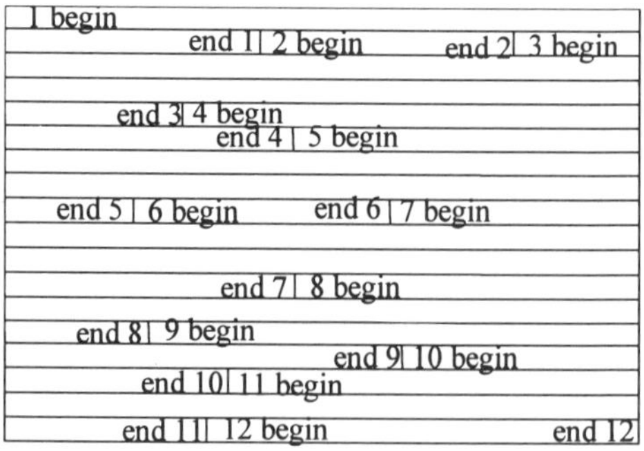

Figure 6.5 Possible arrangement of slices in SIF-625

6.3.4 Macroblock

Slices are divided into *macroblocks* of 16×16 pixels, similar to the division of GOB into macroblocks in H.261. Macroblocks in turn are divided into *blocks*, for coding. In chapter 5, we gave a detailed description of how a macroblock was coded, starting from its type, mode of selection, blocks within the MB, their positional addresses and finally the block-pattern. Since MPEG-1 is also a macroblock based codec, most of these rules are used in MPEG-1. However, due to differences of slice versus GOB, picture type versus a single picture format in H.261, there are bound to be variations in the coding. We first give a general account of these differences, and in the following section, more details are given about the macroblocks in the various picture types.

The first difference is that since a slice has a raster scan structure, macroblocks are addressed in a raster scan order. The top left macroblock in a picture has address 0, the next one on the right has address 1 and so on. If there are M macroblocks in a picture (e.g. $M = 396$), then bottom right macroblock has address $M-1$. To reduce the address overhead, macroblocks are relatively addressed by transmitting the difference between the current macroblock and the previously coded macroblock. This difference is called *macroblock address increment*. In I-pictures, since all the macroblocks are coded, the macroblock address increment is always 1. The exception is that, for the first coded macroblock at the beginning of each slice, the macroblock address is set to that of the right hand macroblock of the previous row. This address at the beginning of each picture is set to -1. If a slice does not start at the left edge of the picture (see the slice structure of Figure 6.5), then the macroblock address increment for the first macroblock in the slice will be larger than one. For example, in the slice structure of Figures 6.4 and 6.5 there are 22 macroblocks per row. For Figure 6.4, at the start of slice 2, the macroblock address is set to 21, which is the address of the macroblock at the right hand edge of the top row of macroblocks. In Figure 6.5, if the first slice contains 30 macroblocks, eight of them would be in the second row, so the address of the first macroblock in the second slice would be 30 and the macroblock increment would be 9. For further reduction of address overhead, macroblock address increments are VLC coded.

There is no code to indicate a macroblock address increment of zero. This is why the macroblock address is set to -1 rather than zero at the top of the picture. The first macroblock will have an increment of one, making its address equal to zero.

6.3.5 Block

Finally, the smallest part of the picture structure is the *block* of 8×8 pixels, for both luminance and chrominance components. DCT coding is applied at this block level. Figure 6.6 illustrates the whole structure of partitioning a video sequence from its GOP level at the top, to the smallest unit of block at the bottom.

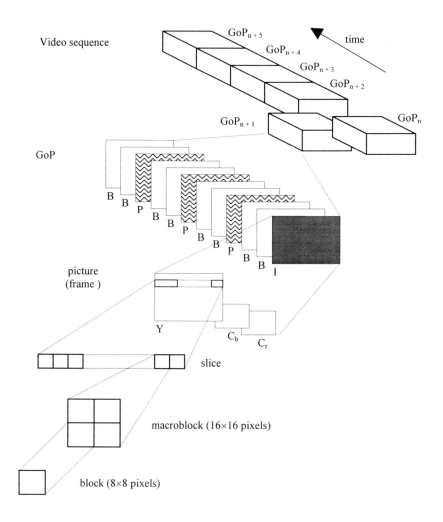

Figure 6.6 MPEG-1 coded video structure

6.4   Encoder

As mentioned, the international standard does not specify the design of the video encoders and decoders. It only specifies the syntax and semantics of the bit-stream and signal processing at the encoder/decoder interface. Therefore, options are left open to the video codec manufacturers to trade-off cost, speed, picture quality and coding efficiency. As a guideline, Figure 6.7 shows a block diagram of an MPEG-1 encoder. Again it is similar to the generic codec of chapter 3 and the H.261 codec of chapter 5. For simplicity the coding flags shown in the H.261 codec are omitted, though they also exist.

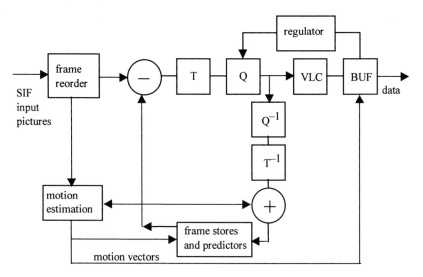

Figure 6.7 A simplified MPEG-1 video encoder

The main differences between this encoder and that defined in H.261 are:

- *Frame re-ordering*: at the input of the encoder coding of B-pictures is postponed to be carried out after coding the anchor I- and P-pictures.
- *Quantisation*: intraframe coded macroblocks are subjectively weighted to emulate perceived coding distortions.
- *Motion estimation*: not only is the search range extended but the search precision is increased to half a pixel. B-pictures use bidirectional motion compensation.
- *No loop filter.*
- *Frame store and predictors*: to hold two anchor pictures for prediction of B-pictures.
- *Rate regulator*: since here there is more than one type of picture, each generating different bit rates.

Before describing how each picture type is coded, and the main differences between this codec and H.261, we can describe the codec on a macroblock basis, as the basic unit of coding. Within each picture, macroblocks are coded in a sequence from left to right. Since 4:2:0 image format is used, then the six blocks of 8×8 pixels, four luminance and one of each chrominance components are coded in turn. Note that the picture area covered by the four luminance blocks is the same as the area covered by each of the chrominance blocks.

First, for a given macroblock, the coding mode is chosen. This depends on the picture type, the effectiveness of motion compensated prediction in that local region and the nature of the signal within the block. Secondly, depending on the coding mode, a motion compensated prediction of the contents of the block based on the past and/or future reference pictures is formed. This prediction is subtracted from the actual data in the current macroblock to form an error signal. Thirdly, this error signal is divided into 8×8 blocks and a DCT is performed on each block. The resulting two-dimensional 8×8 block of DCT coefficients is quantised and is scanned in *zigzag* order to convert into a one-dimensional string of quantised DCT coefficients. Fourthly, the side information for the macroblock, including the type, block-pattern, motion vector and address alongside the DCT coefficients are coded. For maximum efficiency, all the data are variable length coded. The DCT coefficients are run-length coded with the generation of events, as we discussed in H.261.

A consequence of using different picture types and variable length coding is that the overall bit rate is very variable. In applications that involve a fixed rate channel, a FIFO buffer is used to match the encoder output to the channel. The status of this buffer may be monitored to control the number of bits generated by the encoder. Controlling the quantiser index is the most direct way of controlling the bit rate. The international standard specifies an abstract model of the buffering system (the *Video Buffering Verifier*) in order to limit the maximum variability in the number of bits that are used for a given picture. This ensures that a bit-stream can be decoded with a buffer of known size (see Section 6.8).

6.5   Quantisation weighting matrix

The insensitivity of the human visual system to high frequency distortions can be exploited for further bandwidth compression. In this case the higher orders of DCT coefficients are quantised with coarser quantisation step sizes than the lower frequency ones. Experience has shown that for SIF pictures, a suitable distortion weighting matrix for the Intra DCT coefficients is the one shown in Figure 6.8. This Intra matrix is used as the default quantisation matrix for Intraframe coded macroblocks.

If the picture resolution departs significantly from the SIF size, then some other matrix may give perceptively better results. The reason is that this matrix is derived from the vision contrast sensitivity curve, for a nominal viewing distance (e.g. viewing distances of 4–6 times the picture height) [7]. For higher or lower picture resolutions, or changing the viewing distance, the spatial frequency will then change, and hence different weighting will be derived.

It should be noted that different weightings may not be used for interframe coded macroblocks. This is because high frequency interframe error does not necessarily mean high spatial frequency. It might be due to poor motion compensation or block boundary artefacts. Hence interframe coded macroblocks use a flat quantisation matrix. This matrix is called the Inter or non-Intra quantisation weighting matrix.

8	16	19	22	26	27	29	34		16	16	16	16	16	16	16	16
16	16	22	24	27	29	34	37		16	16	16	16	16	16	16	16
19	22	26	27	29	34	34	38		16	16	16	16	16	16	16	16
22	22	26	27	29	34	37	40		16	16	16	16	16	16	16	16
22	26	27	29	32	35	40	48		16	16	16	16	16	16	16	16
26	27	29	32	35	40	48	58		16	16	16	16	16	16	16	16
26	27	29	34	38	46	56	69		16	16	16	16	16	16	16	16
27	29	35	38	46	56	69	83		16	16	16	16	16	16	16	16

INTRA   INTER

Figure 6.8 Default Intra and Inter quantisation weighting matrices

Note that, since in H.261 all the pictures are interframe coded and a very few macroblocks might be intra coded, then only the non-intra weighting matrix is defined. Little work has been performed to determine the optimum non-intra matrix for MPEG-1, but evidence suggests that the coding performance is more related to the motion and the texture of the scene than the non-intra quantisation matrix. If there is any optimum matrix, it should then be somewhere between the flat default Inter matrix and the strongly frequency-dependent values of the default Intra matrix.

The DCT coefficients, prior to quantisation, are divided by the weighting matrix. Note that the DCT coefficients prior to weighting have a dynamic range from -2047 to $+2047$. Weighted coefficients are then quantised by the quantisation step size. At the decoder, reconstructed quantised coefficients are then multiplied to the weighting matrix to reconstruct the coefficients.

6.6   Motion estimation

In chapter 3, block matching motion estimation/compensation and its application in standard codecs was discussed in great detail. We even introduced some fast search methods for estimation, which can be used in software based codecs. As we saw, motion estimation in H.261 was optional. This was mainly due to the assumption that, since motion estimation can reduce correlation, then DCT coding may not be efficient. Investigations since the publication of H.261 have proved that this is not the case. What is expected from a DCT is to remove the spatial correlation within a small area of 8×8 pixels. Measurement of correlations between the adjacent error pixels have shown that there is still strong correlation between the error pixels, which does not impair the potential of DCT for spatial redundancy reduction. Hence motion estimation has become an important integral part of all the later video codecs, such as MPEG-1, MPEG-2, H.263 and MPEG-4. These will be explained in the relevant chapters.

Considering MPEG-1, the strategy for motion estimation in this codec is different from the H.261 in four main respects:

- motion estimation is an integral part of the codec
- motion search range is much larger
- higher precision of motion compensation is used
- B-pictures can benefit from bi-directional motion compensation.

These features are described in the following sections.

6.6.1   Larger search range

In H.261, if motion compensation is used, a search is carried out within every subsequent frame. Also H.261 is normally used for head-and-shoulders pictures, where the motion speed is normally very small. In contrast, MPEG-1 is used mainly for coding of films with much larger movements and activities. Moreover, in search for motion in P-pictures, since they might be several frames apart, the search range becomes many times larger. For example, in a GOP structure with $M{=}3$, where there are two B-pictures between the anchor pictures, the motion speed is three times greater than that for consecutive pictures. Thus in MPEG-1 we expect a much larger search range. Considering that in full search block matching the number of search positions for a motion speed of w is $(2w+1)^2$, then tripling the search range makes motion estimation prohibitively computationally expensive.

In chapter 3 we introduced some fast search methods such as logarithmic step searches and hierarchical motion estimation. Although the hierarchical method can be used here, of course needing one or more levels of hierarchy, use of a logarithmic search may not be feasible. This is because these methods are very prone to large search ranges, and at these ranges the final minima can be very far away from the local minima, so causing the estimation to fail [8].

One way of alleviating this problem is to use a *telescopic* search method. This is unique to MPEG with B-pictures. In this method, rather than searching for the motion between the anchor pictures, the search is carried out on all the consecutive pictures, including B-pictures. The final search between the anchor pictures is then the sum of all the intermediate motion vectors, as shown in Figure 6.9. Note that since we are now searching for motion in successive pictures, the search range is smaller, and even fast search methods can be used.

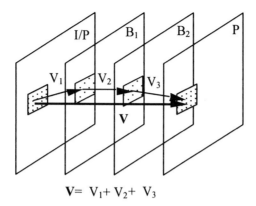

$$V= V_1+ V_2+ V_3$$

Figure 6.9 Telescopic motion search

6.6.2   *Motion estimation with half pixel precision*

In the search process with a half pixel resolution, normal block matching with integer pixel positions is carried out first. Then eight new positions, with a distance of half a pixel around the final integer pixel, are tested. Figure 6.10 shows a part of the search area, where the co-ordinate marked *A* has been found as the best integer pixel position at the first stage.

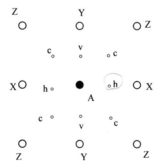

Figure 6.10. Sub-pixel search positions, around pixel co-ordinate A

In testing the eight sub-pixel positions, pixels in the frame previous macroblocks are interpolated, according to the positions to be searched. For sub-pixel positions, marked with *h* in the middle of the horizontal pixels, the interpolation is

$$h = \frac{A + X}{2}$$, where the division is truncated.   (6.1)

pixels in the vertical mid-points, the interpolated values for the pixels

$$v = \frac{A + Y}{2} \tag{6.2}$$

and for sub-pixels in the corner (centre of four pixels), the interpolation is

$$c = \frac{A + X + Y + Z}{4} \tag{6.3}$$

Note that in sub-pixel precision motion estimation, the range of the motion vectors' addresses is increased by 1 bit for each of the horizontal and vertical directions. Thus the motion vector overhead may be increased by 2 bits per vector (in practice due to variable length coding, this might be less than 2 bits.) Despite this increase in motion vector overhead, the efficiency of motion compensation outweighs the extra bits, and the overall bit rate is reduced. Figure 6.11 shows the motion compensated error, with and without half pixel precision, for two consecutive frames of the "Claire" sequence. The motion compensated error has been magnified by a factor of four for better representation. It might be seen that half pixel precision has fewer blocking artefacts and, in general, motion compensated errors are smaller.

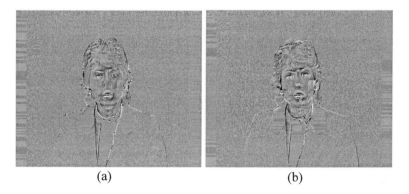

(a)   (b)

Figure 6.11 Motion compensated prediction error, (a) with and (b) without half pixel precision

For further reduction on the motion vector overhead, differential coding is used. The prediction vector at the start of each slice and each Intra coded macroblock is set to zero. Note that the predictively coded macroblocks with no motion vectors also set the prediction vector to zero. The motion vector prediction errors are then variable length coded.

6.6.3 Bi-directional motion estimation

B-pictures have access to both past and future anchor pictures. They can then use either past frame, called *forward* motion estimation, or the future frame for *backward* motion estimation, as shown in Figure 6.12.

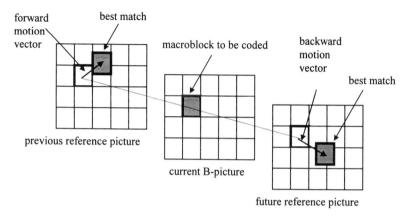

Figure 6.12 Motion estimation in B-pictures

Such an option increases the motion compensation efficiency, particularly when there are occluded objects in the scene. In fact, one of the reasons for the introduction of B-pictures was this fact that the forward motion estimation used in H.261 and P-pictures cannot compensate for the uncovered background of moving objects.

From the two forward and backward motion vectors, the coder has a choice of choosing any of the forward, backward or their combined motion compensated predictions. In the latter case, a weighted average of the forward and backward motion compensated pictures is calculated. The weight is inversely proportional to the distance of the B-picture with its anchor pictures. For example in the GOB structure of I, B1, B2, P, the *bi-directionally* interpolated motion compensated picture for B1 would be two-thirds of the forward motion compensated pixels from the I-picture and one-third from backward motion compensated pixels of the P-picture. This ratio is reversed for B2. Note that B-pictures do not use motion compensation from each other, since they are not used as predictors. Also note that the motion vector overhead in B-pictures is much more than in P-pictures. The reason is that for B-pictures there are more macroblock types, which increase the macroblock type overhead, and for the bi-directionally motion compensated macroblocks two motion vectors have to be sent.

6.7   Coding of pictures

Since the encoder was described in terms of the basic unit of a macroblock, then the picture types may be defined in terms of their macroblock types. In the following each of these picture types are defined.

6.7.1 I-pictures

In I-pictures all the macroblocks are Intra coded. There are two Intra macroblock types: one that uses the current quantiser scale, *Intra-d*, and the other that defines a new value for the quantiser scale, *Intra-q*. Intra-d is the default value when the quantiser scale is not changed. Although these two types can be identified with "0" and "1", and no variable length code is required, the standard has foreseen some possible extensions to the macroblock types in the future. For this reason, they are VLC coded and Intra-d is assigned with "1", and Intra-q, with "01". Extensions to the VLC codes with the start code of "0" are then open. The policy of making the coding tables open in this way was adopted by the MPEG group video committee in developing the international standard. The advantage of future extensions was judged to be worth the slight coding inefficiency.

If the macroblock type is Intra-q, then the macroblock overhead should contain an extra 5 bits, to define the new quantiser scale between 1 and 31. For Intra-d macroblocks, no quantiser scale is transmitted and the decoder uses the previously set value. Therefore the encoder may prefer to use as many Intra-d types as possible. However, when the encoding rate is to be adjusted, which normally causes a new quantiser to be defined, the type is changed to Intra-q. Note that, since in H.261 the bit rate is controlled at either the start of GOBs or rows of a GOB, then, if there is any Intra-q in a GOB, it must be the first MB in that GOB, or rows of the GOB. In I-pictures of MPEG-1, an Intra-q can be any of the macroblocks.

Each block within the MB is DCT coded and the coefficients are divided by the quantiser step size, rounded to the nearest integer. The quantiser step size is derived from the multiplication of the quantisation weighting matrix and the quantiser index (1 to 31). Thus quantiser step size is different for different coefficients and may change from MB to MB. The only exception is the DC coefficients, which are treated differently. This is because the eye is sensitive to large areas of luminance and chrominance errors; then the accuracy of each DC value should be high and fixed. The quantiser step size for the DC coefficient is fixed to 8. Since in the quantisation weighting matrix, the DC weighting element is 8, then the quantiser index for the DC coefficient is always 1, irrespective of the quantisation index used for the remaining AC coefficients.

Due to the strong correlation between the DC values of blocks within a picture, the DC indices are coded losslessly by DPCM. Such a correlation does not exist among the AC coefficients, and hence they are coded independently. The prediction for the DC coefficients of luminance blocks follows the coding order of blocks within a macroblock and the raster scan order. For example in the macroblocks of 4:2:0 format pictures shown in Figure 6.13, the DC coefficient of block Y_2 is used as a prediction for the DC coefficient of block Y_3. The DC coefficient of Block Y_3 is a prediction for the DC coefficient of Y_0 of the next macroblock. For the chrominance, we use the DC coefficients of the corresponding value of the block in the previous macroblock.

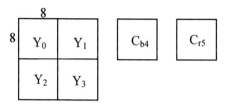

Figure 6.13 Positions of luminance and chrominance blocks within a macroblock in 4:2:0 format

The differentially coded DC coefficient and the remaining AC coefficients are zigzag scanned, in the same manner as was explained for H.261 coefficients of chapter 5. A copy of the coded picture is stored in the frame store to be used for the prediction of the next P- and the past or future B-pictures.

6.7.2 P-pictures

As in I-pictures, each P-picture is divided into slices, which are in turn divided into macroblocks and then blocks for coding. Coding of P-pictures is more complex than for I-pictures, since motion-compensated blocks may be constructed. For inter macroblocks, the difference between the motion compensated macroblock and the current macroblock is partitioned into blocks, and then DCT transformed and coded.

Decisions on the type of macroblock, or whether motion compensation should be used or not, is similar to those of H.261 (see chapter 5). Other H.261 coding tools, such as differential encoding of motion vectors, coded block pattern, zigzag scan, nature of variable length coding, etc. are similar. In fact coding of P-pictures is the same as coding each frame in H.261 with two major differences:

- Motion estimation has a half pixel precision, and due to larger distances between the P-frames, the motion estimation range is much larger.
- In MPEG-1 all Intra-MB use the quantisation weighting matrix, whereas in H.261 all MB use a flat matrix. Also in MPEG-1 the Intra-MB of P-pictures are predictively coded like those of I-pictures, with the exception that the prediction value is fixed at 128×8 if the previous macroblock is not intra coded.

Locally decoded P-pictures are stored in the frame store for further prediction. Note that, if B-pictures are used, two buffer stores are needed to store two prediction pictures.

6.7.3 B-pictures

As in I- and P-pictures, B-pictures are divided into slices, which in turn are divided into macroblocks for coding. Due to the possibility of bi-directional motion compensation, coding is more complex than for P-pictures. Thus the encoder has more decisions to make than in the case of P-pictures. These are: how to divide the picture into slices, determine the best motion vectors to use, decide whether to use forward, backward or interpolated motion compensation or to code intra, and how to set the quantiser scale. These make processing of B-pictures computationally very intensive. Note that motion compensation is the most costly operation in the codecs, and for every macroblock, both forward and backward motion compensations have to be performed.

The encoder does not need to store decoded B-pictures, since they are not used for prediction. Hence B-pictures can be coded with larger distortions. In this regard to reduce the slice overhead, larger slices (fewer slices in the picture) may be chosen.

In P-pictures, as for H.261, there are eight different types of macroblocks. In B-pictures, due to backward motion compensation and interpolation of forward and backward motion compensation, the number of macroblock types is about 14. Figure 6.14 shows the flow chart for macroblock type decisions in B-pictures.

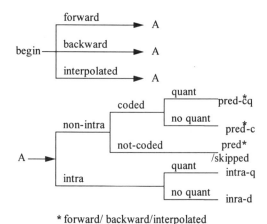

Figure 6.14 Selection of macroblock types in B-pictures

The decision on the macroblock type starts with the selection of a motion compensation mode based on the minimisation of a cost function. The cost function is the mean squared/absolute error of the luminance difference between the motion compensated macroblock and the current macroblock. The encoder first calculates the best forward motion compensated macroblock from the previous anchor picture for forward motion compensation. It then calculates the best motion compensated macroblock from the future anchor picture, as the backward motion compensation. Finally, the average of the two motion compensated errors is calculated to produce the interpolated macroblock. It then selects one that had the smallest error difference with the current macroblock. In the event of a tie, an interpolated mode is chosen.

Another difference between macroblock types in B- and P-pictures is in respect of the skipped macroblock. In P-pictures the skipped macroblocks are the ones that have a zero motion vector and the frame difference error is insignificant. In B-pictures, such an insignificant error signal can have non-zero motion vectors, provided they have the same motion of the previous non-intra coded macroblock. Therefore the macroblock types for these skipped ones are the same as for the previous macroblock.

6.7.4 D-pictures

D-pictures contain only low frequency information, and are coded as the DC coefficients of the blocks. They are intended to be used for fast visible search modes. A bit is transmitted for the macroblock type, although there is only one type. In addition there is a bit denoting the end of the macroblock. D-pictures are not part of the constrained bit-stream.

6.8   Video buffer verifier

A coded bit-stream contains different types of pictures, and each type ideally requires a different number of bits to encode. In addition, the video sequence may vary in complexity with time, and it may be desirable to devote more coding bits to one part of a sequence than to another. For constant bit rate coding, varying the number of bits allocated to each picture requires that the decoder have a buffer to store the bits not needed to decode the immediate picture. The extent to which an encoder can vary the number of bits allocated to each picture depends on the size of this buffer. If the buffer is large an encoder can use greater variations, increasing the picture quality, but at the cost of increasing the decoding delay. The delay is the time taken to fill the input buffer from empty to its current level. An encoder needs to know the size of the decoder's input buffer in order to determine to what extent it can vary the distribution of coding bits among the pictures in the sequence.

In constant bit rate applications (for example decoding a bit-stream from a CD-ROM), problems of synchronisation may occur. In these applications, the encoder should generate a bit-stream that is perfectly matched to the device. The decoder will display the decoded pictures at their specific rate. If the display clock is not locked to the channel data rate, and this is typically the case, then any mismatch between the encoder and channel clock, and the display clock will eventually cause a buffer overflow or underflow. For example, assume that the display clock runs one part per million too slow with respect to the channel clock. If the data rate is 1 Mbit/s, then the input buffer will fill at an average rate of one bit per second, eventually causing an overflow. If the decoder uses the entire buffer to allocate bits between pictures, the overflow could occur more quickly. For example, suppose the encoder fills the buffer completely except for one byte at the start of each picture. Then overflow will occur after only 8 s!

The model decoder is defined to resolve three problems: to constrain the variability in the number of bits that may be allocated to different pictures; it allows a decoder to initialise its buffer when the system is started; and it allows the decoder to maintain synchronisation while the stream is played. At the beginning of this chapter we mentioned multiplexing and synchronisation of audio and video streams. The tools defined in the international standard for the maintenance of synchronisation should be used by decoders when multiplexed streams are being played.

The definition of the parametrised model decoder is known as *Video Buffer Verifier* (VBV). The parameters used by a particular encoder are defined in the bit-stream. This really defines a model decoder that is needed if encoders are to be assured that the coded bit-stream they produce will be decodable. The model decoder looks like Figure 6.15.

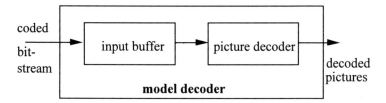

Figure 6.15 Model decoder

A fixed rate channel is assumed to put bits at a constant rate into the buffer, at regular intervals, set by the picture rate. The picture decoder instantaneously removes all the bits pertaining to the next picture from the input buffer. If there are too few bits in the input buffer, i.e. all the bits for the next picture have been received, then the input buffer underflows and there is an underflow error. If during the time between the picture starts, the capacity of the input buffer is exceeded, then there is an overflow error.

Practical decoders may differ from this model in several important ways. They may not remove all the bits required to decode a picture from the *input buffer* instantaneously. They may not be able to control the start of decoding very precisely as required by the buffer fullness parameters in the picture header, and they take a finite time to decode. They may also be able to delay decoding for a short time to reduce the chance of underflow occurring. But these differences depend in degree and kind on the exact method of implementation. To satisfy the requirements of different implementations, the MPEG video committee chose a very simple model for the decoder. Practical implementations of decoders must ensure that they can decode the bit-stream constrained in this model. In many cases this will be achieved by using an input buffer that is larger than the minimum required, and by using a decoding delay that is larger than the value derived from the buffer fullness parameter. The designer must compensate for any differences between the actual design and the model in order to guarantee that the decoder can handle any bit-stream that satisfies the model.

Encoders monitor the status of the model to control the encoder so that overflow does not occur. The calculated buffer fullness is transmitted at the start of each picture so that the decoder can maintain synchronisation.

6.8.1 *Buffer size and delay*

For constant bit rate operation each picture header contains a variable-delay parameter (*vbv_delay*) to enable decoders to synchronise their decoding correctly. This parameter defines the time needed to fill the input buffer of Figure 6.15 from an empty state to the current level immediately before the picture decoder removes all the bits from the picture. This time thus represents a delay and is measured in units of 1/90000 s. This number was chosen because it is almost an exact factor of the picture duration in various original video formats: 1/24, 1/25, 1/29.97 and 1/30 s, and because it is comparable in duration to an audio sample. The delay is given by

$$D = \frac{vbv\_delay}{90000} \text{ s}$$ (6.4)

For example, if *vbv_delay* was 9000, then the delay would be 0.1 s. This means that at the start of a picture the input buffer of the model decoder should contain exactly 0.1 s worth of data from the input bit-stream.

The bit rate, R, is defined in the sequence header. The number of bits in the input buffer at the beginning of the picture is thus given by

$$B = D \times R = \frac{vbv\_delay}{90000} \times R \text{ bits}$$ (6.5)

For example, if *vbv_delay* and *R* were 9000 and 1.2 Mbit/s respectively, then the number of bits in the input buffer would be 120 kbits. The constrained parameter bit-stream requires that the input buffer have a capacity of 327680 bits, and *B* should never exceed this value [3].

6.8.2   *Rate control and adaptive quantisation*

The encoder must make sure that the input buffer of the model decoder is neither overflowed nor underflowed by the bit-stream. Since the model decoder removes all the bits associated with a picture from its input buffer instantaneously, it is necessary to control the total number of bits per picture. In H.261 we saw that the encoder could control the bit rate by simply checking its output buffer content. As the buffer fills up, so the quantiser step size is raised to reduce the generated bit rate, and vice versa. The situation in MPEG-1, due to the existence of three different picture types, where each generates a different bit rate, is slightly more complex. First, the encoder should allocate the total number of bits among the various types of picture within a GOP, so that the perceived image quality is suitably balanced. The distribution will vary with the scene content and the particular distribution of I-, P- and B-pictures within a GOP.

Investigations have shown that for most natural scenes, each P-picture might generate as many as 2–5 times the number of bits of a B-picture, and an I-picture 3 times those of the P-picture. If there is little motion and high texture, then a greater proportion of the bits should be assigned to I-pictures. Similarly, if there is strong motion, then a proportion of bits assigned to P-pictures should be increased. In both cases lower quality from the B-pictures is expected, to permit the anchor I- and P-pictures to be coded at their best possible quality.

Our investigations with variable bit rate (VBR) video, where the quantiser step size is kept constant (no rate control), show that the ratios of generated bits are 6:3:2, for I-, P- and B-pictures respectively [9]. Of course at these ratios, due to the fixed quantiser step size, the image quality is almost constant, not only for each picture, but throughout the image. Again if we lower the expected quality for B-pictures, we can change that ratio in favour of I- and P- pictures.

Although these ratios appear to be very important for a suitable balance in picture quality, one should not worry very much about their exact values. The reason is that it is possible to make the encoder intelligent enough to learn the best ratio. For example, after coding each GOP, one can multiply the average value of the quantiser scale in each picture by the bit rate generated at that picture. Such a quantity can be used as the *complexity index*, since larger complexity indices should be due to both larger quantiser step sizes and larger bit rates. Therefore, based on the complexity index one can derive a new coding ratio, and the target bit rate for each picture in the next GOP is based on this new ratio.

As an example, let us assume that SIF-625 video is to be coded at 1.2 Mbit/s. Let us also assume that the GOP structure of *N*=12 and *M*=3 is used. Therefore there will be one I-picture, three P-pictures and eight B-pictures in each GOP. First of all, the target bit rate for each GOP is $1200 \times \frac{12}{25} = 576$ kbit/GOP. If we assume a coding ratio of 6:3:2, then the target bit rate for each of the I-, P- and B-pictures will be:

I-picture $\qquad \frac{6}{6+3\times3+2\times8} \times 576 = \frac{6}{31} \times 576 = 112$ kbits

P-picture $\qquad \frac{3}{31} \times 576 = 56$ kbits

B-picture $\qquad \frac{2}{31} \times 576 = 37$ kbits

Therefore, each picture is aiming for its own target bit rate. Similar to H.261, one can control the quantiser step size for that picture, such that the required bit rate is achieved. At the end of the GOP, the complexity index for each picture type is calculated. Note that for P- and B-pictures, the complexity index is the average of 3 and 8 complexity indices respectively. These ratios are used to define new coding ratios between the picture type for coding of the next GOP. Also, bits generated in that GOP are added together and the extra bit rate, or the deficit, from the GOP target bit rate is transferred to the next GOP.

Note also that, although at this example (which is typical) the bits per B-pictures are fewer than those of I- and P-pictures, nevertheless the eight B-pictures in a GOP generate almost $8 \times 37 = 296$ kbits, which is more than 50% of the bits in a GOP. The implication of this in the transmission of video over packet networks is that, during periods of congestion, if only the B-pictures are discarded, so reducing the network load by 50%, congestion can be eased without significantly affecting the picture quality. Note that B-pictures are not used for predictions, so their loss will result in only a very brief (480 ms) reduction in quality.

6.9 Decoder

The decoder block diagram is based on the same principle as the local decoder associated with the encoder as shown in Figure 6.16.

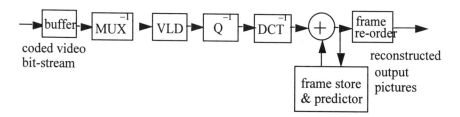

Figure 6.16. A block diagram of an MPEG-1 decoder

The incoming bit-stream is stored in the buffer, and is demultiplexed into the coding parameters such as DCT coefficients, motion vectors, macroblock types, addresses, etc. They are then variable length decoded using the locally provided tables. The DCT coefficients after inverse quantisation are inverse DCT transformed and added to the motion compensated prediction (as required) to reconstruct the pictures. The frame stores are updated by the decoded I- and P-pictures. Finally the decoded pictures are re-ordered to their original scanned form.

At the beginning of the sequence, the decoder will decode the sequence header, including the sequence parameters. If the bit-stream is not constrained, and a parameter exceeds the capability of the decoder, then the decoder should be able to detect this. If the decoder determines that it can decode the bit-stream, then it will set up its parameters to match those defined in the sequence header. This will include horizontal and vertical resolutions and aspect ratio, the bit rate and the quantisation weighting matrices.

Next the decoder will decode the group-of-picture header field, to determine the GOP structure. It will then decode the first picture header in the group of pictures and, for constant bit rate operation, determine the buffer fullness. It will then delay decoding the rest of the sequence until the input buffer is filled to the correct level. By doing this, the decoder can be sure that no buffer overflow or underflow will occur during decoding. Normally, the input buffer size will be larger than the minimum required by the bit-stream, giving a range of fullness at which the decoder may start to decode.

If it is required to play a recorded sequence from a random point in the bit-stream, the decoder should discard all the bits until it finds a sequence start code, a group of pictures start code, or a picture start code which introduces an I-picture. The slices and macroblocks in the picture are decoded and written into a display buffer, and perhaps into another buffer. The decoded pictures may be post-processed and displayed in the order defined by the temporal reference at the picture rate defined in the sequence header. Subsequent pictures are processed at the appropriate times to avoid buffer overflow and underflow.

6.9.1 Decoding for fast play

Fast forward can be supported by D-pictures. It can also be supported by an appropriate spacing of I-pictures in a sequence. For example, if I-pictures were spaced regularly every 12 pictures, then the decoder might be able to play the sequence at 12 times the normal speed by decoding and displaying only the I-pictures. This even simple concept places a considerable burden on the storage media and the decoder. The media must be capable of speeding up and delivering 12 times the data rate. The decoder must be capable of accepting this higher data rate and decoding the I-pictures. Since I-pictures typically require significantly more bits to code than P- and B-pictures, the decoder will have to decode significantly more than the 1/12 of the data rate. In addition it has to search for picture start codes and discard the data for P- and B-pictures. For example, consider a sequence with $N=12$ and $M=3$, such as

I   B   B   P   B   B   P   B   B   P   B   B   I   B   B

Assume that the average bit rate is C, each B-picture requires 0.6C, each P-picture requires 1.4C and the remaining 3C are assigned to the I-picture in the GOP. Then the I-pictures should code $3/12 \times 100\% = 25\%$ of the total bit rate in just 1/12 of the display time.

Another way to achieve fast forward in a constant bit rate application is for the media itself to sort out the I-pictures and transmit them. This would allow the data rate to remain constant. Since this selection process can be made to produce a valid MPEG-1 video bit-stream, the decoder should be able to decode it. If every I-picture of the preceding example were selected, then one I-picture would be transmitted every 3 picture periods, and the speed up rate would be $12/3 = 4$ times.

If alternate I-pictures of the preceding example were selected, then one I-picture would again be transmitted every 3 picture periods, but the speed up rate would be $24/3=8$ times. If one in N I-pictures of the preceding example were selected, then the speed up rate would be $4N$.

6.9.2 Decoding for pause and step mode

Decoding for pause requires the decoder to be able to control the incoming bit-stream, and display a decoded picture without decoding any additional pictures. If the decoder has full control over the bit-stream, then it can be stopped for pause and resumed when play begins. If the decoder has less control, as in the case of a CD-ROM, then there may be a delay before play can be resumed.

6.9.3 Decoding for reverse play

To decode a bit-stream and play in reverse, the decoder must decode each group of pictures in the forward direction, store the entire decoded pictures, then display them in reverse order. This imposes severe storage requirements on the decoder in addition to any problems in gaining access to the decoded bit-stream in the correct order.

To reduce decoder memory requirements, groups of pictures should be small. Unfortunately, there is no mechanism in the syntax for the encoder to state what the decoder requirements are in order to play in reverse. The amount of display buffer storage may be reduced by re-ordering the pictures, either by having the storage unit read and transmit them in another order, or by re-ordering the coded pictures in a decoder buffer. To illustrate this, consider the typical group of pictures shown in Figure 6.17.

B	B	I	B	B	P	B	B	P	B	B	P	Pictures in display order
0	1	2	3	4	5	6	7	8	9	10	11	Temporal reference

I	B	B	P	B	B	P	B	B	P	B	B	Pictures in decoding order
2	0	1	5	3	4	8	6	7	11	9	10	Temporal reference

I	P	P	P	B	B	B	B	B	B	B	B	Pictures in new order
2	5	8	11	10	9	7	6	4	3	1	0	Temporal reference

Figure 6.17 Example of group of pictures, in the display, decoding and new orders

The decoder would decode pictures in the new order, and display them in the reverse of the normal display. Since the B-pictures are not decoded until they are ready to be displayed, the display buffer storage is minimised. The first two B-pictures, 0 and 1, would remain stored in the input buffer until the last P-picture in the previous group of pictures was decoded.

6.10 Postprocessing

6.10.1 Editing

Editing of a video sequence is best performed before compression, but situations may arise where only the coded bit-stream is available. One possible method would be to decode the bit-stream, perform the required editing on the pixels, and recode the bit-stream. This usually leads to a loss in video quality, and it is better, if possible, to edit the coded bit-stream itself.

Although editing may take several forms, the following discussion pertains only to editing at the picture level, that is deletion of the coded video material from a bit-stream and insertion of coded video material into a bit-stream, or re-arrangement of coded video material within a bit-stream.

If a requirement for editing is expected (e.g. clip video is provided analogous to clip art for still pictures), then the video can be encoded with well defined cutting points. These cutting points are places at which the bit-stream may be broken apart or joined. Each cutting point should be followed by a closed group of pictures (e.g. a GOP that starts with an I-picture). This allows smooth play after editing.

To allow the decoder to play the edited video without having to adopt any unusual strategy to avoid overflow and underflow, the encoder should make the buffer fullness take the same value at the first I-picture following every cutting point. This value should be the same as that of the first picture in the sequence. If this suggestion is not followed, then the editor may make an adjustment either by padding (stuffing bits or macroblocks) or by recording a few images to make them smaller.

If the buffer fullness is mismatched and the editor makes no correction, then the decoder will have to make some adjustment when playing over an edited cut. For example, consider a coded sequence consisting of three clips, A, B and C, in order. Assume that clip B is completely removed by editing, so that the edited sequence consists only of clip A followed immediately by clip C, as illustrated in Figure 6.18.

Assume that in the original sequence the buffer is three quarters full at the beginning of clip B, and one quarter full at the beginning of clip C. A decoder playing the edited sequence will encounter the beginning of clip C with its buffer three quarters full, but the first picture in clip C will contain a buffer-fullness value corresponding to a quarter full buffer. In order to avoid buffer overflow, the decoder may try to pause the input bit-stream, or discard pictures without displaying them (preferably B-pictures), or change the decoder timing.

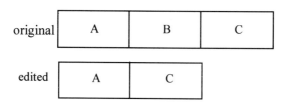

Figure 6.18 Edited sequences

For another example, assume that in the original sequence the buffer is one quarter full at the beginning of clip B, and three quarters full at the beginning of clip C. A decoder playing the edited sequence will encounter the beginning of clip C with its buffer one quarter full, but the first picture in clip C will contain a buffer-fullness value corresponding to a three quarters full buffer. In order to avoid buffer underflow, the decoder may display one or more pictures for longer than the normal time.

If provision for editing was not specifically provided in the coded bit-stream, or if it must be available at any picture, then the editing task is more complex, and places a greater burden on the decoder to manage buffer overflow and underflow problems. The easiest task is to cut at the beginning of a group of pictures. If the group of pictures following the cut is open (e.g. GOP stars with 2 B-pictures), which can be detected by examining the closed-GOP flag in the group of pictures header, then editing must set the broken-link bit to 1 to indicate to the decoder that the previous group of pictures cannot be used for decoding any B-pictures.

6.10.2 Resampling and up-conversion

The decoded sequence may not match the picture rate or the spatial resolution of the display device. In such situations (which occur frequently), the decoded video must be resampled or scaled. In chapter 2 we saw that CCIR-601 video was subsampled into SIF format for coding, hence for display it is appropriate to upsample them back into their original format. Similarly, they have to be temporally converted for proper display, as was discussed in chapter 2. This is particularly important for cases where video was converted from film.

References

[1]   MPEG-1: 'Coding of moving pictures and associated audio for digital storage media at up to about 1.5 Mbit/s', *ISO/IEC 1117-2: video,* (November 1991).

[2]   H.261: 'ITU-T Recommendation H.261, video codec for audiovisual services at p×64 kbit/s', Geneva, (1990).

[3]   'Coding of moving pictures and associated audio for digital storage media at up to about 1.5 Mbit/s', *ISO/IEC 1117-2: Systems,* (November 1991).

[4]   CCIR Rec601, 'Digital methods of transmitting television information', Recommendation 601, Encoding parameters of digital television for studios.

[5]   Wilson D. and Ghanbari M. 'Frame sequence partitioning of video for efficient multiplexing', *Electronics Letters,* **34:15**, pp. 1480-1481, (July 1998).

[6]   Ghanbari M. 'An adapted H.261 two-layer video codec for ATM networks', *IEEE Trans. on Commun.,* **40: 9**, pp. 1481-1490, (September 1992).

[7]   Pearson D.E. 'Transmission and display of pictorial information', Pentech Press, (1975).

[8]   Seferidis V. and Ghanbari M. 'Adaptive motion estimation based on texture analysis', *IEEE Trans. on Commun.,* **42:2/3/4**, pp. 1277-1287, (1994).

[9]   Aldridge R.P., Ghanbari M. and Pearson D.E. 'Exploiting the structure of MPEG-2 for statistically multiplexing video', in *Proc. 1996 International Picture Coding Symposium, PCS'96*, Melbourne, Australia, pp. 111-113, (13-15 March 1996).

Chapter 7

Coding of high quality moving pictures (MPEG-2)

Following the universal success of H.261 and MPEG-1 video codecs, there was a growing need for a video codec to address a wide variety of applications. Considering the similarity between H.261 and MPEG-1, ITU-T and ISO/IEC made a joint effort to devise a generic video codec. Joining the study was a special group in ITU-T Study Group 15, SG15, who were interested in coding of video for transmission over the future Broad-band Integrated Services Digital Networks (B-ISDN) using ATM transport. The devised generic codec was finalised in 1995, and takes the name of MPEG-2/H.262, though it is more commonly known as MPEG-2 [1].

At the time of the development, the following applications for the generic codec were foreseen:

- BSS   Broadcasting Satellite Service (to the home)
- CATV   Cable TV distribution on optical networks, copper, etc.
- CDAD   Cable Digital Audio Distribution
- DAB   Digital Audio Broadcasting (terrestrial and satellite broadcasting)
- DTTB   Digital Terrestrial Television Broadcast
- EC   Electronic Cinema
- ENG   Electronic News Gathering (including SNG, Satellite News Gathering)
- FSS   Fixed Satellite Service (e.g. to head ends)
- HTT   Home Television Theatre
- IPC   Interpersonal Communications (videoconferencing, videophone,...)
- ISM   Interactive Storage Media (optical discs, etc.)
- MMM   Multimedia Mailing
- NCA   News and Current Affairs
- NDS   Networked Database Services (via ATM, etc.)

- RVS   Remote Video Surveillance
- SSM   Serial Storage Media (digital VTR, etc.).

Numerous new applications have been added to the above list. In particular *High Definition Television* (HDTV), and *Digital Versatile Disc* (DVD) for home storage systems appear to be the main beneficiaries of MPEG-2 development.

7.1 MPEG-2 systems

The MPEG-1 standard was targeted for coding of audio and video for storage, where the media error rate is negligible [2]. Hence the MPEG-1 system is not designed to be robust to bit error rates. Also, MPEG-1 was aimed at software oriented image processing, where large and variable length packets could reduce the software overhead [3].

The MPEG-2 standard on the other hand is more generic for a variety of audio-visual coding applications. It has to include error resilience for broadcasting, and ATM networks. Moreover, it has to deliver multiple programs simultaneously without requiring them to have a common time base. These require that the MPEG-2 transport packet length should be short and fixed.

MPEG-2 defines two types of streams: the *Program* stream and the *Transport* stream. The program stream is similar to the MPEG-1 systems stream, but uses a modified syntax and new functions to support advanced functionalities (e.g. scalability). It also provides compatibility with the MPEG-1 systems stream, that is MPEG-2 should be capable of decoding an MPEG-1 bit-stream. Like the MPEG-1 decoder, program stream decoders typically employ long and variable-length packets. Such packets are well suited for software based processing and error free transmission environments, such as coding for storage of video on a disc. Here the packet sizes are usually 1–2 kbytes long, chosen to match the disc sector sizes (typically 2 kbytes). However, packet sizes as long as 64 kbytes are also supported.

The *program stream* also includes features not supported by MPEG-1 systems. These include scrambling of data, assignment of different priorities to packets, information to assist alignment of elementary stream packets, indication of copyright, indication of fast forward, fast reverse and other trick modes for storage devices. An optional field in the packets is provided for testing the network performance, and optional numbering of a sequence of packets is used to detect lost packets.

In the *transport stream*, MPEG-2 significantly differs from MPEG-1 [4]. The transport stream offers robustness for noisy channels as well as the ability to assemble multiple programs into a single stream. The transport stream uses fixed length packets of size 188 bytes with a new header syntax. This can be segmented into four 47-bytes to be accommodated in the payload of four ATM cells, with either of the AAL1 or AAL5 adaptation schemes [5]. It is therefore more suitable for hardware processing and for error correction schemes, such as those required in television broadcasting, satellite/cable TV and ATM networks. Furthermore multiple programs with independent time bases can be multiplexed in one transport stream. The transport stream also allows synchronous multiplexing of programs, fast access to the desired program for channel hopping, multipiexing of programs with clocks unrelated to transport clock and correct synchronisation of elementary streams for playback. It also allows control of the decoder buffers during start-up and playback for both constant and variable bit rate programs.

A basic data structure that is common to the organisation of both the program stream and transport stream is called the *Packetised Elementary Stream* (PES) packet. Packetising the continuous streams of compressed video and audio bit-streams (elementary streams) generates PES packets. Simply stringing together PES packets from the various encoders with other packets containing necessary data to generate a single bit-stream generates a program stream. A transport stream consists of packets of fixed length containing of 4 bytes of header followed by 184 bytes of data, where the data are obtained by segmenting the PES packets.

Figure 7.1 illustrates both types of program and transport stream multiplexes of MPEG-2 systems. Like MPEG-1, the MPEG-2 systems layer is also capable of combining multiple sources of user data along with encoded audio and video. The audio and video streams are packetised to form PES packets that are sent to either a program multiplexer or a transport multiplexer, resulting in a program stream or transport stream, respectively. As mentioned earlier, program streams are intended for an error-free environment such as *digital storage media* (DSM). Transport streams are intended for noisier environments such as terrestrial broadcast channels.

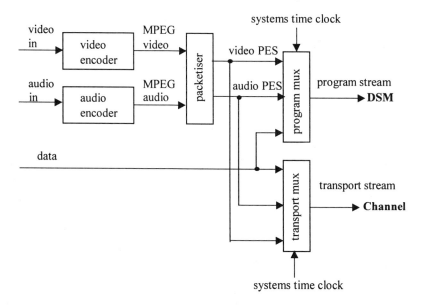

Figure 7.1 MPEG-2 systems multiplex of program and transport streams

At the receiver the transport streams are decoded by a transport demultiplexer (which includes a clock extraction mechanism), unpacketised by a depacketiser, and sent for audio and video decoders for decoding, as shown in Figure 7.2. The decoded signals are sent to the receiver buffer and presentation units that output them to a display device and a speaker at the appropriate time. Similarly if the program streams are used, they are decoded by the program stream demultiplexer, depacketiser, and sent to the audio and the video decoders. The decoded signals are sent to the respective buffer and present and await presentation. Also similar to MPEG-1 systems, the information about systems timing is carried by the clock reference field in the bit-stream that is used to synchronise the decoder systems clock (STC). Presentation time stamps (PTS) that are also carried by the bit-stream control the presentation of the decoded output.

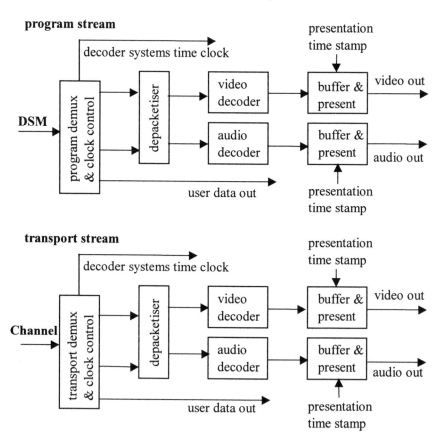

Figure 7.2 MPEG-2 systems demultiplexing of program and transport streams

7.2 Level and profile

MPEG-2 is intended to be generic in the sense that it serves a wide range of applications, bit rates, resolutions, qualities and services. Applications should cover, among other things, digital storage media, television broadcasting and communications. In the course of the development, various requirements from typical applications were considered, and they were integrated into a single syntax. Hence MPEG-2 is expected to facilitate the interchange of bit-streams among different applications. Considering the practicality of implementing the full syntax of the bit-stream, however, a limited number of subsets of the syntax are also stipulated by means of *"profile"* and *"level"* [6].

A *profile* is a subset of the entire bit-stream syntax that is defined by the MPEG-2 specification. Within the bounds imposed by the syntax of a given profile it is still possible to encompass very large variations in the performance of encoders and decoders depending upon the values taken by parameters in the bit-stream. For instance it is possible to specify frame sizes as large as (approximately) 2^{14} samples wide by 2^{14} lines high. It is currently neither practical nor economical to implement a decoder capable of dealing with all possible frame sizes. In order to deal with this problem *levels* are defined within each profile. A level is a defined set of constraints imposed on parameters in the bit-stream. These constraints may be simple limits on numbers. Alternatively they may take the form of constraints on arithmetic combinations of the parameters (e.g. frame width multiplied by frame height multiplied by frame rate). Both profiles and levels have a hierarchical relationship, and the syntax supported by a higher profile or level must also support all the syntactical elements of the lower profiles or levels.

Bit-streams complying with the MPEG-2 specification use a common syntax. In order to achieve a subset of the complete syntax, flags and parameters are included in the bit-stream which signal the presence or otherwise of syntactic elements that occur later in the bit-stream. Then to specify constraints on the syntax (and hence define a profile) it is only necessary to constrain the values of these flags and parameters that specify the presence of later syntactic elements.

In order to parse the bit-stream into specific applications, they are ordered into *layers*. If there is only one layer, the coded video data are called a *non-scalable* video bit-stream. For two or more layers, the bit-stream is called *scalable* hierarchy. In the scalable mode, the first layer, called the *base-layer*, is always decoded independently. Other layers are called *enhancement-layers*, and can only be decoded together with the lower layers.

Before describing how various scalabilities are introduced in MPEG-2, and how many profiles or levels are defined, let us see some examples showing the relations between these parameters. Tables 7.1 and 7.2 summarise some of the most common profiles and levels, with their typical applications.

Table 7.1 MPEG-2 profile

Profile	Typical application	Features
SIMPLE	Broadcast	No B-pictures, No scalability, 4:2:0
MAIN	DSM, Broadcast	All pictures, No scalability, 4:2:0
SNR scalable	ATM networks	Two-layer SNR coding, 4:2:0
SPATIAL scalable	HDTV	Two-layer SS coding, 4:2:0
HIGH	Special applications	Three-level hybrid coding, 4:2:2

Table 7.2 MPEG-2 level

Level	Format	Frame rate (Hz)	Compressed data rate
LOW	SIF	30	< 4 Mbit/s
MAIN	CCIR-601	30	< 15 Mbit/s
HIGH1440	1440×1250	60	< 60 Mbit/s
HIGH	1920×1250	60	< 80 Mbit/s

However, not all profiles and levels are allowed. Table 7.3 shows the allowed combinations of level and profile.

Table 7.3 Allowed combinations of level/profile

Level/ profile	Simple profile	Main profile	SNR scalable	Spatial scalable	High profile
LOW		X	X		
MAIN	X	X	X		X
HIGH1440		X		X	X
HIGH		X			X

7.3   How does the MPEG-2 video encoder differ from MPEG-1?

7.3.1 Major differences

From the profile and level we see that the picture resolutions in MPEG-2 can vary from SIF ($352 \times 288 \times 25\ or\ 30$) to HDTV with $1920 \times 1250 \times 60$. Moreover, most of these pictures are interlaced, whereas in MPEG-1, pictures are non-interlaced (progressive). Coding of interlaced pictures is the first difference between the two coding schemes.

In the MPEG-2 standard, combinations of various picture formats and the interlaced/progressive option create a new range of macroblock types. While each macroblock in a progressive mode has six blocks in the 4:2:0 format, the number of blocks in the 4:4:4 image format is 12. Also the dimensions of the unit of blocks used for motion estimation/compensation can change. In the interlaced pictures, since the number of lines per field is half the number of lines per frame, then with equal horizontal and vertical resolutions, for motion estimation it might be appropriate to choose blocks of 16×8, i.e. 16 pixels over 8 lines. These types of sub-macroblocks have half the number of blocks of the progressive mode.

The second significant difference between the MPEG-1 and the MPEG-2 video encoders is the new function of *scalability*. The scalable modes of MPEG-2 are intended to offer interoperability among different services or to accommodate the varying capabilities of different receivers and networks upon which a single service may operate. They allow a receiver to decode a subset of the full bit-stream in order to display an image sequence at a reduced quality, spatial and temporal resolution.

7.3.2 Minor differences

Apart from the two major distinctions, there are some other minor differences, which have been introduced to increase the coding efficiency of MPEG-2. They are again due to the picture interlacing used in MPEG-2. The first one is the scanning order of DCT coefficients. In MPEG-1, like H.261, *zigzag* scanning is used. MPEG-2 has the choice of using *alternate scan*, as shown in Figure 7.3(b). For interlaced pictures, since the vertical correlation in the field pictures is greatly reduced, should the field prediction be used, an alternate scan may perform better than a zigzag scan.

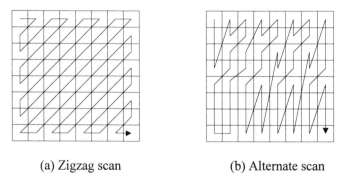

(a) Zigzag scan   (b) Alternate scan

Figure 7.3 Two types of scanning method: (a) zigzag scan; (b) alternate scan

The second minor difference is on the nature of quantisation of the DCT coefficients. MPEG-2 supports both linear and non-linear quantisation of the DCT coefficients. The non-linear quantisation increases the precision of quantisation at high bit rates by employing lower quantiser scale values. This improves picture quality at low contrast areas. At lower bit rates, where larger step sizes are needed, again the non-linear behaviour of the quantiser provides a larger dynamic range for quantisation of the coefficients.

7.3.3   MPEG-1 and MPEG-2 syntax differences

After the inverse quantisation process of the DCT coefficients, the MPEG-1 standard requires that all the non-zero coefficients are added with 1 or −1. In the MPEG-2 standard, only the last coefficient need be added with 1 or −1 provided that the sum of all coefficients is even after inverse quantisation. These are termed the difference standardisation of IDCT mismatch control. Another significant variance is the *run-level* values. In MPEG-1, those that cannot be coded with a variable length code (VLC) are coded with the *escape* code, followed by either a 14-bit or 22-bit *Fixed Length Coding* (FLC), whereas for MPEG-2, they are followed by an 18-bit FLC.

The constraint parameter flag mechanism in MPEG-1 has been replaced by the profile and level structures in MPEG-2. The additional chroma formats (4:2:2 and 4:4:4) and the interlaced related operations (field prediction and scalable coding modes) make MPEG-2 bit-stream syntax different from that of MPEG-1.

The concept of the *group of pictures* (GOP) layer is slightly different. GOP in MPEG-2 may indicate that certain B-pictures at the beginning of an edited sequence comprise a *broken link* which occurs if the forward reference picture needed to predict the current B-pictures is removed from the bit-stream by an editing process. It is an optional structure for MPEG-2 but mandatory for MPEG-1. The final point is that *slices* in MPEG-2 must always start and end on the same horizontal row of macroblocks. This is to assist the implementations in which the decoding process is split into some parallel operations along horizontal strips within the same pictures.

Although these differences may make direct decoding of the MPEG-1 bit-stream by an MPEG-2 decoder infeasible, the fundamentals of video coding in the two codecs remain the same. In fact as we mentioned, there is a need for backward compatibility, such that the MPEG-2 decoder should be able to decode the MPEG-1 encoded bit-stream. Thus MPEG-1 is a subset of MPEG-2. They employ the same concept of a group of pictures, and the interlaced field pictures now become I-, P- and B-fields, and all the macroblock types have to be identified as field or frame based. Therefore in describing the MPEG-2 video codec, we will avoid repeating what has already been said about MPEG-1 in chapter 6. Instead we concentrate on those parts which have risen due to interlacing and scalability of MPEG-2. However, for information on the difference between MPEG-1 and MPEG-2 refer to [7].

7.4   MPEG-2 non-scalable coding modes

This simple non-scalable mode of the MPEG-2 standard is the direct extension of the MPEG-1 coding scheme with the additional feature of accommodating interlaced video coding. The impact of the interlaced video on the coding methodology is that interpicture prediction may be carried out between the fields, as they are closer to each other. Furthermore, for slow moving objects, vertical pixels in the same frame are closer, making frame prediction more efficient.

As usual we define the prediction modes on a macroblock basis. Also to be in line with the MPEG-2 definitions, we define the odd and the even fields as the *Top* and the *Bottom* fields respectively. A field macroblock, similar to the frame macroblock, consists of 16×16 pixels. In the following, five modes of predictions are described [3]. They can be equally applied to P- and B-pictures, unless specified otherwise.

Similar to the reference model in H.261, software-based reference codecs for laboratory testing have also been thought for MPEG-1 and 2. For these codecs, the reference codec is called the *test model* (TM), and the latest version of the test model is TM5 [8].

7.4.1 Frame prediction for frame pictures

Frame prediction for frame pictures is exactly identical to the predictions used in MPEG-1. Each P-frame can make a prediction from the previous anchor frame, and there is *one* motion vector for each motion compensated macroblock. B-frames may use previous, future or interpolated past and future anchor frames. There will be up to *two* motion vectors (forward and backward) for each B-frame motion compensated macroblock. Frame prediction works well for slow to moderate motion as well as panning over a detailed background.

7.4.2 Field prediction for field pictures

This mode of prediction is similar to the frame prediction, except that pixels of the *target* macroblock (MB to be coded) belong to the same field. Prediction macroblocks also should belong to one field, either from the top or the bottom field. Thus for P-pictures the prediction macroblock comes from the two most recent fields, as shown in Figure 7.4. For example the prediction for the target macroblocks in the top field of a P-frame, T_P, may come either from the top field, T_R, or the bottom field, B_R, of the reference frame.

The prediction for the target macroblocks in the bottom field, B_P, can be made from its two recent fields, the top field of the same frame, T_P, or the bottom field of the reference frame, B_R.

For B-pictures the prediction MBs are taken from the two most recent anchor pictures (I/P or P/P). Each target macroblock can make a forward or a backward prediction from either of the fields.

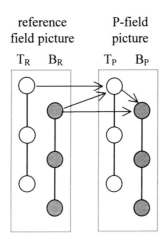

Figure 7.4 Field prediction of field pictures for P-picture MBs

For example in Figure 7.5, the forward prediction for the bottom field of a B-picture, B_B, is either T_P or B_P, and the backward prediction is taken from T_F or B_F.

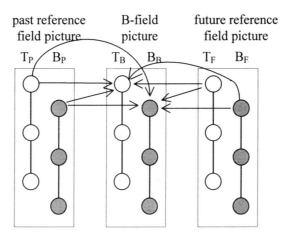

Figure 7.5 Field prediction of field pictures for B-picture MBs

There will be one motion vector for each P-field target macroblock, and two motion vectors for those of B-fields.

7.4.3 Field prediction for frame pictures

In this case the target macroblock in a frame picture is split into two top-field and bottom-field pixels, as shown in Figure 7.6. Field prediction is then carried out independently for each of the 16×8 pixel target macroblocks.

For P-pictures, *two* motion vectors are assigned for each 16×16 pixel target macroblock. The 16×8 predictions may be taken from either of the two most recently decoded anchor pictures. Note that the 16×8 field prediction cannot come from the same frame, as was the case in field prediction for field pictures.

For B-pictures, due to the forward and the backward motion, there can be *two* or *four* motion vectors for each target macroblock. The 16×8 predictions may be taken from either field of the two most recently decoded anchor pictures.

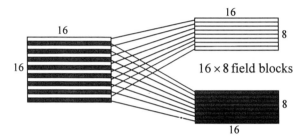

Figure 7.6 A target macroblock is split into two 16×8 field blocks

7.4.4 Dual-prime for P-pictures

This mode is only used in P-pictures where there are no B-pictures in the GOP. Here only one motion vector is encoded (in its full format) in the bit-stream together with a small *differential motion vector* correction. In the case of the field pictures two motion vectors are then derived from this information. These are used to form predictions from the two reference fields (one top, one bottom) which are averaged to form the final prediction. In the case of frame pictures this process is repeated for the two fields so that a total of four field predictions are made.

Figure 7.7 shows an example of *dual-prime* motion compensated prediction for the case of frame pictures. The transmitted motion vector has a vertical displacement of three pixels. From the transmitted motion vector two preliminary predictions are computed, which are then averaged to form the final prediction.

The first preliminary prediction is identical to field prediction, except that the reference pixels should come from the previously coded fields of the same *parity* (top or bottom fields) as the target pixels. The reference pixels, which are obtained from the transmitted motion vector, are taken from two fields (taken from one field for field pictures). In the figure the predictions for target pixels in the top field, T_P, are taken from the top reference field T_R. Target pixels in the bottom field, B_P, take their predictions from the bottom reference field, B_R.

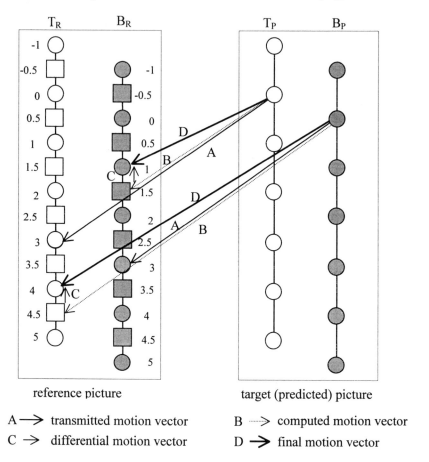

Figure 7.7 Dual-prime motion compensated prediction for P-pictures

The second preliminary prediction is derived using a computed motion vector plus a small differential motion vector correction. For this prediction, reference pixels are taken from the parity field opposite to the first parity preliminary prediction. For the target pixels in the top field T_P, pixels are taken from the bottom reference field B_R. Similarly, for the target pixels in the bottom field B_P, prediction pixels are taken from the top reference field T_R.

The computed motion vectors are obtained by a temporal scaling of the transmitted motion vector to match the field in which the reference pixels lie, as shown in Figure 7.7. For example, for the transmitted motion vector of value 3, the computed motion vector for T_P would be $3 \times 1/2 = 1.5$, since the reference field B_R is mid-way between the top reference field and the top target field. The computed motion vector for the bottom field, is $3 \times 3 / 2 = 4.5$, as the distance between the reference top field and the bottom target field is 3 fields (3/2 frames). The differential motion vector correction, which can have up to one-half pixel precision, is then added to the computed motion vector to give the final corrected motion vector.

In the figure the differential motion vector correction has a vertical displacement of -0.5 pixel. Therefore the corrected motion vector for the top target field, T_P, would be $1.5 - 0.5 = 1$, and for the bottom target field it is $4.5 - 0.5 = 4$, as shown with thicker lines in the figure.

For interlaced video the performance of dual-prime prediction can, under some circumstances, be comparable to that of B-picture prediction and has the advantage of low encoding delay. However, for dual-prime, unlike B-pictures, the decoded pixels should be stored to be used as reference pixels.

7.4.5 16×8 *motion compensation for field pictures*

In this mode, a field of 16×16 pixel macroblock is split into upper half and lower half 16×8 pixel blocks, and a separate field prediction is carried out for each. Two motion vectors are transmitted for each P-picture macroblock and two or four motion vectors for the B-picture macroblock. This mode of motion compensation may be useful in field pictures that contain irregular motion. Note the difference between this mode and the field prediction for frame pictures in Section 7.4.3. Here a field macroblock is split into two halves, while in the field prediction for frame pictures a frame macroblock is split into two top and bottom field blocks.

Thus the five modes of motion compensation in MPEG-2 in relation to field and frame predictions can be summarised in Table 7.4.

Table 7.4. Five motion compensation modes in MPEG-2

Motion compensation mode	Use in field pictures	Use in frame pictures
Frame prediction for frame pictures	No	Yes
Frame prediction for field pictures	Yes	No
Field prediction for frame pictures	No	Yes
Dual-prime for P-pictures	Yes	Yes
16×8 motion compensation for field pictures	Yes	No

7.4.6   *Restrictions on field pictures*

It should be noted that field pictures have some restrictions on I-, P- and B-picture coding type and motion compensation. Normally, the second field picture of a frame must be of the same coding type as the first field. However, if the first field picture of a frame is an I-picture, then the second field can be either I or P. If it is a

P-picture, the prediction macroblocks must all come from the previous I-picture, and dual-prime cannot be used.

7.4.7   *Motion vectors for chrominance components*

As explained, the motion vectors are estimated based on the luminance pixels, hence they are used for the compensation of the luminance component. For each of the two chrominance components the luminance motion vectors are scaled according to the image format:

- 4:2:0 Both the horizontal and vertical components of the motion vector are scaled by dividing by two.
- 4:2:2 The horizontal component of the motion vector is scaled by dividing by two. The vertical component is not altered.
- 4:4:4 The motion vector is unmodified.

7.4.8   *Concealment motion vectors*

Concealment motion vectors are motion vectors that may be carried by the intra macroblocks for the purpose of concealing errors should transmission error result in loss of information. A concealment motion vector is present for all intra macroblocks if, and only if, the *concealment_motion_vectors* flag in the picture header is set. In the normal course of events no prediction is formed for such macroblocks, since they are of intra type. The specification does not specify how error recovery shall be performed. However it is a recommendation that concealment motion vectors should be suitable for use by a decoder that is capable of performing the function. If concealment is used in an I-picture then the decoder should perform prediction in a similar way to a P-picture.

Concealment motion vectors are intended for use in the case that a data error results in information being lost. There is therefore little point in encoding the concealment motion vector in the macroblock for which it is intended be used. This is because, if the data error results in the need for error recovery it is very likely that the concealment motion vector itself would be lost or corrupted. As a result the following semantic rules are appropriate:

- For all macroblocks except those in the bottom row of macroblocks concealment motion vectors should be appropriate for use in the macroblock that lies vertically below the macroblock in which the motion vector occurs.

- When the motion vector is used with respect to the macroblock identified in the previous rule a decoder must assume that the motion vector may refer to samples outside of the slices encoded in the reference frame or reference field.

- For all macroblocks in the bottom row of macroblocks the reconstructed concealment motion vectors will not be used. Therefore the motion vector (0,0) may be used to reduce unnecessary overhead.

7.5 Scalability

Scalable video coding, also called *layered* coding, was originally proposed by the author to increase robustness of video codecs against packet (cell) loss in ATM networks [9]. At the time (late 1980s), H.261 was under development and it was clear that purely interframe coded video by this codec was very vulnerable to loss of information. The idea was that the codec should generate two bit-streams, one carrying the most vital video information named as the *base-layer*, and the other to carry the residual information to enhance the base-layer image quality, named the *enhancement-layer*. In the event of network congestion, only the less important enhancement data should be discarded, and the space made available for the base-layer data. Such a methodology had an influence on the formation of ATM cell structure, to provide two levels of priority for protecting base-layer data [5]. This form of two-layer coding is now known as *SNR scalability* in the MPEG-2 standard, and currently a variety of new two-layer coding techniques have been devised. They now form the basic scalability functions of the MPEG-2 standard.

The concept of scalability has now been extended to other non-telecommunication applications. For example, hierarchical representation of the bit-stream provides the opportunity to extract a video of preferred quality of choice from a single bit-stream. In the following sections, the most common layered coding techniques, known as basic scalability in MPEG-2, are described.

The scalability tools defined in the MPEG-2 specifications are designed to support applications beyond that supported by the single-layer video. Among the noteworthy applications areas addressed are video telecommunications, video on asynchronous transfer mode networks (ATM), interworking of video standards, video service hierarchies with multiple spatial, temporal and quality resolutions, HDTV with embedded TV, systems allowing migration to higher temporal resolution HDTV, etc. Although a simple solution to scalable video is the *simulcast* technique, which is based on transmission/storage of multiple independently coded reproductions of video, a more efficient alternative is scalable video coding, in which the bandwidth allocated to a given reproduction of video can be partially re-utilised in coding of the next reproduction of video. In scalable video coding, it is assumed that given an encoded bit-stream, decoders of various complexities can decode and display appropriate reproductions of the coded video. A scalable video encoder is likely to have increased complexity when compared to a single layer encoder. However, the standard provides several different forms of scalabilities that address non-overlapping applications with corresponding complexities. The basic scalability tools offered are: *data partitioning, SNR scalability, spatial scalability* and *temporal scalability.* Moreover, combinations of these basic scalability tools are also supported and are referred to as *hybrid scalability.* In the case of basic scalability, two layers of video, referred to as the *base-layer* and the *enhancement-layer*, are allowed, whereas in hybrid scalability up to three layers are supported. The following tables provide a few example applications of various scalabilities.

Table 7.5. Applications of SNR scalability

Base-layer	Enhancement-layer	Application
ITU-R-601	Same resolution and format as lower layer	Two quality service for Standard TV
High definition	Same resolution and format as lower layer	Two quality service for HDTV
4:2:0 High definition	4:2:2 chroma simulcast	Video production/distribution

Table 7.6 Applications of spatial scalability

Base	Enhancement	Application
progressive(30Hz)	progressive(30Hz)	CIF/QCIF compatibility or scalability
interlace(30Hz)	interlace(30Hz)	HDTV/SDTV scalability
progressive(30Hz)	interlace(30Hz)	ISO/IECE11172-2/compatibility with this specification
interlace(30Hz)	progressive(60Hz)	Migration to HR progressive HDTV

Table 7.7 Applications of temporal scalability

Base	Enhancement	Higher	Application
progressive(30Hz)	progressive(30Hz)	progressive (60Hz)	Migration to HR progressive HDTV
interlace(30Hz)	interlace(30Hz)	progressive (60Hz)	Migration to HR progressive HDTV

7.5.1 Data partitioning

Data partitioning is a tool intended for use when two channels are available for the transmission and/or storage of a video bit-stream, as may be the case in ATM networks, terrestrial broadcasting, magnetic media, etc. Data partitioning in fact is not a true scalable coding, it is a means of dividing the bit-stream of a single-layer non-scalable MPEG-2 into two parts or two layers. The first layer comprises the critical parts of the bit-stream (such as headers, motion vectors, lower order DCT coefficients) which are transmitted in the channel with the better error performance. The second layer is made of less critical data (such as higher DCT coefficients) and is transmitted in the channel with poorer error performance. Thus, degradations to channel errors are minimised since the critical parts of a bit-stream are better protected. Data from neither channel may be decoded on a decoder that is not intended for decoding data partitioned bit-streams. Even with the proper decoder, data extracted from the second layer decoder cannot be used unless the decoded base-layer data are available.

A block diagram of a data-partitioning encoder is shown in Figure 7.8. The single-layer encoder is in fact a non-scalable MPEG-2 video encoder that may or may not include B-pictures.

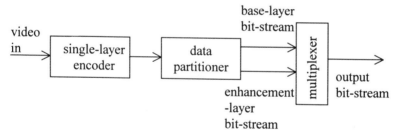

Figure 7.8 Block diagram of a data partitioning encoder

At the encoder, during the quantisation and zigzag scanning of each 8×8 DCT coefficient, the scanning is broken at the *Priority Break Point* (PBP), as shown in Figure 7.9.

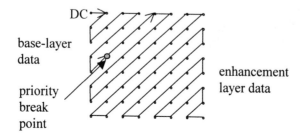

Figure 7.9 Position of the priority break point in a block of DCT coefficients

The first part of the scanned quantised coefficients after variable length coding, with the other overhead information such as motion vectors, macroblock types and addresses, etc., including the priority break point (PBP), are taken as the base-layer bit-stream. The remaining scanned and quantised coefficients plus the end-of-block (EOB) code constitute the enhancement-layer bit-stream. Figure 7.9 also shows the position of the priority break point in the DCT coefficients.

The base and the enhancement-layer bit-streams are then multiplexed for transmission into the channel. For prioritised transmission such as ATM networks, each bit-stream is first packetised into high and low priority cells and the cells are multiplexed. At the decoder, knowing the position of PBP, a block of DCT coefficients is reconstructed from the two bit-streams. Note that PBP indicates the last DCT coefficient of the base. Its position at the encoder is determined based on the portion of channel rate from the total bit rate allocated to the base-layer.

Figure 7.10 shows single shots of an 8 Mbit/s data partitioning MPEG-2 coded video and its associated base-layer picture. The priority breakpoint is adjusted for a base-layer bit rate of 2 Mbit/s. At this bit rate, the quality of the base-layer is almost acceptable. However, some areas in the base-layer show the blocking artefacts and in others the picture is blurred. Blockiness is due to the reconstruction of some macroblocks from only the DC and/or from a few AC coefficients. Blurriness is due to loss of high frequency DCT coefficients.

It should be noted that, since the encoder is a single-layer interframe coder, then at the encoder both the base- and the enhancement-layer coefficients are used at the encoding prediction loop. Thus reconstruction of the picture from the base-layer only can result in a mismatch between the encoder and decoder prediction loops. This causes *picture drift* on the reconstructed picture, that is a loss of enhancement data at the decoder is accumulated and appears as mosquito like noise. Picture drift only occurs on P-pictures, but since B-pictures may use P-pictures for prediction, they suffer from picture drift too. Also, I-pictures reset the feedback prediction, hence they clean up the drift. The more frequent the I-pictures, the less is the appearance of picture drift, but at the expense of higher bit rates.

In summary, data-partitioning is the simplest kind of scalability, which has no extra complexity over the non-scalable encoder, although the base picture suffers from picture drift and may not be usable alone, that of the enhanced (base-layer plus the enhancement-layer) picture with occasional losses is quite acceptable. This is due to normally low loss rates in most networks (e.g. less than 10^{-4}), such that before the accumulation of loss becomes significant, the loss area is cleaned up by I-pictures.

(a)

(b)

Figure 7.10 Data partitioning: (a) enhanced and (b) base picture

7.5.2 SNR scalability

SNR scalability is a tool intended for use in video applications involving telecommunications and multiple quality video services with standard TV and enhanced TV, i.e. video systems with the common feature that a minimum of two layers of video quality are necessary. SNR scalability involves generating two video layers of the same spatio-temporal resolution but different video qualities from a single video source such that the base-layer is coded by itself to provide the basic video quality and the enhancement-layer is coded to enhance the base layer. The enhancement-layer when added back to the base-layer regenerates a higher quality reproduction of the input video. Since the enhancement-layer is said to enhance the *signal-to-noise ratio* (SNR) of the base-layer, this type of scalability is called SNR. Alternatively, as we will see later, SNR scalability could have been called *coefficient amplitude* scalability or *quantisation noise* scalability. These types, although a bit wordy, may better describe the nature of this encoder.

Figure 7.11 shows a block diagram of a two-layer SNR scalable encoder. First, the input video is coded at a low bit rate (lower image quality), to generate the base-layer bit-stream. The difference between the input video and the decoded output of the base-layer is coded by a second encoder, with a higher precision, to generate the enhancement-layer bit-stream. These bit-streams are multiplexed for transmission over the channel. At the decoder, decoding of the base-layer bit-stream results in the base picture. When the decoded enhancement-layer bit-stream is added to the base-layer, the result is an enhanced image. The base- and the enhancement-layers may either use the MPEG-2 standard encoder or the MPEG-1 standard for the base-layer and MPEG-2 for the enhancement-layer. That is, in the latter a 4:2:0 format picture is generated at the base-layer, but a 4:2:2 format picture at the second layer.

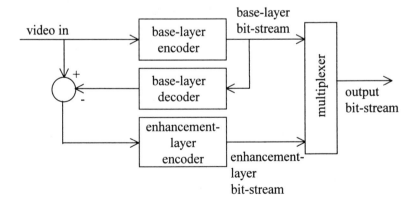

Figure 7.11 Block diagram of a two-layer SNR scalable coder

It may appear that the SNR scalable encoder is much more complex than the data-partitioning encoder is. The former requires at least two non-scalable encoders whereas data-partitioning is a simple single-layer encoder, and partitioning is just carried out on the bit-stream. The fact is that if both layer encoders in the SNR coder are of the same type, e.g. both non-scalable MPEG-2 encoders, then the two-layer encoder can be simplified. Consider Figure 7.12, which represents a simplified non-scalable MPEG-2 of the base-layer [10].

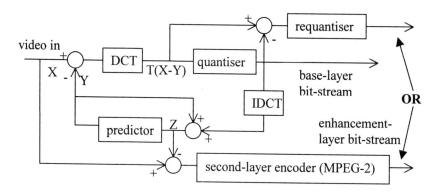

Figure 7.12 A DCT based base-layer encoder

According to the figure, the difference between the input pixels block X and their motion compensated predictions Y are transformed into coefficients $T(X-Y)$. These coefficients after quantisation can be represented with $T(X-Y) - Q$, where Q is the introduced quantisation distortion. The quantised coefficients after the inverse DCT (IDCT) reconstruct the prediction error. They are then added to the motion compensated prediction to reconstruct a locally decoded pixel block Z.

Thus the interframe error signal X-Y after transform coding becomes

$$T(X - Y) \tag{7.1}$$

and after quantisation, a quantisation distortion Q is introduced to the transform coefficients. Then equation 7.1 becomes

$$T(X - Y) - Q \tag{7.2}$$

After the inverse DCT the reconstruction error can be formulated as

$$T^{-1}[T(X - Y) - Q] \tag{7.3}$$

where T^{-1} is the inverse transformation operation. Because transformation is a linear operator, then the reconstruction error can be written as

$$T^{-1}T(X - Y) - T^{-1}(Q) \tag{7.4}$$

Also due to the orthonormality of the transform, where $T^{I}T=1$, equation 7.4 is simplified to

$$X - Y - T^{-1}(Q) \tag{7.5}$$

When this error is added to the motion compensated prediction Y, the locally decoded block becomes

$$Z = Y + X - Y - T^{-1}(Q) = X - T^{-1}(Q) \qquad (7.6)$$

Thus, according to Figure 7.12, what is coded by the second layer encoder is

$$X - Z = X - X + T^{-1}(Q) = T^{-1}(Q) \qquad (7.7)$$

that is the inverse transform of the base-layer quantisation distortion. Since the second layer encoder is also an MPEG encoder (e.g. a DCT based encoder), then DCT transformation of X-Z in equation 7.7 would result in

$$T(X - Z) = TT^{-1}(Q) = Q \qquad (7.8)$$

where again the orthonormality of the transform is employed. Thus the second layer transform coefficients are in fact the quantisation distortions of the base-layer transform coefficients, Q. For this reason the codec can also be called a *coefficient amplitude* scalability or *quantisation noise* scalability unit.

Therefore the second layer of an SNR scalable encoder can be a simple requantiser, as shown in Figure 7.12, without much more complexity than a data partitioning encoder.

The only problem with this method of coding is that, since normally the base-layer is poor, or at least worse than the enhanced image (base plus the second layer), then the used prediction is not good. A better prediction would be a picture of the sum of both layers, as shown in Figure 7.13. Note the second layer is still encoding the quantisation distortion of the base-layer.

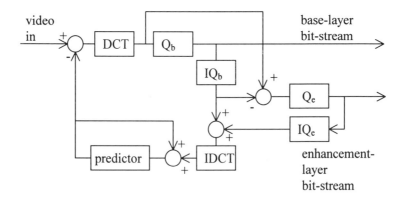

Figure 7.13 A two-layer SNR scalable encoder with drift at the base-layer

In this encoder, for simplicity, the motion compensation, variable length coding of both layers and the channel buffer have been omitted. In the figure Q_b and Q_e are the base- and the enhancement-layer quantisation step sizes respectively. The quantisation distortion of the base-layer is requantised with a finer precision ($Q_e <$ Q_b), and then it is fed back to the prediction loop, to represent the coding loop of the enhancement-layer. Now compared to data partitioning, this encoder only requires a second quantiser, and the complexity is not so great.

Note the tight coupling between the two layer bit-streams. For freedom from drift in the enhanced picture, both bit-streams should be made available to the decoder. For this reason this type of encoder is called an SNR scalable encoder with no drift in the enhancement-layer. If the base-layer bit-stream is decoded by itself, then due to loss of differential refinement coefficients, the decoded picture in this layer will suffer from picture drift. Again, although the drift should only appear in P-pictures, since B-pictures use P-pictures for predictions, this drift is transferred into B-pictures too. I-pictures reset the distortion and drift is cleaned up.

For applications with the occasional loss of information in the enhancement-layer, parts of the picture have the base-layer quality, and other parts that of the enhancement-layer. Therefore picture drift can be noticed in these areas.

If drift free pictures at both layers is the requirement, then the coupling between the two layers must be loosened. Applications such as simulcasting of video with two different qualities need such a requirement. One way to prevent picture drift is not to feed back the enhancement data into the base-layer prediction loop. In this case the enhancement-layer will be intra coded and bit rate would be very high.

In order to reduce the second layer bit rate, the difference between the input to and the output of the base-layer (see Figure 7.11) can be coded by another MPEG encoder [11]. However, here we need two codecs and the complexity is much higher than data partitioning. To reduce the complexity, we need to code only the quantisation distortion. One method is to use a leaky prediction in the enhancement-layer prediction loop, as shown in Figure 7.14.

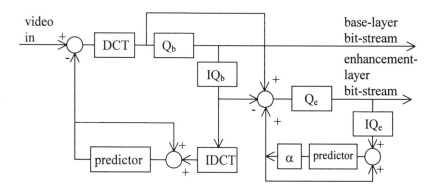

Figure 7.14. A two-layer SNR scalable encoder with no drift at the base- and enhancement-layers

In this case the prediction in the second layer would be a proportion (α) for the interframe loop and ($1-\alpha$) from the intraframe. Our investigations with H.261 type two-layer coding have shown that optimum bit rate versus picture drift can be achieved for $\alpha=0.9$ to 0.95 [11]. Now, since data in the prediction loop are the transform coefficient quantisation distortions, then motion compensation has to be performed in the frequency domain [12].

Note that, even if these methods of coding can reduce the second layer bit rate, coding of the base-layer is still not as efficient as if both layers were fed to the coding loop. For this reason, this type of encoder is not part of the SNR scalability in the MPEG-2 standard. The standard only recommends the SNR scalability compatible with Figure 7.13. Thus picture drift at the base-layer should be reduced by more frequent I-pictures, which reset the drift. In fact, in practice this is the case, where for most MPEG-2 applications, an I-picture is transmitted every half a second. Thus this negligible drift, combined with normally lower quality of the base-layer pictures, is not very noticeable at all.

Figure 7.15 shows the picture quality of the base-layer at 2 Mbit/s. That of the base- plus the enhancement-layer would be similar to those of the data partitioning, albeit with slightly higher bit rate. The extra bit rate would be in the order of 10–15%, due to the overhead of the second layer data [11]. Due to coarser quantisation, some parts of the picture are blocky, as was the case in data partitioning. However, since any significant coefficient can be included at the base-layer, the base-layer picture of this encoder, unlike that of data partitioning, does not suffer from loss of high frequency information.

Figure 7.15 Picture quality of the base-layer of SNR encoder at 2 Mbit/s

Experimental results show that the picture quality of the base-layer of SNR scalable coder is much superior to that of data partitioning, especially at lower bit rates [13]. This is because, at lower base-layer bit rates, data partitioning can only retain DC and possibly one or two AC coefficients. Reconstructed pictures with these few coefficients are very blocky.

7.5.3 Spatial scalability

Spatial scalability involves generating two spatial resolution video streams from a single video source such that the base-layer is coded by itself to provide the basic spatial resolution and the enhancement-layer employs the spatially interpolated base-layer which carries the full spatial resolution of the input video source [14]. The base and the enhancement-layers may either use both the coding tools in the MPEG-2 standard, or the MPEG-1 standard for the base-layer and MPEG-2 for the enhancement-layer, or even an H.261 encoder at the base-layer and an MPEG-2 encoder at the second layer. Use of MPEG-2 for both layers achieves a further advantage by facilitating interworking between video coding standards. Moreover, spatial scalability offers the flexibility in choice of video formats to be employed in each layer. The base-layer can use SIF or even lower resolution pictures at 4:2:0, 4:2:2 or 4:1:1 formats, while the second layer can be kept at CCIR-601 with 4:2:2 format. Like the other two scalable coders, spatial scalability is able to provide resilience to transmission errors as the more important data of the lower layer can be sent over channel with better error performance, while the less critical enhancement-layer data can be sent over a channel with poorer error performance.

Figure 7.16 shows a block diagram of a two-layer spatial scalable encoder.

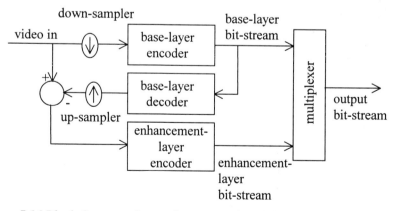

Figure 7.16 Block diagram of a two-layer spatial scalable encoder

An incoming video is first spatially reduced in both the horizontal and vertical directions to produce a reduced picture resolution. For 2:1 reduction, normally a CCIR-601 video is converted into an SIF image format. The filters for the luminance and the chrominance colour components are the 7 and 4 tap filters respectively, described in Section 2.3 of chapter 2. The SIF image sequence is coded at the base-layer by an MPEG-1 or MPEG-2 standard encoder, generating the base-layer bit-stream. The bit-stream is decoded and upsampled to produce an enlarged version of the base-layer decoded video at CCIR-601 resolution. The upsampling is carried out by inserting zero level samples between the luminance and chrominance pixels, and interpolating with the 7 and 4 tap filters, similar to those described in Section 2.3 of chapter 2. An MPEG-2 encoder at the enhancement-layer codes the difference between the input video and the interpolated video from the base-layer. Finally the base- and enhancement-layer bit-streams are multiplexed for transmission into the channel.

If the base- and the enhancement-layer encoders are of the same type (e.g. both MPEG-2), then the two encoders can interact. This is not only to simplify the two-layer encoder, as was the case for the SNR scalable encoder, but also to make the coding more efficient. Consider a macroblock at the base-layer. Due to 2:1 picture resolution between the enhancement- and the base-layers, the base-layer macroblock corresponds to 4 macroblocks at the enhancement-layer. Similarly, a macroblock at the enhancement-layer corresponds to a block of 8×8 pixels at the base-layer. The interaction would be in the form of up-sampling the base-layer block of 8×8 pixels into a macroblock of 16×16 pixels, and using it as a part of the prediction in the enhancement-layer coding loop.

Figure 7.17 shows a block of 8×8 pixels from the base-layer that is up-sampled and is combined with the prediction of the enhancement-layer to form the final prediction for a macroblock at the enhancement-layer. In the figure the base-layer up-sampled macroblock is weighted by w and that of the enhancement-layer by $1-w$.

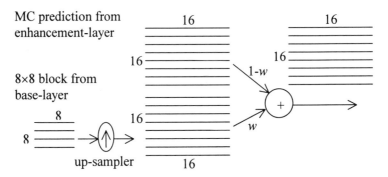

Figure 7.17 Principle of spatio-temporal prediction in the spatial scalable encoder

More details of the spatial scalable encoder are shown in Figure 7.18. The base-layer is a non-scalable MPEG-2 encoder, where each block of this encoder is up-sampled, interpolated and fed to a *weighting table* (WT). The coding elements of the enhancement-layer are shown without the motion compensation, variable length code and the other coding tools of the MPEG-2 standard. A *statistical table* (ST) sets the weighting table elements. Note that the weighted base-layer macroblocks are used in the prediction loop, which will be subtracted from the input macroblocks. This part is similar to taking the difference between the input and the decoded base-layer video and coding their differences by a second layer encoder, as was illustrated in the general block diagram of this encoder in Figure 7.16.

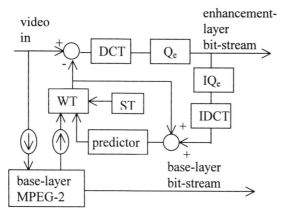

Figure 7.18 Details of spatial scalability encoder

Figure 7.19 shows a single shot of the base-layer picture at 2 Mbit/s. The picture produced by the base- plus the enhancement-layer at 8 Mbit/s would be similar to that resulting for data partitioning, shown in Figure 7.10. Note that since picture size is one quarter of the original, the 2 Mbit/s allocated to the base-layer would be sufficient to code the base-layer pictures at almost identical quality to the base- plus the enhancement-layer at 8 Mbit/s. An up-sampled version of the base-layer picture to fill the display at the CCIR-601 size is also shown in the figure. Comparing this picture with those of data partitioning and SNR scalable coders, it can be seen that the picture is almost free from blockiness, but still some very high frequency information is missing. Note that the base-layer picture can be used alone without picture drift. This was not the case for data partitioning and SNR scalable encoders. However, the price paid is that this encoder is made up of two MPEG encoders, and is more complex than data partitioning and SNR scalable encoders.

(a)

(b)

Figure 7.19 (a) Base-layer picture of a spatial scalable encoder at 2 Mbit/s , and (b) its enlarged version

7.5.4   Temporal scalability

Temporal scalability is a tool intended for use in a range of diverse video applications from telecommunications to HDTV. In such systems migration to higher temporal resolution systems from that of lower temporal resolution systems may be necessary. In many cases, the lower temporal resolution video systems may be either the existing systems or the less expensive early generation systems. The more sophisticated systems may then be introduced gradually.

Temporal scalability involves partitioning of video frames into layers, in which the base layer is coded by itself to provide the basic temporal rate and the enhancement-layer is coded with temporal prediction with respect to the base layer. The layers may have either the same or different temporal resolutions, which, when combined, provide full temporal resolution at the decoder. The spatial resolution of frames in each layer is assumed to be identical to that of the input video. The video encoders of the two layers may not be identical. The lower temporal resolution systems may only decode the base-layer to provide basic temporal resolution, whereas more sophisticated systems of the future may decode both layers and provide high temporal resolution video while maintaining interworking capability with earlier generation systems.

Since in temporal scalability the input video frames are simply partitioned between the base- and the enhancement-layer encoders, the encoder need not be more complex than a single-layer encoder. For example, a single-layer encoder may be switched between the two base- and enhancement-modes to generate the base and the enhancement bit-streams alternately. Similarly a decoder can be reconfigured to decode the two bit-streams alternately. In fact the B-pictures in MPEG-1 and MPEG-2 provide a very simple temporal scalability that is encoded and decoded alongside the anchor I- and P-pictures within a single codec. I- and P-pictures are regarded as the base-layer, and the B-pictures become the enhancement-layer. Decoding of I- and P-pictures alone will result in the base pictures with low temporal resolution, and when added to the decoded B-pictures the temporal resolution is enhanced to its full size. Note that, since the enhancement data do not affect the base-layer prediction loop, both the base and the enhanced pictures are free from picture drift.

Figure 7.20 shows the block diagram of a two-layer temporal scalable encoder. In the figure a temporal demultiplexer partitions the input video into the base- and enhancement-layers, input pictures. For a 2:1 temporal scalability shown in the figure, the odd numbered pictures are fed to the base-layer encoder and the even numbered pictures become inputs to the second layer encoder. The encoder at the base-layer is a normal MPEG-1, MPEG-2, or any other encoder. Again for greater interaction between the two layers, either to make encoding simple or more efficient, both layers may employ the same type of coding scheme.

At the base-layer the lower temporal resolution input pictures are encoded in the normal way. Since these pictures can be decoded independently of the enhancement-layer, they do not suffer from picture drift. The second layer my use prediction from the base-layer pictures, or from its own picture, as shown for frame 4 in the figure. Note that at the base-layer some pictures might be coded as B-pictures, using their own previous, future or their interpolation as prediction, but it is essential that some pictures should be coded as anchor pictures. On the other hand, in the enhancement-layer, pictures can be coded at any mode. Of course, for greater compression, at the enhancement-layer, most if not all the pictures are coded as B-pictures. These B-pictures have the choice of using past, future and their interpolated values, either from the base- or the enhancement-layer.

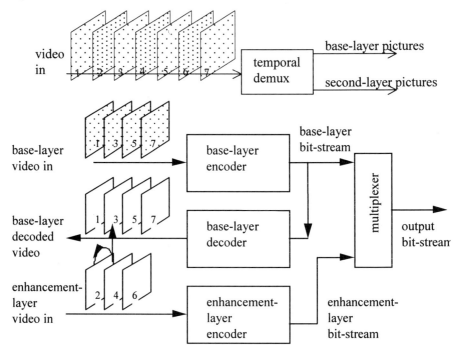

Figure 7.20 A block diagram of a two-layer temporal scalable encoder

7.5.5 Hybrid scalability

MPEG-2 allows combination of individual scalabilities such as spatial, SNR or temporal scalability to form hybrid scalability for certain applications. If two scalabilities are combined, then three layers are generated and they are called the base-layer, *enhancement-layer-1* and *enhancement-layer-2*. Here enhancement-layer-1 is a lower layer relative to enhancement-layer-2, and hence decoding of enhancement-layer-2 requires the availability of enhancement-layer-1. In the following some examples of hybrid scalability are shown.

7.5.5.1 Spatial and temporal hybrid scalability

This is perhaps the most common use of hybrid scalability. In this mode the three-layer bit-streams are formed by using spatial scalability between the base and enhancement-layer-1, while temporal scalability is used between enhancement-layer-2 and the combined base- and enhancement-layer-1, as shown in Figure 7.21.

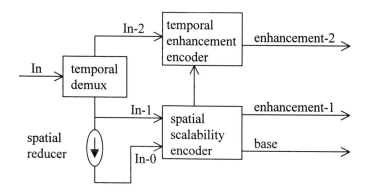

Figure 7.21 Spatial and temporal hybrid scalability encoder

In this figure, the input video is temporally partitioned into two lower temporal resolution image sequences In-1 and In-2. The image sequence In-1 is fed to the spatial scalable encoder, where its reduced version, In-0, is the input to the base-layer encoder. The spatial encoder then generates two bit-streams, for the base- and enhancement-layer-1. In-2 image sequence is fed to the temporal enhancement encoder to generate the third bit-stream, enhancement-layer-2. The temporal enhancement encoder can use the locally decoded pictures of a spatial scalable encoder as predictions, as was explained in Section 7.5.4.

7.5.5.2   SNR and spatial hybrid scalability

Figure 7.22 shows a three-layer hybrid encoder employing SNR scalability and spatial scalability.

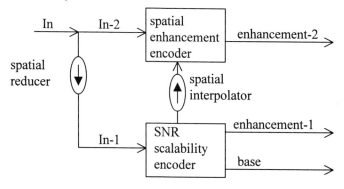

Figure 7.22 SNR and spatial hybrid scalability encoder

In this coder the SNR scalability is used between the base- and the enhancement-layer-1 and the spatial scalability is used between the layer-2 and the combined base- and enhancement-layer-1. The input video is spatially down sampled (reduced) to lower resolution as In-1 is to be fed to the SNR scalable encoder. The output of this encoder forms the base- and enhancement-layer-1 bit-streams. The locally decoded pictures from the SNR scalable coder are up-sampled to full resolution to form prediction for the spatial enhancement encoder.

7.5.5.3 SNR and temporal hybrid scalability

Figure 7.23 shows an example of an SNR and temporal hybrid scalability encoder. The SNR scalability is performed between the base-layer and the first enhancement-layer. The temporal scalability is used between the second enhancement-layer and the locally decoded picture of the SNR scalable coder. The input image sequence through a temporal demultiplexer is partitioned into two sets of image sequences, and are fed to each individual encoder.

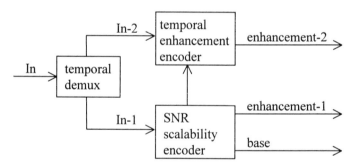

Figure 7.23 SNR and temporal hybrid scalability encoder

7.5.5.4 SNR, spatial and temporal hybrid scalability

The three scalable encoders might be combined to form a hybrid coder with a larger number of levels. Figure 7.24 shows an example of four levels of scalability, using all the three scalability tools mentioned.

The temporal demultiplexer partions the input video into image sequences In-1 and In-2. Image sequence In-2 is coded at the highest enhancement-layer (enhancement-3), with the prediction from the lower levels. The image sequence In-1 is first down-sampled to produce a lower resolution image sequence, In-0. This sequence is then SNR scalable coded, to provide the base- and the first enhancement-layer bit-streams. An up-sampled and interpolated version of the SNR scalable decoded video forms the prediction for the spatial enhancement encoder. The output of this encoder results in the second enhancement-layer bit-stream (enhancement-2).

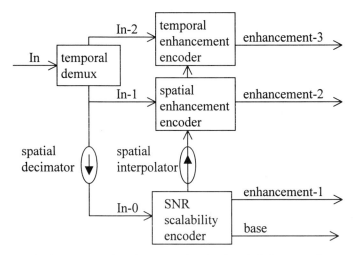

Figure 7.24 SNR, spatial and temporal hybrid scalability encoder

The above figure was just an example of how various scalability tools can be combined to produce bit-streams of various degrees of importance. Of course depending on the application, formation of the base and the level of the hierarchy of the higher enhancement-layers might be defined in a different way to suit the application. For example, when the above scalability methods are applied to each of the I-, P- and B-pictures, since these pictures have different levels of importance, then their layered versions can increase the number of layers even further. In the following section various applications of basic scalability are described.

7.5.6 Applications of scalability

Considering the nature of the basic scalability of data partitioning, SNR, spatial and temporal scalability and their behaviour with regard to picture drift, suitable applications for each method may be summarised in:

(a) **Data partitioning**: This mode is the simplest of all but since it has a poor base-layer quality and is sensitive to picture drift, then it can be used in the environment where there is rarely any loss of enhancement data (e.g. loss rate $<10^{-5}$). Hence the best application would be video over ATM networks, where through admission control, loss ratio can be maintained at low levels [15].

(b)   **SNR scalability**: In this method two pictures of the same spatio-temporal resolutions are generated, but one has lower picture quality than the other. It has generally a higher bit rate over non-scalable encoders, but can have a good base picture quality and can be drift-free. Hence suitable applications can be:

- Transmission of video at different quality of interest, such as multiquality video, video on demand, broadcasting of TV and enhanced TV.
- Video over networks with a high error or packet loss rates, such as Internet, or heavily congested ATM networks.

(c)   **Spatial scalability**: This is the most complex form of scalability, where each layer requires a complete encoder/decoder. Such a loose dependency between the layers has the advantage that each layer is free to use any codec, with different spatio/temporal and quality resolutions. Hence there can be numerous applications for this mode, such as:

- Interworking between two different standard video codecs (e.g. H.263 and MPEG-2).
- Simulcasting of drift-free good quality video at two spatial resolutions, such as standard TV and HDTV.
- Distribution of video over computer networks.
- Video browsing.
- Reception of good quality low spatial resolution pictures over mobile networks.
- Similar to other scalable coders, transmission of error resilience video over packet networks.

(d)   **Temporal scalability**: This is a moderately complex encoder, where either a single-layer coder encodes both layers, such as coding of B- and the anchor I- and P-pictures in MPEG-1 and -2, or two separate encoders operating at two different temporal rates. The major applications can then be:

- Migration to progressive (HDTV) from the current interlaced broadcast TV.
- Internetworking between lower bit rate mobile and higher bit rate fixed networks.
- Video over LANs, Internet and ATM for computer workstations.
- Video over packet (Internet/ATM) networks for loss resilience.

References

[1]   MPEG-2: 'Generic coding of moving pictures and associated audio information', *ISO/IEC 13818-2 Video*, Draft International Standard, (November 1994).

[2]   MPEG-1: 'Coding of moving pictures and associated audio for digital storage media at up to about 1.5 Mbit/s', *ISO/IEC 1117-2: video*, (November 1991).

[3]   Haskel B.G., Puri A. and Netravali A.N. 'Digital video: An introduction to MPEG-2', Chapman and Hall, (1997).

[4]   'Generic coding of moving pictures and associated audio information', *ISO/IEC 13818-1 Systems*, Draft International Standard, (November 1994).

[5]   ITU-T recommendation I.363, 'B-ISDN ATM adaptation layer (AAL) specification', (June 1992).

[6]   Okuba S., McCann K. and Lippman A. 'MPEG-2 requirements, profile and performance verification', *Signal Processing of HDTV*, Elsevier Science, Amsterdam, pp. 65-73, (1994).

[7]   Savatier T. 'Difference between MPEG-1 and MPEG-2 video', ISO/IEC JTC1/SC29/WG11 MPEG94/37, (March 1994).

[8]   Test model editing committee, 'MPEG-2 video test model 5', ISO/IEC JTC1/SC29/WG11 Doc. N0400, (April 1993).

[9]   Ghanbari M. 'Two-layer coding of video signals for VBR networks', *IEEE Journal on Selected Areas in Commun.*, **7:5**, pp. 771-781, (June 1989).

[10] Ghanbari M. 'An adapted H.261 two-layer video codec for ATM networks', *IEEE Transactions on Commun.*, **40:9**, pp. 1481-1490, (September 1992).

[11] Ghanbari M. and Seferidis V., 'Efficient H.261 based two-layer video codecs for ATM networks', *IEEE Transactions on Circuits and Systems for Video Technology*, **5:2**, pp. 171-175, (April 1995).

[12] Assuncao P.A.A. and Ghanbari M. 'A frequency domain video transcoder for dynamic bit rate reduction of MPEG-2 bit-streams', *IEEE Transactions on Circuits and Systems for Video Technology*, **8:8**, pp. 953-967, (December 1998).

[13] Herpel C. 'SNR scalability vs data partitioning for high error rate channels', ISO/IEC JTC1/SC29/WG11 doc. MPEG 93/658, (July 1993).

[14] Morrison G. and Parke I. 'A spatially layered hierarchical approach to video coding', *Signal Processing, Image Commun.* **5:5-6**, pp. 445-462, (December 1995).

[15] ITU-T draft recommendation I.371, 'Traffic control and congestion control in B-ISDN', Geneva, (1992).

Chapter 8

Video coding for low bit rate communications (H.263)

The H.263 Recommendation specifies a coded representation that can be used for compressing the moving picture components of audio-visual services at low bit rates. Detailed specifications and the Test Model (TM) to verify the performance and compliance of this codec were finalised in 1995 [1]. The basic configuration of the video source algorithm in this codec is based on the ITU-T Recommendation H.261, which is a hybrid of interpicture prediction to utilise temporal redundancy and transform coding of the residual signal to reduce spatial redundancy. However, during the course of the development of H.261 and the subsequent advances on video coding in MPEG-1 and MPEG-2 video codecs, substantial experience was gained, which has been exploited to make H.263 an efficient encoder [2–4]. In this chapter those parts of the H.263 standard that make this codec more efficient than its predecessors will be explained.

It should be noted that the primary goal in the H.263 standard codec was coding of video at low or very low bit rates for applications such as mobile networks, public switched telephone network (PSTN) and the narrowband ISDN. This goal could only be achieved with small image sizes such as sub-QCIF and QCIF, at low frame rates. Today, this codec has been found so attractive that higher resolution pictures can also be coded at relatively low bit rates. The current standard recommends operation on five standard pictures of the CIF family, known as sub-QCIF, QCIF, CIF, 4CIF and 16CIF.

Soon after the finalisation of the H.263 in 1995, work began to improve the coding performance of this codec further. The H.263+ is the new codec of this family, which is intended for near-term standardisation of enhancements of H.263 video coding algorithms for real-time telecommunications [5]. The codec for long term standardisation is called H.263L [6]. The H.263L project has the mandate from ITU-T to develop a very low bit rate (less than 64 kbit/s with emphasis on less than 24 kbit/s) video coding recommendation achieving better video quality, lower delay, lower complexity and better error resilience than are currently available. The project also has an objective to work closely with the MPEG-4 committee, in investigating new video coding techniques and technologies as candidates for recommendation [7].

8.1 How does H.263 differ from H.261 and MPEG-1?

The source encoder of H.263 follows the general structure of the generic DCT-based interframe coding technique used in the H.261 and MPEG-1 codecs (see Figure 8.14). The core H.263 employs a hybrid interpicture prediction to utilise temporal redundancy and transform coding of the residual signal to reduce spatial redundancy. The decoder has motion compensation capability, allowing optional incorporation of this technique at the encoder. Half pixel precision is used for the motion compensation, as opposed to the optional full pixel precision and loop filter used in the Recommendation H.261.

Perhaps the most significant differences between the core H.263 and H.261/MPEG-1 are in the coding of the transform coefficients and motion vectors. In the following sections these and some other notable differences such as the additional optional modes are explained.

8.1.1   Coding of H.263 coefficients

In H.261 and MPEG-1, we saw that the transform coefficients are converted via a zigzag scanning process into two-dimensional, *Run* and *Index* events (see Section 5.4, chapter 5). In H.263 these coefficients are represented as a three-dimensional *event* of (*last, run, level*). Similar to the two-dimensional event, the *run* indicates the number of zero-valued coefficients preceding a non-zero coefficient in the zigzag scan, and *level* is the normalised magnitude of the non-zero coefficient which is sometimes called *index*. *last* is a new variable to replace the *End-of-Block* (EOB) code of H.261 and MPEG-1. *last* takes only two values, "0" and "1". *last* "0" means that there are more non-zero coefficients in the block, and "1" means that this is the last non-zero coefficient in the block.

The most likely events of (*last, run, level*) are then variable length coded. The remaining combinations of (*last, run, level*) are coded with a fixed 22-bit word consisting of 7 bits *escape*, 1 bit *last*, 6 bits *run* and 8 bits *level*.

8.1.2   Coding of motion vectors

The motion compensation in the core H.263 is based on one motion vector per macroblock of 16×16 pixels, with half pixel precision. The macroblock motion vector is then differentially coded with predictions taken from three surrounding macroblocks, as indicated in Figure 8.1. The predictors are calculated separately for the horizontal and vertical components of the motion vectors, MV1, MV2 and

MV3. For each component, the predictor is the median value of the three candidate predictors for this component:

$$pred_x = median~(MV1_x, MV2_x, MV3_x)$$
$$pred_y = median~(MV1_y, MV2_y, MV3_y) \qquad (8.1)$$

The difference between the components of the current motion vector and their predictions are variable length coded. The vector differences are defined by:

$$MVD_x = MV_x - pred_x$$
$$MVD_y = MV_y - pred_y \qquad (8.2)$$

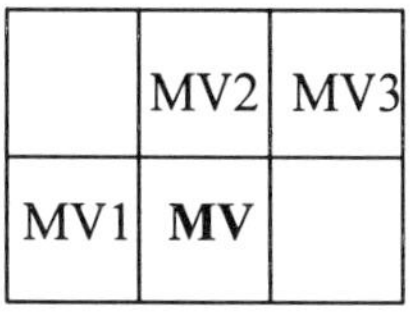

	MV2	MV3
MV1	**MV**	

MV : current motion vector
MV1 : previous motion vector
MV2 : above motion vector
MV3 : above right motion vector

Figure 8.1 Motion vector prediction

In the special cases at the borders of the current group of blocks (GOB) or picture, the following decision rules are applied in order as follows:

1. The candidate predictor MV1 is set to zero if the corresponding macroblock is outside the picture at the left side (Figure 8.2(a)).

2. The candidate predictors MV2 and MV3 are set to MV1 if the corresponding macroblocks are outside the picture at the top, or if the GOB header of the current GOB is non-empty (Figure 8.2(b)).

3. The candidate predictor MV3 is set to zero if the corresponding macroblock is outside the picture at the right side (Figure 8.2(c)).

4. When the corresponding macroblock is coded INTRA or was not coded, the candidate predictor is set to zero.

The values of the difference components are limited to the range [-16 to 15.5]. Since, in H.263, the source images are of the CIF family with the 4:2:0 format, then each macroblock comprises four luminance and two chrominance components, C_b and C_r. Hence the motion vector of the macroblock is used for all four luminance blocks in the macroblock. Motion vectors for both chrominance blocks are derived by dividing the component values of the macroblock vector by two, due to the lower chrominance resolution. The resulting values of the quarter pixel resolution vectors are modified towards the nearest half pixel position (note: the macroblock motion vector has half pixel resolution).

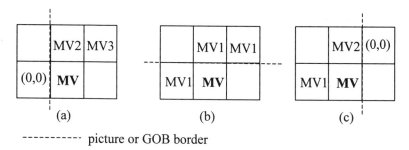

                    (a)   (b)   (c)

-------- picture or GOB border

Figure 8.2 Motion vector prediction for the border macroblocks

8.1.3 Source pictures

The source encoder operates on non-interlaced pictures at approximately 29.97 frames per second. These pictures can be one of the five standard picture formats of the CIF family: Sub-QCIF, QCIF, CIF, 4CIF and 16CIF. Since in CIF the luminance and chrominance sampling format is 4:2:0, then for either of these pictures, the horizontal and vertical resolutions of the chrominance components are half the luminance. Table 8.1 summarises pixel resolutions of the CIF family used in H.263.

Table 8.1 Number of pixels per line and number of lines per picture for each of the H.263 picture formats

Picture format	Number of pixels for luminance per line	Number of lines for luminance per picture	Number of pixels for chrominance per line	Number of lines for chrominance per picture
Sub-QCIF	128	96	64	48
QCIF	176	144	88	72
CIF	352	288	176	144
4CIF	704	576	352	288
16CIF	1408	1152	704	576

Each picture is divided into a *group of blocks* (GOBs). A GOB comprises $k \times 16$ lines, depending on the picture format ($k=1$ for Sub-QCIF, QCIF and CIF; $k=2$ for 4CIF; $k=4$ for 16CIF). The number of GOBs per picture is 6 for Sub-QCIF, 9 for QCIF, and 18 for CIF, 4CIF and 16CIF. Each GOB is divided into 16×16 pixel macroblocks, of which there are four luminance and one each of chrominance blocks of 8×8 pixels.

8.1.4 Picture layer

The picture layer contains the picture header, the GOB header together with various coding decisions on macroblocks in a GOB and finally the coded transform coefficients, which are also used in H.261 and MPEG-1 and -2. The most notable difference in the header information for H.263 is in the *type information*, called PTYPE. This is a 13-bit code that gives information about the complete picture, in the form of [1]:

Bit 1   Always "1", in order to avoid start code emulation,
Bit 2   Always "0", for distinction with H.261,
Bit 3   Split screen indicator, "0" off, "1" on,
Bit 4   Document camera indicator, "0" off, "1" on,
Bit 5   Freeze picture release, "0" off, "1" on,
Bit 6-8   Source format, "000" forbidden "001" Sub-QCIF, "010" QCIF, "011" CIF, "100" 4CIF, "101" 16CIF, "110", reserved, "111" extended PTYPE.
Bit 9   Picture coding type, "0" INTRA, "1" INTER,
Bit 10   Optional unrestricted motion vector mode, "0" off, "1" on,
Bit 11   Optional syntax-based arithmetic coding mode, "0" off, "1" on,
Bit 12   Optional advanced prediction mode, "0" off, "1" on,
Bit 13   Optional PB-frame mode, "0" normal picture, "1" PB-frame.

The *split screen* indicator is a signal that indicates the upper and lower half of the decoded picture could be displayed side-by-side. This has no direct effect on the encoding and decoding of the picture.

The *freeze picture release* is a signal from an encoder which responds to a request for packet retransmission (if not acknowledged) or fast update request, and allows a decoder to exit from its freeze picture mode and display decoded picture in the normal manner.

Bits 10-13 refer to *optional modes* that are only used after negotiation between encoder and decoder. These four negotiable options are:

- Unrestricted motion vector mode
- Advanced prediction mode
- Syntax-based arithmetic coding
- PB-frames mode.

All these options can be used together or separately, except that the advanced prediction mode should be used at the same time as the unrestricted motion vector mode. This means that if Bit-12 is set to "1", Bit-10 shall be set to "1" as well. Also if Picture Code Type is in INTRA mode, i.e. the whole picture is coded as an I-picture (Bit-9 is set to "0"), there will not be a PB-frames mode (Bit-13 is set to

"0"). In the next sections details of these options, which improve the compression performance of H.263, are explained.

Another header information that is unique to H.263 is the quantisation information for B-pictures in relation to the P-pictures in the PB-frames mode. In normal mode the quantisation parameter QUANT is used for each macroblock. In PB-frames mode, QUANT is used for P-blocks only, while for the B-blocks a different quantisation parameter BQUANT is used. In the header information a relative quantisation parameter known as DBQUANT is sent which indicates the relation between QUANT and BQUANT, as defined in Table 8.2.

Table 8.2 DBQUANT codes and relation between QUANT and BQUANT

DBQUANT	BQUANT
00	$(5 \times QUANT)/4$
01	$(6 \times QUANT)/4$
10	$(7 \times QUANT)/4$
11	$(8 \times QUANT)/4$

Division is done by truncation, and BQUANT ranges from 1 to 31. If the range exceeds these values they are clipped to their limits. Note that since DBQUANT is a 2-bit code-word whereas quantisation information, such as QUANT, is a 5-bit word (indicating quantisation indices in the range of 1 to 31), such a strategy significantly reduces the overhead information.

Also for further reduction in the overhead, the code for macroblock type and coded block pattern are combined. For example the combined code of macroblock type & coded block pattern for chrominance is called MCBPC. Similarly combined codes are defined for luminance and for B-blocks, known as CBPY and CBPB respectively. MCBPC is always present for each macroblock, irrespective of its type and the options used. Note that in H.261, MPEG-1 and -2 these patterns are defined separately from the macroblock type.

8.2   Switched multipoint

In H.263 the decoder can be instructed to alter its normal decoding mode and provide some extra display functions. Instructions for the alterations may be issued by an external device such as Recommendation H.245, which is a control protocol for multimedia communications [8]. Some of the commands and the actions are as follows.

8.2.1 Freeze picture request

This signal causes the decoder to freeze its displayed picture until a freeze release signal is received or a time-out period of at least 6 s has expired.

8.2.2 Fast update request

This command causes the encoder to encode its next picture in INTRA mode, with coding parameters to avoid buffer overflow. This mode in conjunction with the back-channel reduces the probability of error propagation into the subsequent pictures.

8.2.3 Freeze picture release

Freeze picture release is a signal from the encoder which has responded to a fast update request and allows a decoder to exit from its freeze mode and display decoded pictures in the normal manner. This signal is transmitted by the PTYPE in the picture header of the first picture coded in response to the fast update request.

8.2.4 Continuous presence multipoint

In a multipoint connection, a *multipoint control unit* (MCU) can assemble two to four video bit-streams into one video bit-stream, so that at the receiver up to four different video signals can be displayed simultaneously. In H.261, this can be done on a quad-screen by only editing the GOB header, but in H.263 it is more complex due to a different GOB structure, overlap motion estimation, multiple motion vectors, etc. Therefore, in H.263 a special *continuous presence multipoint* mode is provided in which four independent video bit-streams are transmitted in the four logical channels of a single H.263 video bit-stream.

8.3   Optional modes of H.263

8.3.1 Unrestricted motion vector mode

In the default prediction mode of H.263, motion vectors are restricted such that all pixels referenced by them are within the coded picture area. In the optional *unrestricted motion vector* mode this restriction is removed and therefore motion vectors are allowed to point outside the picture. When a pixel referenced by a motion vector is outside the coded picture area, an edge pixel is used instead. This edge pixel is found by limiting the motion vector to the last full pixel position inside the coded picture area. Limitation of the motion vector is performed on a pixel-by-pixel basis and separately for each component of the motion vector.

8.3.2 Advanced prediction mode

The optional *advanced prediction* mode of H.263 employs overlapped block motion compensation and may have four motion vectors per macroblock. The use of this mode is indicated in the macroblock type header. This mode is only used in combination with the *unrestricted motion vector* mode, described above.

8.3.2.1   Four motion vectors per macroblock

In H.263, one motion vector per macroblock is used except in the advanced prediction mode, where either one or four motion vectors per macroblock are employed. In this mode, the motion vectors are defined for each 8×8 pixel block. If only one motion vector for a certain macroblock is transmitted, this is represented as four vectors with the same value. When there are four motion vectors, the information for the first motion vector is transmitted as the code-word MVD (motion vector data), and the information for the three additional vectors in the macroblock is transmitted as the code-word MVD_{2-4}.

The vectors are obtained by adding predictors to the vector differences indicated by MVD and MVD_{2-4}, as was the case when only one motion vector per macroblock was present (see Section 8.1.2). Again the predictors are calculated separately for the horizontal and vertical components. However, the candidate predictors MV1, MV2 and MV3 are *redefined* as indicated in Figure 8.3.

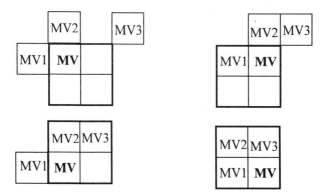

Figure 8.3 Redefinition of the candidate predictors MV1, MV2 and MV3 for each luminance block in a macroblock

As Figure 8.3 shows, the neighbouring 8×8 blocks that form the candidates for the prediction of the motion vector MV take different forms, depending on the position of the block in the macroblock. Note, if only one motion vector in the neighbouring macroblocks is used, then MV1, MV2 and MV3 are defined as 8×8 block motion vectors, possessing the same motion vector of the macroblock.

8.3.2.2   Overlapped motion compensation

The overlapped motion compensation is only used for the 8×8 luminance blocks. Each pixel in an 8×8 luminance prediction block is the weighted sum of three prediction values, divided by 8 (with rounding). To obtain the prediction values, three motion vectors are used. They are the motion vector of the current luminance block and two out of four *remote* vectors, as follows:

- the motion vector of the block at the left or right side of the current luminance block
- the motion vector of the block above or below the current luminance block.

The remote motion vectors from other *groups of blocks* (GOBs) are treated the same way as the remote motion vectors inside the GOB.

For each pixel, the remote motion vectors of the block at the two nearest block borders are used. This means that for the upper half of the block the motion vector corresponding to the block above the current block is used, while for the lower half of the block the motion vector corresponding to the block below the current block is used, as shown in Figure 8.4. In this figure, the neighbouring pixels closer to the pixels in the current block take greater weights.

2	2	2	2	2	2	2	2	bottom of the current block
1	2	2	2	2	2	2	1	
1	1	1	1	1	1	1	1	
1	1	1	1	1	1	1	1	
1	1	1	1	1	1	1	1	
1	1	1	1	1	1	1	1	top of the current block
1	2	2	2	2	2	2	1	
2	2	2	2	2	2	2	2	

Figure 8.4 Weighting values for prediction with motion vectors of the luminance blocks on top or bottom of the current luminance block, $H_1(i,j)$

Similarly, for the left half of the block, the motion vector corresponding to the block at the left side of the current block is used, while for the right half of the block the motion vector corresponding to the block at the right side of the current block is used, as shown in Figure 8.5.

	2	1	1	1	1	1	1	2	
	2	2	1	1	1	1	2	2	
	2	2	1	1	1	1	2	2	
right of the current block	2	2	1	1	1	1	2	2	left of the current block
	2	2	1	1	1	1	2	2	
	2	2	1	1	1	1	2	2	
	2	2	1	1	1	1	1	2	
	2	1	1	1	1	1	1	2	

Figure 8.5 Weighting values for prediction with motion vectors of luminance blocks to the left or right of current luminance block, $H_2(i,j)$

The creation of each pixel, $p(i,j)$, in an 8×8 luminance block is governed by:

$$p(i, j) = [q(i, j) \times H_0(i, j) + r(i, j) \times H_1(i, j) + s(i, j) \times H_2(i, j) + 4] // 8 \qquad (8.3)$$

where $q(i,j)$, $r(i,j)$ and $s(i,j)$ are the pixels from the reference picture as defined by:

$$q(i, j) = p(i + MV_x^0, j + MV_y^0)$$
$$r(i, j) = p(i + MV_x^1, j + MV_y^1)$$
$$s(i, j) = p(i + MV_x^2, j + MV_y^2)$$

(MV_x^0, MV_y^0) denotes the motion vector for the current block, (MV_x^1, MV_y^1) denotes the motion vector of the block either above or below, and (MV_x^2, MV_y^2) denotes the motion vector of the block either to the left or right of the current block. The matrices $H_0(i,j)$, $H_1(i,j)$ and $H_2(i,j)$ are the current, top-bottom and left-right weighting matrices, respectively. Weighting matrices of $H_1(i,j)$ and $H_2(i,j)$ are shown in Figures 8.4 and 8.5 respectively, and the weighting matrix for prediction with the motion vector of the current block, $H_0(i,j)$, is shown in Figure 8.6.

If one of the surrounding blocks was not coded or was in INTRA mode, the corresponding remote motion vector is set to zero. However, in PB-frames mode (to be explained later), a candidate motion vector predictor is not set to zero if the corresponding macroblock was INTRA mode.

If the current block is at the border of the picture and therefore a surrounding block is not present, the corresponding remote motion vector is replaced by the current motion vector. In addition, if the current block is at the bottom of the macroblock, the remote motion vector corresponding with an 8×8 luminance block in the macroblock below the current macroblock is replaced by the motion vector for the current block.

4	5	5	5	5	5	5	4
5	5	5	5	5	5	5	5
5	5	6	6	6	6	5	5
5	5	6	6	6	6	5	5
5	5	6	6	6	6	5	5
5	5	6	6	6	6	5	5
5	5	5	5	5	5	5	5
4	5	5	5	5	5	5	4

Figure 8.6 Weighting values for prediction with motion vector of current block, $H_0(i,j)$

8.3.3 Syntax-based arithmetic coding mode

In the optional arithmetic coding mode of H.263, all the corresponding variable length coding/decoding operations are replaced with binary arithmetic coding/decoding. The use of this mode is indicated by the type information, PTYPE. Details of binary arithmetic coding including a "C"-program were given in chapter 3. The model for the arithmetic coding of each symbol is specified by the cumulative frequency of that symbol.

8.3.4 PB-frames mode

A PB-frames consists of two pictures coded as *one* unit. The name PB comes from the name of picture types in MPEG, where there are P-pictures and B-pictures.

Thus a PB-frame consists of one P-picture which is predicted from the last decoded P-picture and one B-picture which is predicted both from the last decoded P-picture and the P-picture *currently* being decoded. This picture is called the B-picture, because parts of it may be bi-directionally predicted from the past and current P-pictures. The prediction process is illustrated in Figure 8.7.

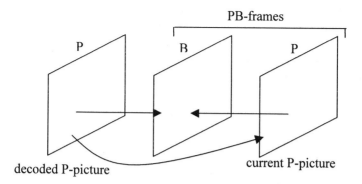

Figure 8.7 Prediction in PB-frames mode

8.3.4.1 Macroblock type

Since in the PB-frames mode a unit of coding is a combined macroblock from P- and B-pictures, then the composite macroblock comprises 12 blocks. First the data for the six P-blocks are transmitted as the default H.263 mode then the data for the six B-blocks. The composite macroblock may have various combinations of coding status for the P- and B-blocks, which are dictated by the combined macroblock block pattern MCBPC. One of the modes of the MCBPC is the INTRA macroblock type that has the following meaning:

- The P-blocks are INTRA coded.
- The B-blocks are INTER coded with prediction as for an INTER block.

The motion vector data (MVD) is also included for INTRA blocks in pictures for which the type information PTYPE indicates INTER. In this case the vector is used for the B-block only. The code-words MVD_{2-4} are never used for INTRA. The candidate motion vector predictor is not set to zero if the corresponding macroblock was coded in INTRA mode.

8.3.4.2 Motion vectors for B-pictures in PB-frames

In the PB-frames mode, the motion vectors for the B-pictures are calculated as follows. Assume we have a motion vector component MV in half pixel units to be used in the P-pictures. This MV represents a vector component for an 8×8 luminance block. If only one motion vector per macroblock is transmitted, then MV has the same value for each of the 8×8 luminance blocks.

For prediction of the B-picture we need both forward and backward vector components MV_F and MV_B. Assume also that MV_D is the delta vector component given by the motion vector data of a B-picture (MVDB) and corresponds to the vector component MV. Now MV_F and MV_B are given in half pixel units by the following formulae:

$$MV_F = \frac{TR_B \times MV}{TR_D} + MV_D$$

$$MV_B = \frac{(TR_B - TR_D) \times MV}{TR_D} \qquad \text{if } MV_D = 0 \qquad\qquad (8.4)$$

$$MV_B = MV_F - MV \qquad\qquad \text{if } MV_D \neq 0$$

Here TR_D is the increment of temporal reference TR from the last picture header. In the optional PB-frames mode, TR only addresses P-pictures. TR_B is the temporal reference for the B-pictures, which indicates the number of non-transmitted pictures since the last P- or I-picture and before the B-picture.

Division is done by truncation and it is assumed that the scaling reflects the actual position in time of P- and B-pictures. Care is also taken that the range of MV_F should be constrained. Each variable length code for MVDB represents a pair of difference values. Only one of the pairs will yield a value for MV_F falling within the permitted range of −16 to +15.5. The above relations between MV_F, MV_B and MV are also used in the case of INTRA blocks, where the vector is used for predicting B-blocks.

For chrominance blocks, the forward and backward motion vectors, MV_F and MV_B, are derived by calculating the sum of the four corresponding luminance vectors and dividing this sum by 8. The resulting one 16th pixel resolution vectors are modified towards the nearest half pixel position.

8.3.5 Prediction for a B-block in PB-frames

In PB-frames mode, predictions for the 8×8 pixel B-blocks are related to the blocks in the corresponding P-macroblock. First, it is assumed that the forward and backward motion vectors MV_F and MV_B are calculated. Secondly, it is assumed that the luminance and chrominance blocks of the corresponding P-macroblock are decoded and reconstructed. This macroblock is called P_{REC}. Based on P_{REC} and its prediction, the prediction for the B-block is calculated.

The prediction of the B-block has two modes that are used for different parts of the block:

- For pixels where the backward motion vector MV_B points to inside P_{REC}, use bi-directional prediction. This is obtained as the average of the forward prediction using MV_F relative to the previously decoded P-picture, and the backward prediction using MV_B relative to P_{REC}. The average is calculated by dividing the sum of the two predictions by two with truncation.

- For all other pixels, forward prediction using MV_F relative to the previously decoded P-picture is used.

Figure 8.8 shows forward and bi-directionally predicted B-blocks. Part of the block that is predicted bi-directionally is shaded and the part that uses forward prediction only is shown unshaded.

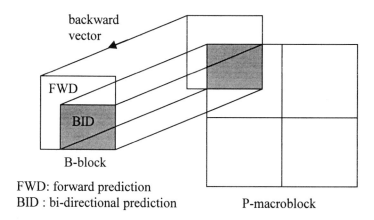

FWD: forward prediction
BID : bi-directional prediction

Figure 8.8 Forward and bi-directional prediction for a B-block

8.4   Coding efficiency of H.263

In order to demonstrate the video compression superiority of H.263 over H.261 and MPEG-1, the CIF test image sequence "Claire" was coded at 256 kbit/s with the following encoders:

- H.261
- MPEG-1, with a GOP length of 12 frames and two B-frames between the anchor pictures, i.e. $N=12$ and $M=3$ (MPEG-GOP)
- MPEG-1, with only P-pictures, i.e. $N=\infty$ and $M=1$ (MPEG-IPPPP..)
- H.263 with advanced mode, but no arithmetic coding, (H.263-ADV).

Figure 8.9 illustrates the Peak-Signal-to-Noise-Ratio (PSNR) of the coded sequence. At this bit rate, the worst performance is that of MPEG-1, with a GOP structure of 12 frames per GOB, and 2 B-frames between the anchor pictures, (IBBPBBPBBPBBIBB...). The main reason for the poor performance of this codec at this bit rate is that I-pictures consume most of the bits, and compared to the other coding modes, relatively lower bits are assigned to the P- and B-pictures.

The second poorest is the H.261, where all the consecutive pictures are interframe coded. The second best performance is the MPEG-1 with only P-pictures. It is interesting to note that this mode is similar to H.261 (every frame is predictively coded), except that motion compensation is carried out with half pixel precision. Hence this mode shows the advantage of using half pixel precision motion estimation. The amount of improvement for the used sequence at 256 kbit/s is almost 2 dB.

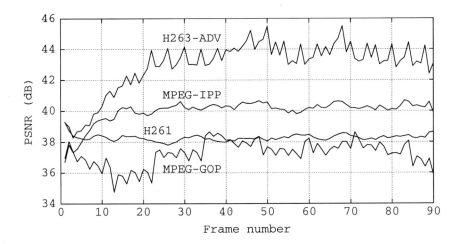

Figure 8.9 PSNR of "Claire" sequence coded at 256 kbit/s, with MPEG-1, H.261 and H.263

Finally, the best performance comes from the advanced mode of H.263, which results in an almost 4 dB improvement over the best of MPEG-1 and 6 dB over H.261. The following are some of the factors that may have contributed to such a good performance:

- Motion compensation on smaller block sizes of 8×8 pixels results in smaller error signals than for the macroblock compensation used in the other codecs.
- Overlapped motion compensation; by removing the blocking artefacts on the block boundaries, the prediction picture has a better quality, so reducing the error signal, and hence the number of significant DCT coefficients.
- Use of PB-frames; where not only B-pictures need fewer bits than P-pictures, but also much less overhead is required when they are coded as a single unit.
- Efficient coding of DCT coefficients through three-dimensional (*last, run, level*).
- Efficient representation of macroblock type and block patterns.

Note that, in this experiment arithmetic coding was not used. Had it been used, it is expected that the picture quality would be further improved by 1–2 dB. Experimental results have confirmed that arithmetic coding has almost 5–10% better compression efficiency over the Huffman [9].

8.5   Video coding for very low bit rates

The video coding group within the Low Bit rate Coding (LBC) Experts Group of Study Group 15 of the ITU-Telecommunications standardisation sector currently has two ongoing activities. The aim is to develop very low bit rate video coding at bit rates less than 64 kbit/s and more particularly at less than 24 kbit/s. One group is looking at the *video coding for very low bit rates*, under the name of H.263+ [5]. The other group is working on *advanced low bit rate video coding*, under the name of H.263L [6].

The H.263+ development effort is intended for short-term standardisation of enhancements of the H.263 video coding algorithm for real-time telecommunication and related non-conversational services. The H.263L development effort is aimed at identifying new video coding technology beyond the capabilities of enhancements to H.263 by the H.263+ coding algorithm.

These two groups also have a close co-operation in the development of their codecs, since the core codec is still H.263. They also work closely with the other bodies of ITU. For example, the collaboration between the H.263+ with the mobile group has led to the consideration for greater video error resilience capability. The *back-channel* error resilience in H.263+ is especially designed to address the needs of mobile video and other such unreliable bit-stream transport environments. The H.263L group work very closely with the MPEG-4 group, as this group has the mandate of developing advanced video coding for storage and broadcasting applications.

One of the key features of the H.263+ and H.263L is the real-time audio-visual conversational services. In a real-time application, information is simultaneously acquired, processed and transmitted and is usually used immediately at the receiver. This feature implies critical delay and complexity constraints on the codec algorithm.

An important component in any application is the transmission media over which it will need to operate. The transmission media for H.263+/H.263L applications include PSTN, ISDN (1B), dial-up switched-56/64 kbit/s service, LANs, mobile networks (including GSM, DECT, UMTS, FLMPTS, NADC, PCS, etc.), microwave and satellite networks, digital storage media (i.e. for immediate recording), and concatenation of the above media. Due to the large number of likely transmission media and the wide variations in the media error and channel characteristics, error resiliency and recovery are critical requirements for this application class.

8.5.1   Scope and goals of H.263+

The expected enhancements of H.263+ over H.263 fall into two basic categories:

- Enhancing quality within existing applications
- Broadening the current range of applications.

A few examples of the enhancements are:

- Improving perceptual compression efficiency
- Reducing video coding delay
- Providing greater resilience to bit errors and data losses.

Note that H.263+ has all the features of H.263, and further tools are added to this codec to increase its coding efficiency and its robustness to errors. In the following sections some of the most important added tools are explained. The group of blocks (GOB) in H.263 is now called "slice" in H.263+.

8.5.2   Advanced intra coding

In this optional mode of H.263+, intra blocks are predictively coded using nearby blocks in the image to predict values in each intra block. A separate VLC is used for the INTRA VLC coefficients, and also the quantisation of the DC coefficient for INTRA is different. These are all done to improve the coding efficiency of the intra-macroblocks.

The prediction may be made from the block above or the block to the left of the current block being decoded. An exception occurs in the special case of an isolated intra coded macroblock in an inter coded frame with neither macroblock above or to the left being intra coded. In this case, no prediction is made. In prediction, DC coefficients are always predicted in some manner, while either the first row or column of AC coefficients may or may not be predicted as signalled on a macroblock-by-macroblock basis. Inverse quantisation of the INTRA DC coefficient is identical to the inverse quantisation of AC coefficients for predicted blocks, unlike the H.263 standard where a fixed quantiser of 8 bits is used for INTRA DC coefficients.

Also in addition to zigzag scanning, two more scans are employed, *alternate-horizontal* and *alternate-vertical* scans, as shown in Figure 8.10. Alternate-vertical is similar to the alternate-scan mode of MPEG-2. For intra predicted blocks, if the prediction mode is set to zero, a zigzag scan is selected for all blocks in a macroblock, otherwise the prediction direction is used to select a scan on a block basis. For instance, if the prediction refers to the horizontally adjacent block, an alternate-vertical scan is selected for the current block, otherwise (for DC prediction referring to vertically adjacent block), alternate-horizontal scan is used for the current block.

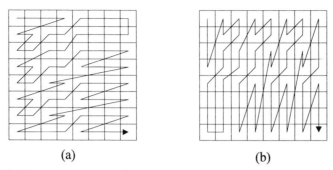

(a)   (b)

Figure 8.10 Alternate scans: (a) horizontal, (b) vertical

For non-intra blocks, the 8×8 blocks of transform coefficients are always scanned with zigzag scanning, similar to all the other standard codecs. A separate VLC table is used for all INTRA DC and AC coefficients.

Depending on the value of INTRA_MODE, either one or eight coefficients are the prediction residuals that must be added to a predictor. Figure 8.11 shows three 8×8 blocks of quantised DC levels and prediction residuals labelled $A(u,v)$, $B(u,v)$ and $E(u,v)$, where u and v are row and column indices, respectively.

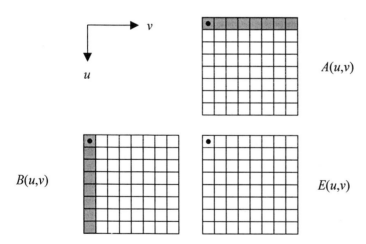

Figure 8.11 Three neighbouring blocks in the DCT domain

$E(u,v)$ denotes the current block that is being decoded. $A(u,v)$ denotes the block immediately above $E(u,v)$ and $B(u,v)$ denotes the block immediately to the left of $E(u,v)$. Define $C(u,v)$ to be the actual quantised DCT coefficient. The quantised level $C(u,v)$ is recovered by adding $E(u,v)$ to the appropriate prediction as signalled in the INTRA_MODE field.

The reconstruction for each coding mode is given next.

Mode 0: DC prediction only

$$C(0,0) = E(0,0) + \frac{1}{2}(\frac{A(0,0) \times QP_A}{QP_C} + \frac{B(0,0) \times QP_B}{QP_C})$$

$$C(u,v) = E(u,v) \qquad u \neq 0, v \neq 0, u = 0...7, v = 0...7$$

(8.5)

Mode 1: DC and AC prediction from the block above

$$C(0,v) = E(0,v) + \frac{A(0,v) \times QP_A}{QP_C} \qquad v = 0...7$$

$$C(u,v) = E(u,v) \qquad u = 1...7, v = 0...7$$

(8.6)

Mode 2: DC and AC prediction from the block to the left

$$C(u,0) = E(u,0) + \frac{B(u,0) \times QP_B}{QP_C} \qquad u = 0...7$$

$$C(u,v) = E(u,v) \qquad u = 0...7, v = 1...7$$

(8.7)

where QP_A, QP_B and QP_C denote the quantisation parameter (taking values between 1 and 31) used for $A(u,v)$, $B(u,v)$ and $C(u,v)$, respectively.

8.5.3   *Advanced inter coding with switching between two VLC tables*

The idea is that INTRA VLC use the same code-words as in the INTER VLC (from H.263) but with different interpretation of *level* and *run*. The INTRA VLC is better suited in cases where there are many and/or large coefficients.

   The INTRA VLC is constructed so that code-words have the same value for *last* (0 or 1) in both the INTER and INTRA tables. The INTRA table is therefore produced by *reshuffling* the meaning of the code-words with the same value of *last*. Furthermore, for *events* with large *level*, the INTRA table uses a code-word which in the INTER table has large *run*.

Encoder action:
   The encoder uses the INTRA VLC table for coding an INTER block if the following two criteria are satisfied:

* The INTRA VLC results in fewer bits than INTER VLC.

- If the coefficients are coded with the INTRA VLC table, but the decoder assumes that the INTER VLC is used, coefficients outside the 64 coefficients of a 8×8 block are addressed.

With many large coefficients, this will easily happen due to the way the INTRA VLC is used.

Decoder action:
At the decoder the following actions are taken:

- The decoder first receives all coefficient codes of a block.
- The code-words are then interpreted assuming that INTER VLC is used. If the addressing of coefficients stays inside the 64 coefficients of a block, the decoding is ended.
- If coefficients outside the block are addressed, the code-words are interpreted according to the INTRA VLC.

8.5.4 Improved PB-frames mode

This mode is an improved version of the optional PB-frames mode of H.263. Most parts of this mode are similar to the PB-frames mode, and the main difference is that in the improved PB-frames mode, the B part of the composite PB-macroblock, known as B_{PB}-macroblock, may have a separate motion vector for *forward* and *backward* prediction. These are in addition to the bi-directional prediction mode that is also used in the normal PB-frames mode.

Hence there are three different ways of coding a B_{PB}-macroblock. The coding type is signalled by the MODB parameter, as listed in Table 8.3. The B_{PB}-macroblock coding modes are:

1. **Bi-directional prediction**: In the bi-directional prediction mode, prediction uses the reference pictures before and after the B_{PB}-picture. These references are the P-picture part of the temporally previous Improved PB-frames and the P-picture part of the current Improved PB-frame. This prediction is equivalent to the prediction in normal PB-frames mode when $MV_D=0$. Note that in this mode motion vector data (MVD) of the PB-macroblock must be included if the P-macroblock is INTRA coded

2. **Forward prediction**: In the forward prediction mode the vector data contained in MVDB are used for forward prediction from the previous reference picture (an INTRA or INTER picture, or the P-picture part of PB- or Improved PB-frames). This means that there is always only one 16×16 vector for the B_{PB}-macroblock in this prediction mode. A simple prediction is used for coding of the forward motion vector. The rule for this predictor is that if the current macroblock is not at the far left edge of the current picture or slice and the macroblock to the left has a forward motion vector, then the predictor of the

forward motion vector for the current macroblock is set to the value of the forward motion vector of the lock to the left; otherwise the predictor is set to zero. The difference between the predictor and the desired motion vector is then VLC coded in the same way as vector data to be used for the P-picture (MVD).

3. **Backward prediction**: In the backward prediction mode the prediction of B_{PB}-macroblock is identical to B_{REC} of normal PB-frames mode. No motion vector data is used for the backward prediction.

The motion vector for the bi-directional prediction of the B_{PB}-macroblocks consists of the scaled forward and backward vectors, similar to that in H.263. The new table for MODB is given in Table 8.3. The symbol "x" in the table indicates that the associated syntax element is present.

Table 8.3 MODB table for Improved PB-frames mode

Index	CBPB	MVDB	Number of bits	Code	Coding mode
0			1	0	Bidirectional prediction
1	x		2	10	Bidirectional prediction
2		x	3	110	Forward prediction
3	x	x	4	1110	Forward prediction
4			5	11110	Backward prediction
5	x		5	11111	Backward prediction

8.6 Deblocking filter mode

The main purpose of the block edge filter is to reduce the blocking artefacts of coded pictures. This type of distortion is common at very low bit rates and subjectively is very annoying, since pictures break into blocks with sharp boundaries between them. To remove blockiness, the filtering is performed on 8×8 block edges and assumes that 8×8 DCT is used and the motion vectors may have either 8×8 or 16×16 resolutions. In case the PB-frames or any kind of B-frame option mode is selected, the present option also applies to the P- and I-frames.

Filtering is performed on the complete reconstructed image, for both luminance and chrominance data. No filtering is performed on the frame and slice edges.

Consider four pixels A, B, C and D on a line (horizontal or vertical) of the reconstructed picture, where A and B belong to block-1 and C and D belong to a neighbouring, block-2 , which is either to the right of or below block-1, as shown in Figure 8.12.

In order to turn the filter on for a particular edge, either block-1 or block-2 should be an INTRA or a coded macroblock with the code COD=0. In this case B_1 and C_1 replace values of the boundary pixels B and C, respectively, where

$$B_1 = B + d_1$$
$$C_1 = C - d_1$$
$$d_1 = sign(d) \times (Max(0, |d| - Max(0, 2 \times |d| - QP))) \qquad (8.8)$$
$$d = (3A - 8B + 8C - 3D)/16$$
$$QP = \text{quantisation parameter of block - 2}$$

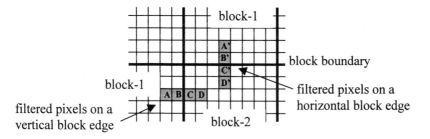

Figure 8.12 Filtering of pixels at the block boundaries

Figure 8.13 shows how the value of d is modified into d_1 to make sure that only block edges which may suffer from blocking artefacts are filtered, and not the natural edges. As a result of this modification, only those pixels on the edge are filtered so that their luminance changes are less than the quantisation parameter, QP.

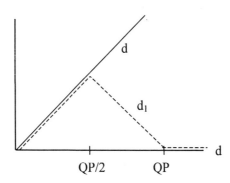

Figure 8.13 d_1 as a function of d

8.7   Protection against error

8.7.1   Error correction

The forward error correction for H.263 is the same as for H.261, and is optional. However, since the main usage of H.263 will be in the mobile environment with harsh error characteristics, forward error correction is particularly important. In most cases (e.g. the GSM system), the error correction will be an integral part of the transmission channel. If it is not, or if additional protection is required, then it should be built into the H.263 system.

To allow the video data and error correction parity information to be identified by the decoder, an error correction *framing pattern* is included. This pattern consists of multiframes of eight frames, each frame comprising 1 bit framing, 1 bit *fill indicator* (Fi), 492 bits of coded data and 18 bits parity.

The error detection/correction code is a BCH (511, 493) [10]. Use of this by the decoder is optional. The parity is calculated against a code of 493 bits, comprising a bit fill-indicator (Fi) and 492 bits of coded video data. The generator polynomial is given by

$$g(x) = (x^9 + x^4 + 1)(x^9 + x^6 + x^4 + x^3 + 1) \tag{8.9}$$

For example, for the input data of "01111...11" (493 bits), the resulting correction parity bits are "011011010100011011" (18 bits).

8.7.2   Error resilience

The optional error resilience mode of H.263 as well as H.263+ requires additional picture memory to be provided at the encoder. The amount of additional picture memory accommodated in the decoder may be signalled by external means to help memory management at the encoder. In order to use this mode, an additional channel for messages in the backward direction is required.

The source encoder for this mode is similar to the generic interframe coder, but several picture memories are provided, in order that the encoder may keep a copy of several past pictures. The complete block diagram of the encoder is shown in Figure 8.14.

The source encoder selects one of the picture memories according to the backward channel message GOB-by-GOB to suppress the temporal error propagation due to the interframe coding. The information to signal which picture is selected for prediction is included in the encoded bit-stream. The decoder of this mode also has an additional plural number of picture memories, to store the correctly decoded video signals with its temporal reference (TR) information. The decoder uses the stored picture whose TR is TRP as the reference picture for interframe decoding, instead of the last decoded picture, if the TRP field exists in the forward message. When the picture whose TR is TRP is not available at the decoder, the decoder may send the forced intra update signal to the encoder.

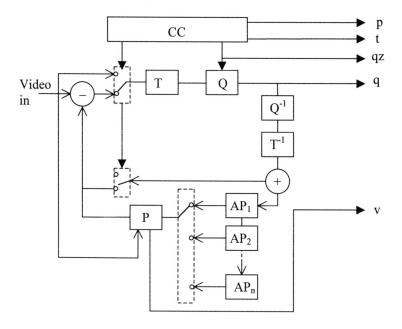

T: Transform   Q: Quantiser   CC: Coding control
P: Picture memory with motion compensated variable delay
AP: Additional picture memory   v: Motion vector
p: Flag for INTRA/INTER   t: Flag for transmitted or not
qz: Quantisation indication   q: Quantisation index for DCT coefficients

Figure 8.14 A block diagram of H.263 encoder with additional picture memory

A positive acknowledgment (ACK) and a negative-acknowledgment (NACK) are defined as backward channel messages. The ACK will be returned when the decoder successfully decodes a GOB. The NACK will be returned when it fails to decode a GOB.

8.7.3 Decoder with error concealment

Due to the interframe coding nature of standard video codecs, bit errors in the video bit-stream can cause severe picture degradation at the decoder. In H.263 three methods for alleviating the problem of channel errors are considered:

- Forward error correction
- Request for retransmission
- Error concealment.

Forward error correction and request for retransmission were discussed in sections 8.7.1 and 8.7.2 respectively. These methods are used to restore the exact value of the encoded bit-stream. If none of these methods is possible, then the loss concealment is used as the last resort.

In the loss concealment, the decoder tries to hide or conceal the effect of received corrupted data. The main idea behind the concealment is to detect the erroneous data and prevent it from being used by the decoder. In parts of the picture where the data are lost (not available to the decoder), pixels from the previous frame are used, either by direct substitutions or by their motion compensated versions, using estimated motion vectors. This method has been successfully applied to video over packet networks to conceal packet losses [11,12]. Loss concealment for H.263 has not been standardised yet, but here we explain how such a method can be used in H.263 type codecs.

Considering that in H.263 the coded macroblocks are relatively addressed to each other and the generated data are variable length coded, then any error in the bit-stream will cause the remaining bit-stream up to the end of GOB (Slice) to be non-decodable. The decoder then stops decoding, and waits for the next GOB header to resume decoding. Non-decoded data are then regarded as lost information. The effect of error on the reconstructed picture can be seen in Figure 8.15(b).

(a)   (b)

Figure 8.15 Effect of error and error concealment on the picture quality: (a) with and (b) without error concealment

8.8 Video over ATM networks

In the transmission of video over ATM networks, due to network congestion, cells carrying visual information might be excessively delayed. There is a maximum tolerable delay beyond which late arrival cells will be of no use. Either the switching nodes or the receiver can discard these cells. In the former case, the cell discard is done by the switching multiplex buffer due to its limited capacity, and in the later, the received information is too late to be of any use by the decoder. In both cases, loss of cells leads to degradation in picture quality.

In recent years several cell loss concealment methods have been devised to improve the quality of decoded pictures (e.g. [11]). All the methods exploit the high correlation between pixels in natural images by interpolating the missing information from other parts of the picture, with similar content. It should be noted that the efficiency of cell loss concealment is greatly influenced by the size of the areas of lost information. This inevitably depends on the packetisation method used to fill the payload of packets with visual information. One form of packetisation may confine the effect of a lost packet to a small area of the picture, while other methods may spread degradation to a larger area. These effects will be addressed later.

However, regardless of the packetisation method, not all parts of the picture are coded for transmission. In DCT based codecs such as H.261, H.263 and MPEG-1, it is more likely that coded macroblocks are separated by many non-coded ones, because only active parts of the pictures are coded. Hence in the event of cell loss, the receiver has no way of discriminating the coded from non-coded macroblocks in the lost area. Attempts to improve picture quality by concealment, may degrade the picture quality of those macroblocks which did not require such concealment. In the following section, after the introduction of loss concealment the effect of packetisation and supervised concealment on the picture quality will be shown.

8.8.1 Loss concealment

Since in the standard codecs, the coding unit is based on macroblocks, then loss concealment should be carried out on a macroblock basis. Assume that a macroblock C_0 from the current frame is lost. Such a macroblock is normally surrounded by eight neighbouring macroblocks, forming a 3 by 3 grid, as shown in Figure 8.16.

For homogenous and uniform motion, the motion vector of the lost macroblock can be estimated by using the average motion vectors of six macroblocks, three from the previous GOB and three from the next GOB. The two macroblocks from the current GOB are not used as they may not be available. Also when the macroblock is the first or the last macroblock of a GOB or when it falls in the first or last GOB of the frame, where it is surrounded by fewer macroblocks. The non-available macroblocks are ignored.

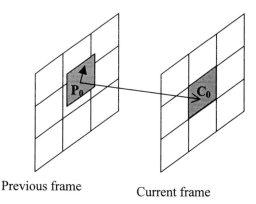

Previous frame   Current frame

Figure 8.16 A grid of 3 × 3 *macroblocks in the current and previous frame*

The estimated average motion vector is then used as the lost motion vector for the current macroblock. For concealment, the macroblock at the same position in the previous frame, P_0, is motion compensated by the estimated motion vector, and the motion compensated P_0 replaces missing C_0.

To demonstrate the image enhancement due to loss concealment, the "Salesman" test image sequence coded at 144 kbit/s, 10 Hz, was exposed to channel errors at a rate of 10^{-2} bit rate. Figure 8.15 showed the reconstructed picture quality with and without error concealment. In this figure, due to variable length coding, any error in the bit-stream causes the remaining data not to be decodable, until the VLC decoder is initialised at the next GOB. The figure also shows how error concealment improves the degraded parts of the picture.

Figure 8.17 shows the objective quality of the entire decoded picture sequence with loss and loss concealment. As the figure shows while the quality of the decoded video due to loss is impaired by more than 10 dB, loss concealment enhances degraded image quality by around 7 dB. It should be noted that, during the encoding, not all parts of the picture are coded. The best concealment for non-coded macroblocks is the direct copy of the previous macroblock without any motion compensation. However, the information as to which macroblock was or was not coded is not available at the decoder. It is obvious that any attempt to replace the missing macroblock by the motion compensated macroblock will degrade the image quality rather than improve it. Our simulations have confirmed this [12].

In order to properly conceal the lost macroblocks, our simulations indicate that, if a macroblock at the previous frame was coded, it is more likely to be coded at the next frame and vice versa. Hence, knowing the coding status of a macroblock in the previous frame, P_0, will indicate whether the current macroblock should be concealed with a motion compensated or non-motion compensated P_0. We call this method *selective concealment*. Figure 8.17 also shows the improvement due to selective concealment versus the *full concealment*, where a lost macroblock is always replaced by the motion compensated previous macroblock, irrespective of whether a macroblock was coded or not.

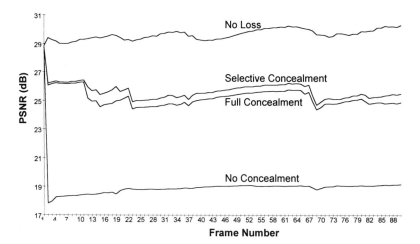

Figure 8.17 Quality of decoded video with and without loss concealment with a bit error ratio of 10^{-2}

8.8.2   Effect of packetisation

The effect of cell loss and hence the cell loss concealment strategy depends on the packetisation method used. With AAL1 packetisation [13], where every 47 bytes of the bit-stream are packed into the ATM cell payload without any further processing, if a cell is lost, the following cells may not be recoverable until the next slice or GOB. Thus a large part of a picture slice may be degraded, depending on the location of the lost macroblock. This problem can be overcome by making the first macroblock of each cell absolutely addressed, hence the loss can be confined to a smaller area of the picture [14]. Let us call this method of packing AALx, as shown in Figure 8.18.

In block based codecs such as H.261, H.263 and MPEG-1,-2, in order to reduce the bit rate, the coded macroblocks are relatively addressed. The address of each coded macroblock is referenced to the last coded macroblock, taking into account all non-coded or skipped macroblocks. For AAL1 packetisation, the generated bit-stream is then packed into the 47 byte payload of the ATM cells.

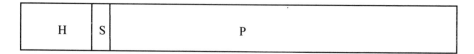

AAL1: H: header, 5 bytes
       S: cell sequency number , 1 byte
       P: payload, 47 bytes

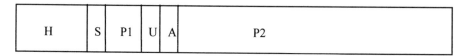

AALx: H: header, 5 bytes
       S:cell sequency number, 1 byte
       U: unique pttern, 11 bits
       A: absolute address, 9 bits
       P1& P2: payload, 45.5 bytes

Figure 8.18 Structure of ALL1 and AALx cells

In AALx, where the first macroblock in each ATM cell is absolutely addressed, the lost area could be confined to the area covered by the lost cell. All following cells could then be decodable. For the decoder to be able to recognise the absolute address, an additional 11-bit header (absolute address header) must be inserted before the address. Also the average length of the relative addressing is normally 2 bits long, whereas the length of the absolute address can be 9 bits long, resulting in an additional 7 bits [14]. Thus AALx has an almost 5% extra overhead compared to AAL1. Referring to the multiplex cell discard graphs, this can result in 5 to 10 times more cell loss, depending on the network load and the number of channels in the multiplex [15].

In an experiment, 90 frames of the "Salesman" image sequence were MPEG-2 coded with the first frame being intra (I-frame) coded and the remaining frames predictively (P-frame) coded ($N=\infty$, $M=1$). Two types of packetisation methods, AALx and AAL1 were used. The AALx type cells were discarded with the ITU-T cell loss model with a cell loss rate of 10^{-2} and a mean burst length of 1 [16]. Those of AAL1 were discarded at cell loss rates of 10^{-3} (10 times lower) and 10^{-4} (100 times lower) with the same mean burst length. In both cases selective concealment has been employed. From Figure 8.19, it can be seen that AALx outperforms AAL1 at 10 times lower cell loss rate, but is inferior to AAL1 with a cell loss rate of 100 times lower. Considering that in the experiment AALx is more likely to experience 5–10 times more loss than AAL1, AALx is a better packetisation scheme for this type of image format (e.g. H.261or H.263).

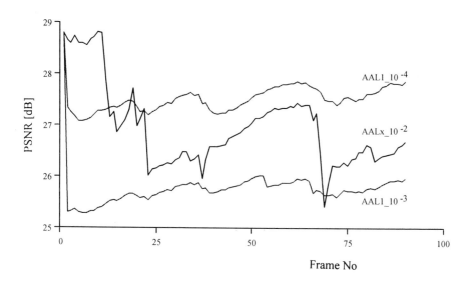

Figure 8.19 PSNR of MPEG-2 coded video sequence of full concealment with 90 frames per GOP (IPPPPPP...) using different error rates: (a) AALx with error rate of 10^{-2}; (b) AAL1 with error rate of 10^{-3}; (c) AAL1 with error rate of 10^{-4}

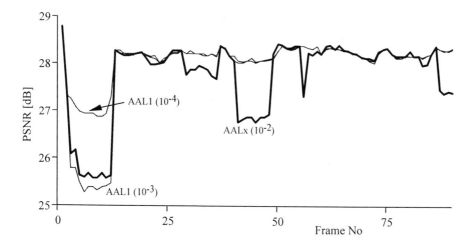

Figure 8.20 PSNR of MPEG-2 coded video sequence of full concealment with 12 frames per GOP (IPP...IPPP...IP...) using different error rates: (a) AALx with error rate of 10^{-2}; (b) AAL1 with error rate of 10^{-3}; (c) AAL1 with error rate of 10^{-4}

In another experiment the same 90 frames of the "Salesman" image sequence were MPEG-2 coded with a GOP structure of N=12, M=1.

The packetisation techniques, the cell loss rates and the cell loss concealment method were similar to the previous experiment. In this case, shown in Figure 8.20, AALx does not show the same improvement over AAL1, as was the case for Figure 8.19. In fact its performance, due to higher overhead, is worse than AAL1 with 10 times lower cell loss rate.

The implications of these two experiments are that with MPEG-1 and -2 structures, where there are regular I-pictures every N frames, AAL1 outperforms AALx. But for very large N (e.g. in H.261 and H.263) AALx is better than AAL1. Note also that since selective concealment is consistently better than full concealment (Figure 8.17), the same conclusions can be drawn for prediction in the full concealment.

8.9 Buffer regulation

Regulation of output bit rates for better distribution of the target bit rate among the encoding parameters is an important part of any video encoder. This is particularly vital in the H.263 encoder, at least for the following reasons:

- Better bit rate regulation requires larger buffer sizes, hence longer delays.
- H.263 is intended for visual telephony, and the encoding delay should be limited, hence smaller buffer sizes are preferred.
- The target bit rate is in the order of 24 kbit/s, and even small size buffers can introduce long delays.

There is no best known method for buffer regulation, and the Recommendation H.263 does not standardise any method (neither do other standard encoders). However, at least for the laboratory simulations, one can use those methods designed for the test models. The following is a method that can be used in the simulations [5]. The bit rate is controlled at a macroblock level, by changing the quantiser parameter, QP, depending on the bit rate, the source and target frame rates.

For the first picture, which is intraframe coded, the quantisation parameter is set to its mid-range QP=16 (QP varies from 1 to 31). After the first picture, the buffer content is set to:

$$\frac{R}{f_{target}} + 3 \times \frac{R}{FR} \quad \text{and} \quad B_{i-1} = \overline{B} \tag{8.10}$$

For the following pictures the quantiser parameter is updated at the beginning of each new macroblock line. The formula for calculating the new quantiser parameter is:

$$QP_{new} = \overline{QP_{i-1}}\left(1 + \frac{\Delta_1 B}{2\overline{B}} + \frac{12\Delta_2 B}{R}\right)$$

$$\Delta_1 B = B_{i-1} - \overline{B} \hspace{4cm} (8.11)$$

$$\text{and } \Delta_2 B = B_{i,mb} - \frac{mb}{MB} \times \overline{B}$$

where:

$\overline{QP_{i-1}}$	= mean quantiser parameter for the previous picture
B_{i-1}	= number of bits spent for the previous picture
$\overline{B}$	= target number of bits per picture
mb	= present macroblock number
MB	= number of macroblocks in a picture
$B_{i,mb}$	= number of bits spent until now for the picture
R	= bit rate
FR	= frame rate of the source picture (typically 25 or 30 Hz)
f_{target}	= target frame rate.

The first two terms of the above formula are fixed for macroblocks within a picture. The third term adjusts the quantiser parameter during coding of the picture.

The calculated new quantisation parameter, QP_{new}, must be adjusted so that the difference fits within the definition of DQUANT (see Section 8.1.4). The buffer content is updated after each complete picture by using the following "C" function:

```
buffer_content=buffer_content+B_{i,99} ;
while(buffer_content>(3R/FR)){
   buffer_content=buffer_content - (R/FR);
frame_incr++;
}
```

The variable `frame_incr` indicates how many times the last coded picture must be displayed. It also indicates which picture from source is coded next.

To regulate the frame rate, f_{target}, a new $\overline{B}$ is calculated at the start of each frame:

$$f_{target} = 10 - \frac{\overline{QP_{i-1}}}{4} \hspace{2cm} 4 < f_{target} < 10$$

$$\overline{B} = \frac{R}{f_{target}} \hspace{4cm} (8.12)$$

For this buffer regulation, it is assumed that the process of encoding is temporarily stopped when the physical transmission buffer is nearly full, preventing buffer overflow. However, this means that no minimum frame rate and delay can be guaranteed.

8.10 Scalability

H.263+ also supports temporal, SNR and spatial scalability. This mode is normally used in conjunction with the error control scheme. The capability of this mode and the extent to which its features are supported is signalled by external means such as H.245 [8].

There are three types of enhancement pictures in the H.263+ codec that are known as B, EI and EP pictures [5]. Each of these has an enhancement layer number, ELNUM, that indicates to which layer it belongs to, and a reference layer number, RLNUM, that indicates which layer is used for its prediction. The encoder may use either of its basic scalability of temporal, SNR , spatial or their combinations in a multilayer scalability mode. Details of the basic and multilayer scalabilities were given in Section 7.5 of chapter 7. However, due to the different nature and application of H.263 to MPEG-2, there are some differences.

8.10.1 Temporal scalability

Temporal scalability is achieved using bi-directionally predicted pictures or B-pictures. As usual, B-pictures use prediction from either or both of a previous and subsequent reconstructed picture in the reference layer. These B-pictures differ from the B-picture part of a PB or Improved PB frames, in that they are separate entities in the bit-stream. They are not syntactically intermixed with a subsequent P or its enhancement part EP.

B-pictures and the B part of PB or Improved PB frames are not used as reference pictures for the prediction of any other pictures. This property allows for B-pictures to be discarded if necessary without adversely affecting any subsequent pictures, thus providing temporal scalability. There is no limit to the number of B-pictures that might be inserted between the pairs of the reference pictures in the base layer. A maximum number of such pictures may be signalled by external means (e.g. H.245). However, since H.263 is normally used for low frame rate applications (low bit rates, e.g. mobile), then due to larger separation between the base layer I- and P-pictures, there is normally one B-picture between them. Figure 8.21 shows the position of Base-layer I- and P-pictures and the B-pictures of the enhancement layer for most applications.

8.10.2 SNR scalability

In SNR scalability, the difference between the input picture and lower quality base-layer picture is coded. The picture in the base layer which is used for the prediction of the enhancement layer pictures may be an I-picture, a P-picture, or the P part of a PB- or Improved PB-frames, but shall not be a B-picture or the B part of a PB or its improved version.

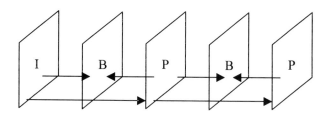

Figure 8.21 B-picture prediction dependency in the temporal scalability

In the enhancement layer two types of pictures are identified, EI and EP. If prediction is only formed from the base-layer, then the enhancement layer picture is referred to an EI-picture. In this case the base layer picture can be an I- or a P-picture (or the P part of a PB-frames). It is possible, however, to create a modified bi-directionally predicted picture using both a prior enhancement layer picture and temporally simultaneous base layer reference picture. This type of picture is referred to EP-picture or "Enhancement" P-picture. Figure 8.22 shows the positions of the base and enhancement layer pictures in an SNR scalable coder. The figure also shows the prediction flow for the EI and EP enhancement pictures.

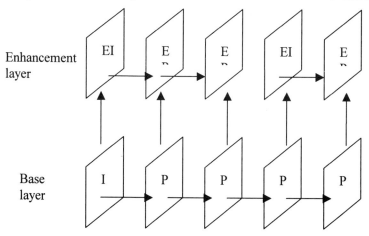

Figure 8.22 Prediction flow in SNR scalability

For both EI- and EP-pictures, the prediction from the reference layer uses no motion vectors. However, as with normal P-pictures, EP pictures use motion vectors when predicting from their temporally-prior reference picture in the same frame.

8.10.3 Spatial scalability

The arrangement of the enhancement layer pictures in the spatial scalability is similar to that of SNR scalability. The only difference is that before the picture in the reference layer is used to predict the picture in the spatial enhancement layer, it is down-sampled by a factor of two either horizontally or vertically (1-D spatial scalability), or both horizontally and vertically (2-D spatial scalability). Figure 8.23 shows the flow of the prediction in the base and enhancement layer pictures of a spatial scalable encoder.

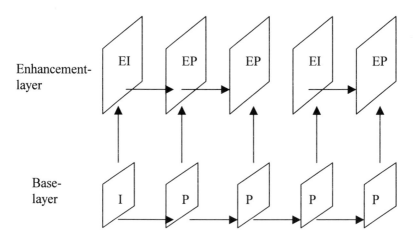

Figure 8.23 Prediction flow in an spatial scalability

8.10.4 Multilayer scalability

Undoubtedly multilayer scalability will increase the robustness of H.263+ agaisnt the channel errors. In the multilayer scabale mode, it is possible not only for B-pictures to be temporally inserted between the base layer pictures of type I, P, PB and Improved PB, but also between the enhancement pictyures types of EI and EP, whether these consist of SNR or spatial enhancement pictures. It is also possible to have more than one SNR or spatial enhanecment layer in conjunction with the base layer. Thus a multilayer scalable bit-stream can be a combination of SNR layers, spatial layers and B-pictures. With increasing the layer number, the size of a picture cannot decrease. Figure 8.24 illustrates the prediction flow in a multilayer scalable encoder.

As with the two-layer case, B-pictures may occur in any layer. However, any picture in an enhancement alyer which is temporally simultanous with a B-picture in its reference layer must be a B-picture or the B-picture part of an PB- or Improved PB-frames. This is to preserve the disposable natute of B-pictures. Note, however, that B-pictures may occur in any layers that have no corresponding picture in the lower layers. This allows an encoder to send enhancement video with a higher picture rate than the lower layers.

The enhancement layer number and the reference layer number of each enhancement picture (B, EI, or EP) are indicated in the ELNUM and RLNUM fields, respectively, of the picture header (when present). If a B-picture appears in an enhancement layer in which temporally-surrending SNR or spatial pictures also appear, the reference layer number (RLNUM) of the B-picture shall be the same as the enhancement layer number (ELNUM). The picture height, width and pixel aspect ratio of a B-picture shall always be equal to those of its temporally-subsequent reference layer picture.

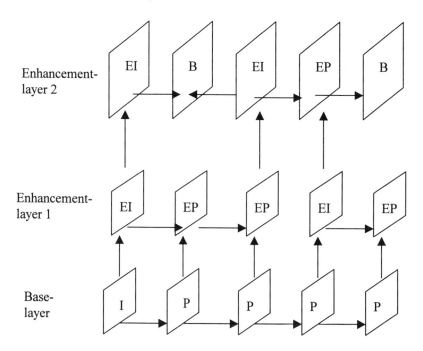

Figure 8.24 Positions of the base and enhancement-layer pictures in a multilayer scalable bit-stream

8.10.5 Transmission order of pictures

Pictures, which are dependent on other pictures, shall be located in the bit-stream after the pictures on which they depend. The bit-stream syntax order is specified such that for reference pictures (i.e. pictures having types I, P, EI, EP, or the P part of PB or Improved PB), the following two rules shall be obeyed:

1. All reference pictures with the same temporal reference shall appear in the bit-stream in increasing enhancement layer order. This is because each lower layer reference picture is needed to decode the next higher layer reference picture.

2. All temporally simultaneous reference pictures as discussed in item 1 above shall appear in the bit-stream prior to any B-pictures for which any of these reference pictures is the fist temporally subsequent reference picture in the reference layer of the B-picture. This is done to reduce the delay of decoding all reference pictures, which may be needed as references for B-pictures.

Then, the B-pictures with earlier temporal references shall follow (temporally ordered within each enhancement layer). The bit-stream location of each B-picture shall comply with the following rules:

1. Be after that of its first temporally subsequent reference pictures in the reference layer. This is because, the decoding of the B-pictures generally depends on the prior decoding of that reference picture.

2. Be after that of all reference pictures that are temporally simultaneous with the first temporally subsequent reference picture in the reference layer. This is to reduce the delay of decoding all reference pictures, which may be needed as references for B-pictures.

3. Precede the location of any additional temporally subsequent pictures other than B-pictures in its reference layer. Otherwise, it would increase picture-storage memory requirement for the reference layer pictures.

4. Be after that of all EI and EP pictures that are temporally simultaneous with the first temporally subsequent reference picture.

5. Precede the location of all temporally subsequent pictures within its same enhancement layer. Otherwise, it would introduce needless delay and increase picture-storage memory requirements for the enhancement layer.

Figure 8.25 shows two allowable picture transmission orders given by the rules above for the layering structure shown as an example. Numbers next to each picture indicate the bit-stream order, separated by commas for the two alternatives.

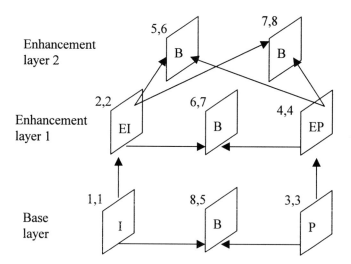

Figure 8.25 Example of picture transmission order

8.11 Advanced video coding (H.263L)

The long-term objective of the ITU-U video experts group, under the Advanced Video Coding project, is to provide a video coding recommendation which performs at *very low bit rates* with performance which is substantially better than that achievable with the existing standards (e.g. H.263+). The adopted technology should provide for:

- Enhanced visual quality at very low bit rates and particularly at PSTN rates (e.g. at rates below 24 kbit/s).
- Enhanced error robustness in order to accommodate the error prone environments experienced when operating for example over mobile links.
- Low complexity as would be appropriate for small, relatively inexpensive, audio-visual terminals.
- Low end-to-end delay as required in a bi-directional personal communications environment.

In addition, the group is closely working with the MPEG-4 experts group, to include new coding methods and promote interoperability. Advances in this direction will be discussed in the next chapter, on MPEG-4.

References

[1]   Draft ITU-T Recommendation H.263, 'Video coding for low bit rate communication', (July 1995).

[2]   H.261: 'ITU-T Recommendation H.261, video codec for audiovisual services at p×64 kbit/s', Geneva, (1990).

[3]   MPEG-1: 'Coding of moving pictures and associated audio for digital storage media at up to about 1.5 Mbit/s', *ISO/IEC 1117-2: video*, (November 1991).

[4]   MPEG-2: 'Generic coding of moving pictures and associated audio information', *ISO/IEC 13818-2 Video*, Draft International Standard, (November 1994).

[5]   Draft ITU-T Recommendation H.263+, 'Video coding for very low bit rate communication', (September 1997).

[6]   ITU- Document for very low bit rate visual telephony, 'Advanced video coding', (April 1996).

[7]   MPEG-4: 'Testing and evaluation procedures document', ISO/IEC JTC1/SC29/WG11, N999, (July 1995).

[8]   ITU-T Recommendation H.245, 'Control protocol for multimedia communication', (September 1998).

[9]   Wallace G.K. 'The JPEG still picture compression standard', *Communications of the ACM*, **34**, pp. 30-44, (1991).

[10] Blahut, R.E. 'Theory and practice of error control codes', Addison-Wesley, (1983).

[11] Ghanbari M. and Seferidis V. 'Cell loss concealment in ATM video codecs', *IEEE Transactions on Circuits and Systems for Video Technology*, Special Issue on Packet Video, **3:3**, pp. 238-247, (June 1993).

[12] Lim C.P., Tan E.A.W., Ghanbari M. and Ghanbari S. 'Cell loss concealment and packetisation in packet video', *International Journal of Imaging Systems*, **10**, pp. 54-58, (1999).

[13] ITU-T recommendation I.363, 'B-ISDN ATM adaptation layer (AAL) specification', (June 1992).

[14] Ghanbari M. and Hughes C.J. 'Packing coded video signals into ATM cells', *IEEE Transaction on Networking*, **1:5**, pp. 505-509, (October 1993).

[15] Hughes C.J., Ghanbari M., Pearson D.E., Seferidis V. and Xiong J., 'Modelling and subjective assessment of cell discard in ATM Video', *IEEE Transactions on Image Processing*, **2:2**, pp. 212-222, (April 1993).

[16] ITU SGXV working party XV/I, Experts Group for ATM video coding, working document AVC-205, (January 1992).

Chapter 9

Content-based video coding
(MPEG-4)

MPEG-4 is another ISO/IEC standard, developed by MPEG (Moving Picture Experts Group), the committee which also developed the Emmy Award winning standards of MPEG-1 and MPEG-2. While MPEG-1 and MPEG-2 video aimed at devising coding tools for CD-ROM and digital television respectively, MPEG-4 video aims at providing tools and algorithms for efficient storage, transmission and manipulation of video data in *multimedia* environments [1,2]. The main motivations behind such a task are the proven success of digital video in three fields of digital television, interactive graphics applications (synthetic image content) and the interactive multimedia (World Wide Web, distribution and access to image content). The MPEG-4 group believe these can be achieved by emphasising the *functionalities* of the proposed codec, which include efficient compression, object scalability, spatial and temporal scalability, error resilience, etc.

The approach taken by the experts group in coding of video for multimedia applications relies on a *content-based* visual data representation of scenes. In content-based coding, in contrast to the conventional video coding techniques, a scene is viewed as a composition of *video objects* (VO) with intrinsic properties such as shape, motion and texture. It is believed that such a content-based representation is a key to facilitating *interactivity* with objects for a variety of multimedia applications. In such applications, the user can access arbitrarily shaped objects in the scene and manipulate these objects.

The MPEG-4 group has defined the specifications of their intended video codec in the form of *verification models* (VM) [3]. The verification model in MPEG-4 has the same role as the reference and test models defined for H.261 and MPEG-2 respectively. The verification model has evolved over time by means of core experiments in various laboratories round the world. It is regarded as a common platform with a precise definition of the encoding and decoding algorithms that can be represented as tools addressing specific functionalities of

MPEG-4. New algorithms/tools are added to the VM and old algorithms/tools are replaced in the VM by successful core experiments.

So far the verification model has been gradually evolved from version 1.0 to version 11.0, and during each evolution new functionalities have been added to the latest model. In this chapter we do not intend to review all of them, but instead to address those funtionalities that have made MPEG-4 video coding radically different from its predecessors. Hence, it is intended to look at the fundamentals of new coding algorithms that have been introduced in MPEG-4. The chapter will end with new technological advances within the MPEG group on the areas of image retrieval and video data bases, under the name of MPEG-7.

9.1   Video object plane (VOP)

In object-based coding the video frames are defined in terms of layers of *video object planes* (VOP). Each video object plane is then a video frame of a specific object of interest to be coded, or to be interacted with. Figure 9.1(a) shows a video frame that is made of three VOPs. In this figure, the two objects of interest are the balloon and the aeroplane. They are represented with their video object planes of VOP_1 and VOP_2. The remaining part of the video frame is regarded as a background, represented with VOP_0. For coding applications, the background is coded only once, and the other object planes are encoded through the time. At the receiver the reconstructed background is repeatedly added to the other decoded object planes. Since in each frame the encoder only codes the objects of interest (e.g. VOP_1 and/or VOP_2), and usually these objects represent a small portion of the video frame, then the bit rate of the encoded video stream can be extremely low. Note that, had the video frame of Figure 9.1(a) been coded with a conventional codec such as H.263, since clouds in the background move, then the H.263 encoder will inevitably encode most parts of the picture, with a much higher bit rate than that generated from the two objects.

The VOP can be a semantic object in the scene, such as the balloon and aeroplane in Figure 9.1. It is made of Y, U and V components plus theirs *shapes*. The shapes are used to mask the background, and help to identify object boarders.

In MPEG-4 video, the VOPs are either known by construction of the video sequence (hybrid sequence based on blue screen composition or synthetic sequences) or are defined by semi-automatic *segmentation*. In the former, the shape information is represented by 8 bits, known as *grey scale alpha plane*. This plane is used to blend several video object planes to form the video frame of interest. Thus with 8 bits, up to 256 objects can be identified within a video frame. In the second case, the shape is a binary mask, to identify individual object borders and their positions in the video frames.

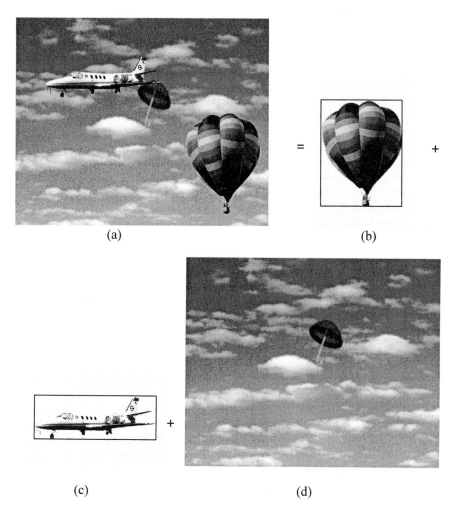

Figure 9.1 (a) A video frame composed of (b) balloon VOP$_1$, (c) aeroplane VOP$_2$ and (d) the background VOP$_0$

Figure 9.2 shows the binary shapes of the balloon and aeroplane in the above example. Both cases are currently considered in the encoding process. The VOP can have an arbitrary shape. When the sequence has only one rectangular VOP of fixed size displayed at a fixed interval, it corresponds to the *frame-based* coding. Frame-based coding is similar to H.263.

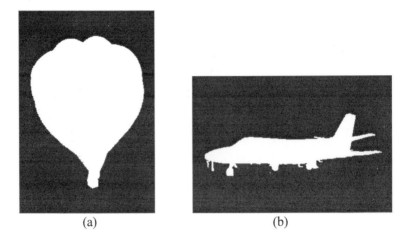

(a)   (b)

Figure 9.2. Shape of objects: (a) balloon and (b) aeroplane

9.1.1 Coding of objects

Each video object plane corresponds to an entity that after being coded is added to the bit-stream. The encoder sends together with the VOP, composition information to indicate where and when each VOP is to be displayed. Users are allowed to trace objects of interest from the bit-stream. They are also allowed to change the composition of the entire scene displayed by *interacting* with the composition information.

Figure 9.3 illustrates a block diagram of an object-based coding verification model (VM). After defining the video object planes, each VOP is encoded and the encoded bit-streams are multiplexed to a single bit-stream. At the decoder the chosen object planes are extracted from the bit-stream and then are composed into an output video to be displayed.

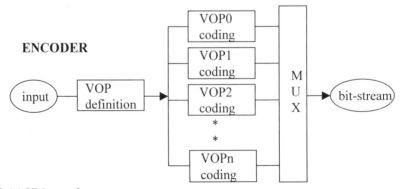

Figure 9.3 (a) VM encoder

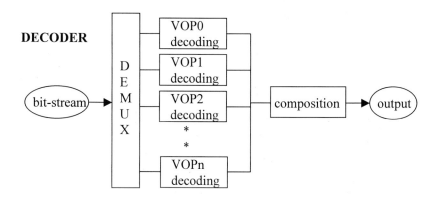

Figure 9.3 (b) VM decoder structure

9.1.2 Encoding of VOPs

Figure 9.4 shows a general overview of the encoder structure for each of the video object planes (VOPs). The encoder is mainly composed of two parts: the *shape* encoder and the traditional *motion and texture* encoder (e.g. H.263) applied to the same VOP.

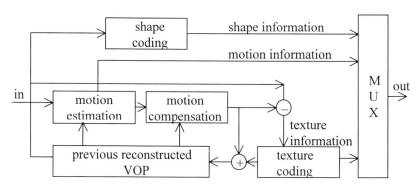

Figure 9.4 VOP encoder structure

Before explaining how the shape and the texture of the objects are coded, in the following we first explain how a VOP should be represented for efficient coding.

9.1.3   *Formation of VOP*

The shape information is used to form a VOP. For maximum coding efficiency, the arbitrary shape VOP is encapsulated in a bounding rectangle such that the object contains the minimum number of macroblocks. To generate the bounding rectangle, the following steps are followed:

1. Generate the tightest rectangle around the object, as shown in Figure 9.5. Since the dimensions of the chrominance VOP are half of the luminance VOP (4:2:0), then the top left position of the rectangle should be an even numbered pixel.

2. If the top left position of this rectangle is the origin of the frame, skip the formation procedure.

3. Form a control macroblock at the top left corner of the tightest rectangle, as shown in Figure 9.5.

4. Count the number of macroblocks that completely contain the object, starting at each even numbered point of the control macroblock. Details are as follows:
    (i)   Generate a bounding rectangle from the control point to the right bottom side of the object that consists of multiples of 16×16 pixel macroblocks.
    (ii) Count the number of macroblocks in this rectangle that contain at least one object pixel.

5. Select that control point which results in the smallest number of macroblocks for the given object.

6. Extend the top left co-ordinate of the tightest rectangle to the selected control co-ordinate.

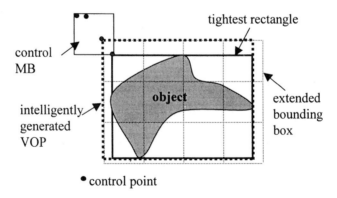

Figure 9.5 Intelligent VOP formation

This will create a rectangle that completely contains the object but with the minimum number of macroblocks in it. The VOP horizontal and vertical spatial references are taken directly from the modified top-left co-ordinate.

9.2 Image segmentation

If VOPs are not available, then video frames need to be *segmented* into objects and a VOP to be derived for each one. In general, segmentation consists of extracting image regions of similar properties such as brightness, colour or texture. These regions are then used as masks to extract the objects of interest from the image. Before describing the object segmentation, a brief overview of image segmentation in general is given.

9.2.1 Segmentation

Segmentation methods can be categorised according to the used processing strategy into the following classes [4] :

- **Region merging**: Starting with tiny uniform regions, merge similar regions until no further merging is possible. The starting regions in the finest level could be pixels themselves. They are called *atomic* regions. Usually atomic regions are chosen as such regions with grey levels within a predefined range. A suitable atomic region can be constructed from the edges, where closed contour edges form the boundary of the object of interest. Edges are extracted by edge extraction methods, such as double differentiation by the Sobel operator [5], where the image pixels are convolved with a 3×3 masking array, and then thresholded to segregate the edge from the non-edge image content. The masking elements are defined such that the slope of the edge is amplified, and can easily be thresholded. In order to obtain many atomic regions, the threshold for edge extraction must be low enough so that the edges with low contrasts may be also detected.
- **Region splitting**: Starting with large regions, split them into multiple regions. Continue the splitting process until no further splitting is required. The key in this method is the criterion for deciding how a region should be split. Most techniques determine the criteria on the basis of statistics of pixel values within a region. These methods are based on the assumption that foreground and background can be discriminated by their grey level values, or that the background is almost uniform. Although these techniques are based on simplistic assumptions, they are very important and fundamental in real-time applications in which only techniques with very low degrees of complexity can be implemented. *Thresholding* is perhaps the most common technique for elementary image segmentation by splitting. The determination of suitable

threshold values involves the analysis of some function of the image intensity values. From a computational point of view, techniques based on the analysis of the *histogram* present a high degree of efficiency [6]. Moreover, the distribution of the intensity values contains essential information about the position of optimal thresholds. To detect them in an easy but efficient manner, a peak detection function has to be generated. Using this function, modes and local maxima and minima in the histogram are detected. After detecting the histogram extremes, the image is quantised by assigning the histogram mode to all values between the start and the end of the respective peaks.

- **Split and merge:** Starting with medium size regions, such as blocks of fixed size, merge similar regions and then split regions which are not merged.

9.2.2 Object segmentation

Object segmentation in computer vision consists of the extraction of the shape of the physical objects projected onto the image plane, ignoring edges due to texture inside the object borders. This extremely difficult image processing task differs from the most basic segmentation problems usually formulated as separation of image areas containing pixels with similar intensity, in the objective of the task itself. While the result of general segmentation can be a large number of irregular segments (based only on intensity similarity), object segmentation tries to recognise the shapes of complete physical objects present in the scene. It is intuitively clear that this more general segmentation cannot be carried out without any additional information about the structure or dynamics of the scene. In this context most approaches for object segmentation can be included in two broad classes. The first one concerns methods for extraction of object masks by means of multiview image analysis on sequences taken from different perspectives, e.g. stereoscopic images, exploiting the 3D structure of the scene. The second is motion-based segmentation when only monoscopic sequences are available. In the latter case the dynamics of objects present in the scene is exploited in order to group pixels that undergo the same or similar motion. Because most natural scenes consist of locally rigid objects and moving objects deform continuously in time, it is expected that connected image regions with similar motion belong to a single object.

Let us consider a composite video frame, such as the scene shown in Figure 9.6(a). Obviously, a general segmentation method based on pixel similarity would split the image into several regions without any physical meaning. Even with a very good edge detection strategy, the best one can achieve is shown in Figure 9.6(b). As can be seen any edge, irrespective of belonging to the object of interest or not, is detected. In this figure, in order to extract only edges representing physical surface characteristics and not those due to the texture or noise, a scale-space based approximation is applied [7]. This is a form of edge selection, where edges are selected by convolving the image with a Gaussian function of decreasing variance. They are then detected at the location where the second derivative of the smoothed image crosses zero. Now if the object of the interest is just the CAR, then additional information, such as motion, is required to discriminate the car's borders from the rest of the edges of Figure 9.6(b).

(a)   (b)

Figure 9.6 (a) composite frame of a BBC-CAR and (b) edge selection with thresholding

For example, image edges that undergo similar motion in connected regions enclosed by a contour can be merged to form a rigid body object. Hence, a foreground mask can be made from the merged region of uniform motion, and is used to extract the CAR from the rest of the image, as shown in Figure 9.6(c).

Figure 9.6(c) Segmented car with the constraint on motion

In certain cases, human interaction might even be required to select the chosen object. For example, in scenes with multiple moving objects, complete automatic object segmentation is not possible. In this situation, the user normally chooses the object by, say, hand drawing a contour round the object as a rough guess, then refines it by object segmentation.

9.3   Shape coding

The binary and grey scale shapes are normally referred to binary and grey scale *alpha planes*. Binary alpha planes are encoded with one of the binary shape coding methods (to be explained later), while the grey scale alpha planes are encoded by motion compensated DCT similar to texture coding (e.g. H.263). An alpha plane is bounded by a rectangle that includes the shape of the VOP, as described in the formation of VOP, in Section 9.1.3. The bounding rectangle of the VOP is then extended on the right-bottom side to multiples of 16×16 pixel macroblocks. The extended alpha samples are set to zero. Now the extended alpha plane can be partitioned into exact multiples of 16×16 pixel macroblocks. Hereafter, these macroblocks are referred to *alpha blocks*, and the encoding and decoding process for block-based shape coding is carried out per alpha block.

   If the pixels in an alpha block are all transparent (all zero), the block is skipped before motion and/or texture coding. No overhead is required to indicate this mode since this transparency information can be obtained from shape coding. This skipping applies to all I-, P- and B-VOPs. Since shape coding is unique to MPEG-4 (no other standard codecs use it), then in the following sections we pay special attention to various shape coding methods.

9.3.1   Coding of binary alpha planes

A binary alpha plane is encoded in the INTRA mode for I-VOPs and the INTER mode for P-VOPs and B-VOPs. During the development of MPEG-4 several methods for coding of the binary alpha planes have been considered. These include *Chain* coding of the object contours, *Quad-tree* coding, *Modified Modified Reed* (MMR) and *Content-based Arithmetic Encoding* (CAE) [3, 8]. It appears that CAE, recommended in the latest version of the verification model (VM-11) [3], is the best. Hence in the introduction of these methods, more details are given on the CAE.

9.3.2   Chain code

In the chain code method, the object boundaries are represented by a closed *contour*, as shown in Figure 9.7, and the chain codes are then applied to the contour. Derivation of the contour from the binary alpha plane is similar to detection of the edge, as discussed in Section 9.2. For coding, it involves moving on the contour in one of eight directions, as shown in the figure, and coding the direction. The chain code terminates when the starting point is revisited.

Each chain code contains a start point data followed by the first chain code, and the subsequent differential chain codes. If VOP contains several closed contours, then plural chain codes are coded following the data for the number of regions.

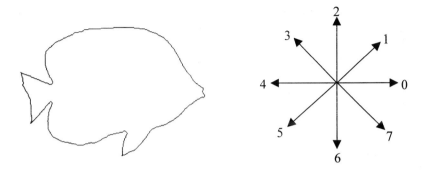

Figure 9.7 Object boundaries for chain coding and the eight directions of the chain around the object

Since a chain code has a cyclic property, a differential chain code in eight directions can be expressed in the range from -3 to 4 by the following definition:

$$d = \begin{cases} c_n - c_{n-1} + 8, & \text{if } c_n - c_{n-1} < -3 \\ c_n - c_{n-1} - 8, & \text{if } c_n - c_{n-1} > 4 \\ c_n - c_{n-1}, & \text{otherwise} \end{cases} \qquad (9.1)$$

where d is the differential chain code, c_n is the current chain code, and c_{n-1} is the previous chain code. Huffman code is used to encode the differential chain code d. The Huffman table is shown in Table 9.1.

Table 9.1 Huffman table for the differential chain code

d	code
0	1
1	00
−1	011
2	0100
−2	01011
3	010100
−3	0101011
4	0101010

At the receiver, after the variable length decoding of d, the current chain code, c_n, is then reconstructed as follows:

$$c_n = (c_{n-1} + d + 8) \mod 8 \tag{9.2}$$

9.3.3 Quad-tree coding

Each *binary alpha block* (BAB) of 16×16 pixels, represented by binary data (white 255 and black 0), is first *quadtree* segmented. The indices of the segments, according to the rules to be explained, are calculated and then Huffman coded. Figure 9.8 shows the quadtree structure employed for coding of a binary alpha block.

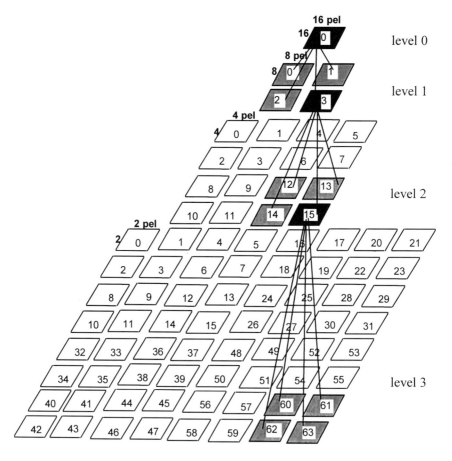

Figure 9.8 Quadtree representation of a shape block

At the bottom level (level-3) of the quadtree, a 16×16 alpha block is partitioned into 64 sub-blocks of 2×2 samples. Each higher level as shown also contains 16×16 pixels, but in groups of 4×4, 8×8 and 16×16 sub-blocks.

The calculation of the indices is as follows:

- The indexing of sub-blocks starts at level-3, where an index is assigned to each 2×2 sub-block pixel.
- For the four pixels of the sub-block b[0] to b[3] of Figure 9.9, the index is calculated as:

$$index = (27 \times b[0]) + (9 \times b[1]) + (3 \times b[2]) + b[3] \tag{9.3}$$

where $b[i] = 2$ if the sample value is 255 (white) and $b[i]=0$ if it is black. Hence there are 16 different index values with a minimum of 0 and a maximum of 80.

b[0]	b[1]
b[2]	b[3]

Figure 9.9 A sub-block of 2×2 pixels

Step 1. Indexing of sub-blocks at level 3

These indices then become inputs to level-2 for the generation of a new set of indices at this level. However, to increase inter-block correlation, the sub-blocks are swapped in decreasing order of indices. The swapping also causes the distribution of index values to be predominantly low and hence this non-uniform distribution is more efficiently variable length coded. Arrangement for the swap of the four sub-blocks is carried out according to the relationship of the neighbouring indices in the following order. The upper and left neighbouring indices are shown in Figure 9.10.

	upper_ index[0]	upper_ index[1]
left_ index[0]	index[0]	index[1]
left_ index[1]	index[2]	index[3]

Figure 9.10 Upper and left level indices of a sub-block

(a) If upper_index[0] is less than upper_index[1], then swap index[0] with index[1] and index[2] with index[3], except for sub-blocks numbered 0,1,4,5,16,17,20 and 21.

(b) If left_index[0] is less than left_index[1], then swap index[0] with index[2] and index[1] with index[3] except for subblocks numbered 0,2,8,10,32,34,40 and 42.

(c) If upper_index[0] + upper_index[1] is less than left_index[0] + left_index[1], then swap index[1] with index[2] except for sub-blocks numbered 0,1,2,4,5,8,10,16,17,20,21,32,34,40,and 42,

(d) The index of level-2 is computed from index[0], index[1], index[2] and index[3] after swapping according to:

$index\_level\_2 =$

$$27 \times f(index[0]) + 9 \times f(index[1]) + 3 \times f(index[2]) + f(index[3])$$

where

$$
\begin{array}{lll}
f(x) = 0 & \text{if } x = 0 & \\
f(x) = 2 & \text{if } x = 80 & (9.4) \\
f(x) = 1 & \text{otherwise} &
\end{array}
$$

The current sub-block is then reconstructed and used as a reference when processing subsequent sub-blocks.

Step 2. Grouping process for higher levels

The grouping process of blocks at the higher level first starts at level-2 where four sub-blocks from level-3 are grouped to form a new sub-block. The grouping process involves swapping and indexing similarly to that discussed for level-3, except that in this level a 4 × 4 pixel block is represented by a 2 × 2 sub-block whose elements are indices rather than pixels. The current sub-block is then reconstructed and used as a reference when processing subsequent sub-blocks. At the decoder swapping is done following a reverse sequence of steps as at the encoder.

The grouping process is also performed similarly for level-1 where four sub-blocks from level-2 are grouped to form a new sub-block. The swapping, indexing and reconstruction of a sub-block follows grouping, the same as that for other levels.

Now arrangement of sub-blocks in decreasing order of their indices at level-2, to utilise inter-block correlation, is done as follows:

(a) If f(upper_index[0]) is less than f(upper_index[1]), then swap index[0] with index[1] and index[2] with index[3], except for sub-blocks numbered 0,1,4 and 5.

(b) If f(left_index[0]) is less than f(left_index[1]), then swap index[0] with index[2] and index[1] with index[3] except for sub-blocks numbered 0,2,8 and 10.

(c) If f(upper_index[0]) + f(upper_index[1]) is less than f(left_index[0]) + f(left_index[1]), then swap index[1] with index[2] except for sub-blocks numbered 0,1,2,4,5,8 and 10.

(d) The index of level-1 is computed from index[0], index[1], index[2] and index[3] after swapping, according to equation 9.4.

At level-1 no swapping is required.

Step 3. Encoding process
The encoding process involves use of results from the grouping process which produces a total of 85 (= 1 + 4 + 16 + 64) indices for a 16 × 16 alpha block. Each index is encoded from the topmost level (level 0). At each level, the order for encoding and transmission of indices is shown by numbers in Figure 9.8. Indices are Huffman coded. Note that indices at level-3 can take only 16 different values, while at the other levels they take 80 different values. Hence for efficient variable length coding, two different Huffman tables are used, one with 16 symbols at level-3 and the other with 80 symbols at levels 0 to 2. These tables are shown in Appendix C.

9.3.4 *Modified modified Reed (MMR)*

During the course of MPEG-4 development, another shape coding method named *modified modified Reed* (MMR) was also investigated [8]. The basic idea in this method is to detect the pixel intensity changes (from opaque to transparent and vice versa) within a block, and to code the positions of the changing pixels. The changing pixels are defined by pixels whose colour changes while scanning an alpha block in raster-scan order. Figure 9.11 illustrates the changing pixels in an Intra and motion compensated Inter alpha block. Also in the figure are the Top and Left reference row and column of pixels respectively.

To code the position of the changing pixels, the following parameters, as shown in Figure 9.11, are defined.

For each length, the starting pixel is denoted by a_0. Initially a_0 is positioned at the right end in the Top reference and addressed as abs_a_0 = −1. The first changing pixel appearing after a_0 is called a_1. For Intra blocks, the pixel located above a_0 is called b_0. The area from the next pixel to b_0 down to a_0 is called the reference area in IntraMMR. In this case the reference changing pixel is called b_1. This pixel is found in reference area r_1 or r_2, shown in Figure 9.12(a). Searching in r_1, the first changing pixel whose colour is the opposite of a_0 is named b_1; if not found, the first changing pixel in r_2 is named b_1. Thus b_1 might become identical to a_0. Exceptionally b_1 may not be found when abs_$a_0 = -1$.

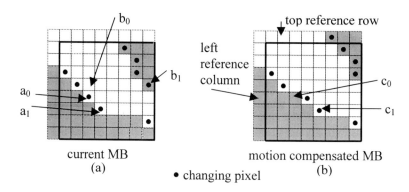

Figure 9.11 Changing pixels of (a) Intra and (b) Inter alpha block

For InterMMR, the pixel at the corresponding position to a_0 is called c_0. The area from the next pixel to c_0 down to the end of alpha block is called *reference area* in InterMMR. The reference changing pixel in this mode is called c_1. This pixel is found in the reference area r_1 or r_2, shown in Figure 9.12(b). Searching in r_1, the first changing pixel whose colour is opposite of a_0 is named c_1; if not found, the first changing pixel in r_2 is named c_1.

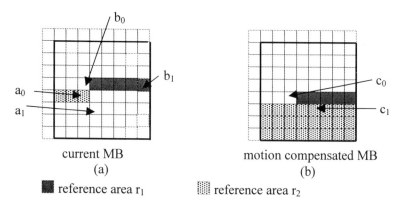

Figure 9.12 Reference area for detecting reference changing pixel: (a) b_1 and (b) c_1

Given a_0, the eventual task is to identify a_1 by referring to either b_1 or c_1, depending on the IntraMMR or InterMMR mode respectively. This is achieved in three different modes as *vertical*, *horizontal* and *vertical pass* modes. The vertical mode is the first option that is considered and if it is decided not to be applicable, the horizontal mode or the vertical pass mode is employed in turn.

In the vertical mode the position of a_1 is identified relative to that of b_1. It is invoked only when the absolute value of the relative distance defined by the relative address DIST $= r\_a_1 - r\_b_1$, is equal to or less than a predefined threshold [8]. The DIST is then variable length coded using the appropriate InteraMMR and InterMMR VLC tables.

If the vertical mode is not used (DIST > threshold), then the horizontal mode is considered for coding. In this mode the position of a_1 is identified on the basis of the absolute distance from a_0. If this distance is less than the width of the alpha block, then it is used; otherwise the vertical pass mode is used, which implies that the one row of the pixels in the alpha block is passed (not coded).

Finally, the decision to use IntraMR or InterMMR is to first scan the alpha block in the horizontal and vertical scanning directions. The one requiring the least of bits is chosen. In the case of a tie, the horizontal scanning is chosen. For the final decision between IntraMMR and InterMMR, again the one is selected that gives the least coding bits.

9.3.5 Context based arithmetic coding

In this method each INTRA binary alpha block (BAB) and the INTER one after being motion compensated by block-based motion compensation, is *context-based arithmetic encoded* (CAE). In general each binary alpha block is coded according to one of the following seven modes (in 'C' terminology):

1. MVDs ==0 && No_Update

2. MVDs !=0 && No_Update

3. All_0

4. All_255

5. IntraCAE

6. MVDs ==0 && InterCAE

7. MVDs !=0 && InterCAE

The first and second modes indicate that the shape will not be updated, and the All_0 and All_255 indicate that the BAB contains only black and white pixels respectively. None of these modes are required to be arithmetic coded. Also in the Quadtree and MMR methods, All_0 and All-255 are not coded further.

IntraCAE is the mode for context-based arithmetic coding of BABs that contain a mixture of black and white pixels. In modes 6 and 7, the interframe BABs (mixed black and white pixels) with and without motion compensation respectively, are arithmetic coded.

The motion vector difference of shape, represented by MVDS, is the difference between the shape motion vector and its predictor, MVP. The prediction procedure is similar to that of the motion vector difference for texture, described in chapter 8, Section 8.1.2. However, there are differences, such as:

- The prediction motion vectors can be derived from the candidate motion vectors of shape MVs1, MVs2, MVs3 or the candidate motion vectors of the texture, MV1, MV2 and MV3, similar to those of H.263 illustrated in Figure 8.1 of chapter 8. The prediction motion vector is determined by taking the first encountered motion vector that is valid. If no candidate is valid, the prediction is set to zero.
- Overlapped, half pixel precision and 8×8 motion compensation is not carried out.
- In the case that the region outside the VOP is referred to, the value for that is set to zero.
- For B-VOPs, only forward motion compensation is used and neither backward nor interpolated motion compensation is allowed.

It should be noted that when the shape prediction motion vector MVPS is determined, the difference between the motion compensated BAB indicated with MVPS and the current BAB is calculated. If the motion compensated error is less than a certain threshold (AlphaTH) for any 4×4 sub-block of the BAB, the MVPS is directly employed as the best prediction. If this condition is not met, MV is searched around the prediction vector MVPS, by comparing the BAB indicated by the MV and the current BAB. The MV that minimises the error is taken as the best motion vector for shape, MVS, and the motion vector difference for shape (MVDS) is given by MVDS=MVS–MVPS.

9.3.5.1 Size conversion

Rate control and rate reduction in MPEG-4 is realised through size conversion of the binary alpha information. This method is also applicable to Quadtree and MRR. It is implemented in two successive steps.

In the first step, if required, the size of the VOP can be reduced by half in each of the horizontal and vertical directions. This is indicated in the VOP header, as the video object plane conversion ratio, VOP_CR, which takes a value either 1 or ½. When VOP_CR is ½, the size conversion is carried out on the original bounding box of Figure 9.5.

In the case that the value of VOP_CR is ½, the locally decoded shape which is size converted at the VOP level is stored in the frame memory of the shape frame.

For the shape motion estimation and compensation, if VOP_CR of the reference shape VOP is not equal to that of the current shape VOP, the reference shape frame (not VOP) is size converted corresponding to the current shape VOP.

For P-VOPs, if the VOP_CR is ½, the components of the shape motion information vector are measured on the down-sampled shape frame. The predicted motion vector for the shape, MVPS, is calculated only using the shape motion vectors MVS1, MVS2 and MVS3.

In the second step, when required, the size conversion is carried out for every binary alpha block, BAB, except for All_0, All_255 and No_Update. At the block level the conversion ratio (CR) can be one of ¼, ½ and 1 (the original size).

For CR = ½, if the average of pixel values in a 2×2 pixel block is equal to or larger than 128, the pixel value of the down-sampled block is set to 255, otherwise it is set to zero. For CR = ¼, if the average of pixels in a 4×4 pixel block is equal to or larger than 128, the pixel value of the down-sampled block is set to 255, otherwise it is set to zero. In either of these cases, up-sampling is carried out for the BAB. The values of the interpolated pixels are calculated from their neighbouring pixels, according to their Euclidean distances.

Selection of a suitable value for the conversion ratio (CR) is done based on the conversion error between the original BAB and the BAB which is once down-sampled and then reconstructed by up-sampling. The conversion error is computed for each 4×4 sub-block, by taking the absolute difference of pixels in the corresponding sub-blocks of the original and reconstructed BABs. If this difference is greater than a certain threshold, this sub-block is called an error pixel block (Error_PB). Size-conversion at a certain conversion ratio is accepted if there is no Error_PB at that ratio. Figure 9.13 summarises determination of the conversion ratio, CR.

If a down-sampled BAB turns out to be "All transparent" or "All opaque" while the conversion error in any 4×4 sub-blocks in the BAB is equal to or lower than the threshold, the shape information is coded as shape_mode = All_0 or All_255. Unless this is the case, the BAB is coded with a context-based arithmetic coding at the size determined by the algorithm for the rate control.

9.3.5.2 Generation of context index

The pixels in the binary alpha blocks (BABs) are context-based arithmetic coded for both INTRA and INTER modes. The number of pixels in the BAB is determined by the conversion ratio (CR), which is either 16×16, 8×8 or 4×4 pixels for CR values of 1, ½ and ¼ respectively.

The context-based arithmetic encoding (CAE) is a binary arithmetic coding, where the symbol probability is determined from the context of the neighbouring pixels. Such a coding is applied to each pixel of the BAB in the following manner. First, prior to encoding of each BAB, the arithmetic encoder is initialised. Each binary pixel is then encoded in the raster scan order. The process for coding a given pixel is carried out using the following steps:

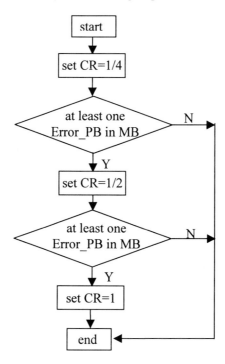

Figure 9.13 CR determination algorithm

1. Compute the context number.

2. Index a probability table using the context number.

3. Use the indexed probability to derive an arithmetic encoder.

When the final pixel has been encoded the arithmetic code is terminated.

Figure 9.14 shows the template of the neighbouring pixels that contribute to the creation of the context number for INTRA and INTER shape pixels.

For INTRA coded BABs, a 10-bit context $C = \sum_{k=0}^{9} c_k \cdot 2^k$ is calculated for each pixel, as shown in Figure 9.14(a). In this figure the pixel to be encoded is represented by "?" and the 10 neighbouring pixels are ordered as shown. For INTER coded BABs, in addition to spatial redundancy, temporal redundancy is exploited by using pixels from the bordered motion compensated BAB, to make up part of the context, as shown in Figure 9.14(b). In this mode, only 9 bits are required to calculate the context number, e.g. $C = \sum_{k=0}^{8} c_k 2^k$.

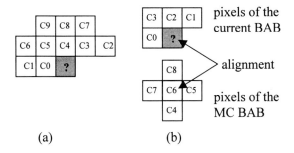

(a)   (b)

Figure 9.14   Template for the construction of the pixels of (a) the INTRA and (b) INTER BABs. The pixel to be coded is marked with "?"

In both modes there are some special cases to note:

- In building contexts, any pixel outside the bounding box of the current VOP to the left and above are assumed to be zero.
- The template may cover pixels from BABs which are not known at the decoding time. The values of these unknown pixels are estimated by template padding in the following manner:

  (a) When constructing the INTRA context, the following steps are taken in sequence:

    1. If (C7 is unknown) C7=C8.

    2. If (C3 is unknown) C3=C4.

    3. If (C2 is unknown) C2=C3.

  (b) When constructing the INTER context, the following conditional assignment is performed:

    1. If (C1 is unknown) C1=C2.

Once the context number is calculated, it is used to derive a probability table for binary arithmetic coding. Two probability tables, a 10-bit for INTRA and a 9-bit for INTER BABs, are given in Appendix D. These tables contain the probabilities for a binary alpha pixel being equal to 0 for intra and inter shape coding using the context-based arithmetic coding. All probabilities are normalised to the range of $[1, 65535]$.

As an example let us assume the neighbouring pixels for an INTRA BAB template has a black and white pattern as shown in Figure 9.15.

In this figure, C0=C1=C2=C3=C4=C7=1, and C5=C6=C8=C9=0. Hence the context number for coding of pixel "?" is $C = 2^0 + 2^1 + 2^2 + 2^3 + 2^4 + 2^7 = 159$.

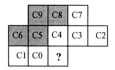

Figure 9.15 An example of an INTRA BAB template

If pixel "?" was a black pixel it would have been coded with an Intra_prob[159]. This value according to Appendix D is 74 out of 65535. If it was a white pixel, its probability would have been 65535−74=65461 out of 65535. Such a high probability for a white pixel in this example is expected, since this pixel is surrounded by many white pixels. Note also, although the given probability table is fixed, as the pattern of neighbouring pixels changes, the calculated context number changes such that the assigned probability to the pixel is better suited for that pattern. This is a form of adaptive arithmetic coding which only looks at the limited number of past coded symbols. It has been shown that adaptive arithmetic coding with limited past history has more efficient compression over fixed rate arithmetic coding [9].

9.3.6   Grey scale shape coding

The grey level alpha plane is encoded as its support function and the alpha values on the support. The support is obtained by thresholding the grey level alpha plane by 0, and the remaining parts constitute the alpha values, as shown in Figure 9.16.

The support function is encoded by binary shape coding, as described in Section 9.3.5. The alpha values are partitioned into 16×16 blocks and encoded the same way as the luminance of texture is coded.

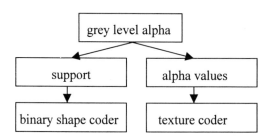

Figure 9.16 Grey scale shape coding

9.4   Motion estimation and compensation

The texture of each VOP is motion compensated prior to coding. The motion estimation and compensation is similar to that of H.263 with the exception that the blocks on the VOP borders have to be modified to cater for the arbitrary shapes of the VOPs. These modified macroblocks are referred to as *polygons*, and the motion estimation is called *polygon based matching*. Furthermore, since shapes change from time to time, some conversion is necessary to ensure the consistency of the motion compensation.

A macroblock that lies on the VOP boundary, called a *boundary macroblock*, is padded by replicating the boundary samples of the VOP towards the exterior. This process is carried out by repetitive padding in the horizontal and vertical directions. In case there are macroblocks completely outside the VOP, they are padded by extended padding.

In horizontal padding, each sample at the boundary of a VOP is replicated horizontally in the left or right direction in order to fill the transparent region outside the VOP of a boundary macroblock. If there are two boundary sample values for filling a sample outside a VOP, the two boundary samples are averaged. A similar method is used for vertical padding of the boundary macroblocks in the vertical direction.

Exterior macroblocks immediately next to boundary macroblocks are filled by replicating the samples at the border of the boundary macroblocks. The boundary macroblocks are numbered in a prioritised order according to Figure 9.17.

The exterior macroblock is then padded by replicating upwards, downwards, lefwards or rightwards the rows of sampling from the horizontal, vertial border of the boundary macroblock having the largest priority number. Note that the boundary macroblocks have already been padded by horizontal and vertical repetitive padding. The remaining macroblocks (not located next to any boundary macroblock) are filled with 128. The original alpha plane for the VOP is used to exclude the pixels of the macroblocks that are outside the VOP.

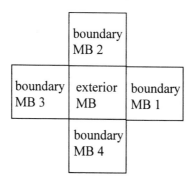

Figure 9.17 Priority of boundary macroblocks surrounding an exterior macroblock

The reference VOP is padded based on its own shape information. For example, when the reference VOP is smaller than the current VOP, the reference is not padded up to the size of the current VOP.

The motion estimation and compensation with the padded VOPs can be carried out in several different forms, such as integer pixel motion estimation, half and quarter sample search, unrestricted motion estimation/compensation, overlapped motion compensation and advanced mode prediction. Motion vectors are then differentially encoded, similar to H.263.

9.5   Texture coding

The intra VOPs and motion compensated inter VOPs are coded with 8×8 block DCT. The DCT is performed separately for each of the luminance and chrominance planes.

For an arbitrarily shaped VOP, the macroblocks that completely reside inside the VOP shape are coded with a technique identical to H.263. For the boundary macroblocks, if it is of intra type, it is padded with horizontal and vertical repetition. For inter macroblocks, not only is the macroblock repeatedly padded, but also the region outside the VOP within the block is padded with zeros. Transparent blocks are skipped and therefore are not coded. These blocks are then coded in a manner identical to the interior blocks. Blocks that lie outside the original shape are padded with 128, 128 and 128 for the luminance and the two chrominances in the case of intra and 0, 128 and 128 for inter macroblocks. Blocks that belong neither to the original nor the coded arbitrary shape but to the inside of the bounding box of the VOP are not coded at all.

9.5.1 Shape adaptive DCT

At the boundary macroblocks, the horizontally/vertically padded blocks can be coded with a standard 8×8 block DCT. This padding removes any abrupt transitions within a block, and hence reduces the number of significant DCT coefficients. At the decoder the added pixels are removed by the help of shape parameters from the decoded BABs.

Since the number of opaque pixels in the 8×8 blocks of some of the boundary macroblocks is usually less than 64 pixels, it would have been more efficient if these opaque pixels could have been DCT coded without padding. This method of DCT coding is called *shape adaptive DCT* (SA-DCT). The internal processing of SA-DCT is controlled by the shape information that has to be derived from the decoded BAB. Hence only opaque pixels within the boundary blocks are actually coded. As a consequence, in contrast to standard DCT, the number of DCT coefficients in a SA-DCT is equal to the number of opaque pixels.

There are two types of shape adaptive DCT, one used for inter blocks, known as SA-DCT and the other for intra blocks, known as ΔSA-DCT, which is an extension of SA-DCT. For both cases, a two-dimensional separable DCT with a varying length of basis vectors is used.

The basic concept of SA-DCT is shown in Figure 9.18. Segments of the opaque pixels are encapsulated in the picture grids of 8×8 pixel blocks as shown in Figure 9.18(a). Each row of the pixels is then shifted and aligned to the left, as shown in Figure 9.18(b). The aligned pixels are then one-dimensionally DCT coded in the horizontal direction with variable basis functions, where the lengths of the basis functions are determined by the number of pixels in each line. For example the first pixel of the segment is represented by itself, as a DC coefficient. The second line of the pixels is DCT coded with a 3-point transform, and the third line, with a 5-point transform, and so on. The coefficients of the N-point DCT, c_j, are defined by:

$$c_j = \sqrt{\frac{2}{N}} \, c_0 \cos\left[p(k + 0.5)\frac{\pi}{N} \right]$$

(9.5)

and $c_0 = \dfrac{\sqrt{2}}{2}$ if $p = 0$; $c_0 = 1$ otherwise

Figure 9.18(c) illustrates the horizontal DCT coefficients, where the DC values are represented with a dot. These coefficients now become the input to the second stage one-dimensional DCT in the vertical direction. Again they are shifted upwards and aligned to the upper border, and the N-point DCT is applied to each vertical column, as shown in Figure 9.18(e). The final two-dimensional DCT coefficients are shown in Figure 9.18(f). Note that, since the shape information from the decoded BABs is known, these processes of shifting and alignments in the horizontal and vertical directions are reversible.

The ΔSA-DCT algorithm that is used for intra coded macroblocks is similar to SA-DCT but with extra processing. This additional processing is simply calculating the mean of the opaque pixels in the block, and subtracting the mean from each individual pixel. The resultant zero mean opaque pixels are then SA-DCT coded. The mean value is separately transmitted as the DC coefficient.

Zigzag scanning, quantisation and the variable length coding of the SA-DCT coefficients operations are similar to those of standard DCT used in H.263.

9.6 Coding of synthetic objects

Synthetic images form a subset of computer graphics, that can be supported by MPEG-4. Of particular interest in synthetic images is the animation of head-and-shoulders or cartoon-like images. Currently animation of synthetic faces has been extensively studied, and the three-dimensional body animation will be addressed in the second phase of MPEG-4 development.

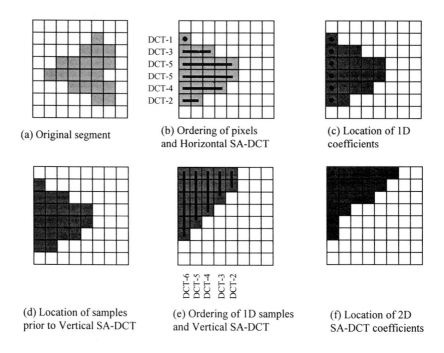

Figure 9.18 An example of shape adaptive DCT

The animation parameters are derived from a two-dimensional *mesh*, which is a tessellation of a two-dimensional region into polygonal patches. The vertices of the polygonal patches are referred to as the *node points* or vertices of the mesh. In coding of the objects, these points are moved according to the movement of the body, head, eyes, lips and changes in the facial expressions. A two-dimensional mesh matched to the "Claire" image is shown in Figure 9.19(a). Since the number of nodes representing the movement can be very small, this method of coding, known as *model-based* coding, requires a very low bit rate, possibly in the range of 1–10 bit/s [10].

In order to make synthetic images look more natural, the texture of the objects is mapped into the two-dimensional mesh, as shown in Figure 9.19(b). For coding of the animated images, triangular patches in the current frame are deformed by the movement of the node points to be matched into the triangular patches or facets in the reference frame. The texture inside each patch in the reference frame is thus *warped* onto the current frame, using a parametric mapping, defined as a function of the node point motion vectors.

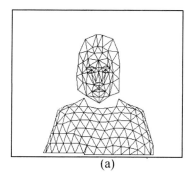 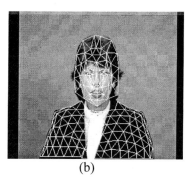

(a)   (b)

Figure 9.19 (a) A two-dimensional mesh, and (b) the mapped texture

For triangular meshes, the affine mapping with six parameters (three node points or vertices) is a common choice [11]. Its linear form implies that texture mapping can be accomplished with a low computational complexity. This mapping can model a general form of motion including translation, rotation, scaling, reflection, shear, and preserves straight lines. This implies that the original two-dimensional motion field can be compactly represented by the motion of the node points, from which a continuous, piece-wise affine motion field can be reconstructed. At the same time, the mesh structure constrains movements of adjacent image patches. Therefore, meshes are well suited to represent mildly deformable but spatially continuous motion fields.

However, if the movement is more complex, like the motion of lips, then affine modelling may fail. For example, Figure 9.20 shows the reconstructed picture of "Claire", after nine frames of affine modelling. The accumulated error due to model failure around the lips is very evident.

Figure 9.20 Reconstructed model-based image with the affine transform

For a larger complex motion, requiring a more severe patch deformation, one can use quadrilateral mappings with 8 degrees of freedom. *Bilinear* and

Perspective mappings are these kinds of mappings, which have a better deformation capability over the affine mapping [12, 13].

9.7 Coding of still images

MPEG-4 also supports coding of still images with a high coding efficiency as well as spatial and SNR scalability. This coding method is compatible with the new method of coding of still images under the JPEG-2000 [14].

The coding principle is based on the *discrete wavelet transform*, which is a sub-class of *sub-band* coding. The lowest sub-band after quantisation is coded with a differential pulse code modulation (DPCM) and the higher bands with a novel technique, called *zero-tree* coding [15]. The quantised DPCM and zero-tree data are then entropy coded with an arithmetic encoder. Figure 9.21 shows a block diagram of the still image encoder.

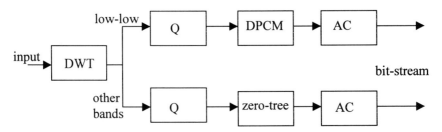

Figure 9.21 Block diagram of a wavelet-based still image encoder

In the following sections each part of the encoder is described.

9.7.1 Discrete wavelet transform

Discrete wavelet transform, under the generic name of sub-band coding, was first introduced by Crochiere *et al.* in 1976 [16], and has since proved to be a simple and powerful technique for speech and image compression. The basic principle is the partitioning of the signal spectrum into several frequency bands, then coding and transmitting each band separately. This is particularly suited to image coding. Firstly, natural images tend to have a non-uniform frequency spectrum, with most of the energy being concentrated in the lower frequency band. Secondly, according to the human visual system, noise visibility tends to fall off at both high and low frequencies and this enables the designer to adjust the compression distortion according to perceptual criteria. Thirdly, since images are processed in their entirety, and not in artificial blocks, there is no block structure distortion in the coded picture, as occurs in the transform based image encoders.

In wavelet coding the band splitting is done by passing the image data through a bank of bandpass *analysis filters*, as shown in Figure 9.22. In order to adapt the frequency response of the decomposed pictures to the characteristics of the human visual system, filters are arranged into octave-bands.

Since the bandwidth of each filtered version of the image is reduced, they can now in theory be down-sampled at a lower rate, according to the Nyquist criteria, giving a series of reduced size sub-images. The sub-images are then quantised, coded and transmitted. The received sub-images are restored to their original sizes and passed through a bank of *synthesis filters*, where they are interpolated and added to reconstruct the image.

In the absence of quantisation error, it is required that the reconstructed picture should be an exact replica of the input picture. This can only be achieved if the spatial frequency response of the analysis filters *tile* the spectrum without overlapping, which requires infinitely sharp transition regions and cannot be realised practically. Instead, the analysis filter responses have finite transition regions and do overlap, as shown in Figure 9.22, which means that the down-sampling/up-sampling processes introduce *aliasing* distortion into the reconstructed picture.

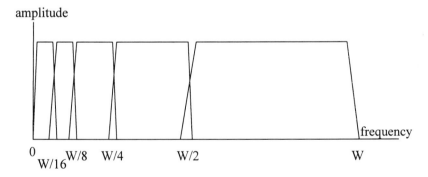

Figure 9.22 A bank of bandpass filters

In order to eliminate the aliasing distortion, the synthesis and analysis filters have to have certain relationships such that the aliased components in the transition regions cancel each other out. To see how such a relation can make alias-free wavelet coding possible, consider a two-band wavelet transform, as shown in Figure 9.23.

The corresponding two-band wavelet transform encoder/decoder is shown in Figure 9.24. In this diagram, filters $H_0(z)$ and $H_1(z)$ represent the z-transform transfer functions of the respective low pass and high pass analysis filters. Filters $G_0(z)$ and $G_1(z)$ are the corresponding synthesis filters. The down-sampling and up-sampling factors are 2.

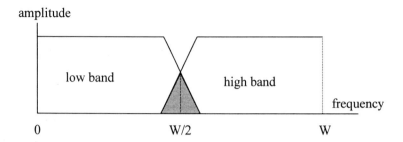

Figure 9.23 A two-band analysis filter

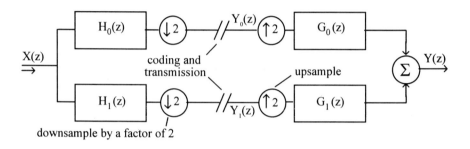

Figure 9.24 A two-band wavelet transform encoder/decoder

At the encoder, down-sampling by 2 is carried out by discarding alternate samples, the remainder being compressed into half the distance occupied by the original sequence. This is equivalent to compressing the source image by a factor of 2, which doubles all the frequency components present. The frequency domain effect of this down-sampling/compression is thus to double the width of all components in the sampled spectrum.

At the decoder, the up-sampling is a complementary procedure: it is achieved by inserting a zero-valued sample between each input sample, and is equivalent to a spatial expansion of the input sequence. In the frequency domain, the effect is as usual the reverse and all components are compressed towards zero frequency.

The problem with these operations is the impossibility of constructing ideal, sharp-cut analysis filters. This is illustrated in Figure 9.25(a). Spectrum A shows the original sampled signal which has been low pass filtered so that some energy remains above $F_s/4$, the cut-off of the ideal filter for the task. Down-sampling compresses the signal and expands to give B, while C is the picture after expansion or up-sampling. As well as those at multiples of F_s, this process generates additional spectrum components at odd multiples of $F_s/2$. These cause aliasing when the final sub-band recovery takes place as at D.

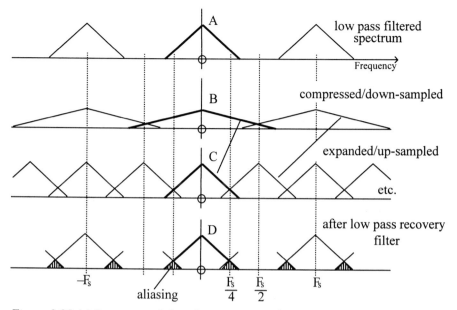

Figure 9.25 (a) Low pass sub-band generation and recovery

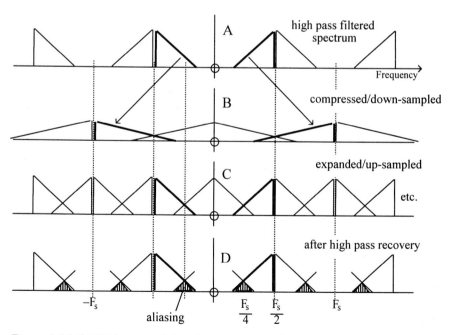

Figure 9.25 (b) High pass sub-band generation and recovery

In the high pass case, Figure 9.25(b), the same phenomena occur, so that on recovery there is aliased energy in the region of $F_s/4$. The final output image is generated by adding the low pass and high pass sub-bands regenerated by the up samplers and associated filters. The aliased energy would normally be expected to cause interference. However, if the phases of the aliased components from the high and low pass sub-bands can be made to differ by π, then cancellation occurs and the recovered signal is alias-free.

How this can be arranged is best analysed by reference to z-transforms. Referring to Figure 9.24, after the synthesis filters, the reconstructed output in z-transform notation can be written as:

$$Y(z) = G_0(z) \cdot Y_0(z) + G_1(z) \cdot Y_1(z) \tag{9.6}$$

where $Y_0(z)$ and $Y_1(z)$ are inputs to the synthesis filters after up-sampling. Assuming there are no quantisation and transmission errors, the reconstructed samples are given by

$$Y_0(z) = \frac{1}{2}[H_0(z) \cdot X(z) + H_0(-z) \cdot X(-z)]$$

$$Y_1(z) = \frac{1}{2}[H_1(z) \cdot X(z) + H_1(-z) \cdot X(-z)] \tag{9.7}$$

where the aliasing components from the down-sampling of the lower and higher bands are given by $H_0(-z)X(-z)$ and $H_1(-z)X(-z)$ respectively. By substituting these two equations in the previous one, we get

$$Y(z) = \frac{1}{2}[H_0(z) \cdot G_0(z) + H_1(z) \cdot G_1(z)]X(z)$$

$$+ \frac{1}{2}[H_0(-z) \cdot G_0(z) + H_1(-z) \cdot G_1(z)]X(-z) \tag{9.8}$$

The first term is the desired reconstructed signal, while the second term is aliased components. The aliased components can be eliminated regardless of the amount of overlap in the analysis filters by defining the synthesis filters as

$$G_0(z) = H_1(-z) \qquad \text{and} \quad G_1(z) = -H_0(-z) \tag{9.9}$$

With such a relation between the synthesis and analysis filters, the reconstructed signal now becomes

$$Y(z) = \frac{1}{2}[H_0(z) \cdot H_1(-z) - H_0(-z) \cdot H_1(z)]X(z) \tag{9.10}$$

If we define $P(z) = H_0(z)H_1(-z)$, then the reconstructed signal can be written as

$$Y(z) = \frac{1}{2}[P(z) - P(-z)]X(z) \qquad (9.11)$$

Now the reconstructed signal can be a perfect, but an m-sample delayed, replica of the input signal, if

$$P(z) - P(-z) = 2z^{-m} \qquad (9.12)$$

Thus the z-transform input/output signals are given by

$$Y(z) = z^{-m}X(z) \qquad (9.13)$$

This relation in the pixel domain implies that the reconstructed pixel sequence $\{y(n)\}$ is an exact replica of the delayed input sequence $\{x(n–m)\}$.

In these equations $P(z)$ is called the *product filter* and m is the delay introduced by the filter banks. The design of analysis/synthesis filters is based on factorisation of the product filter $P(z)$ into linear phase components $H_0(z)$ and $H_1(-z)$, with the constraint that the difference between the product filter and its image should be a simple delay. Then the product filter must have an odd number of coefficients. LeGall and Tabatabai [17] have used a product filter $P(z)$ of the kind

$$P(z) = \frac{1}{16}(-1 + 9z^{-2} + 16z^{-3} + 9z^{-4} - z^{-6}) \qquad (9.14)$$

and by factorising have obtained several solutions for each pair of the analysis and synthesis filters

$$H_0(z) = \frac{1}{4}(-1 + 3z^{-1} + 3z^{-2} - z^{-3}),\ H_1(-z) = \frac{1}{4}(1 + 3z^{-1} + 3z^{-2} + z^{-3})$$

or

$$H_0(z) = \frac{1}{4}(1 + 3z^{-1} + 3z^{-2} + z^{-3}),\ H_1(-z) = \frac{1}{4}(-1 + 3z^{-1} + 3z^{-2} - z^{-3})$$

or

$$(9.15)$$

$$H_0(z) = \frac{1}{8}(-1 + 2z^{-1} + 6z^{-2} + 2z^{-3} - z^{-4}),\ H_1(-z) = \frac{1}{2}(1 + 2z^{-1} + z^{-2})$$

The synthesis filters $G_0(z)$ and $G_1(z)$ are then derived using their relations with the analysis filters. Each of the above equation pairs give the results $P(z)–P(-z)=2z^{-3}$, which implies that the reconstruction is perfect with a delay of three samples.

9.7.2 Higher order systems

Multidimensional and multiband wavelet coding can be developed from the two-band low pass and high pass analysis/synthesis filter structure of Figure 9.24. For example, wavelet coding of a two-dimensional image can be performed by carrying out a one-dimensional decomposition along the lines of the image and then down each column.

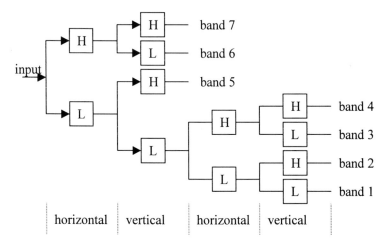

Figure 9.26 Multiband wavelet transform coding using repeated two-band splits

A seven-band wavelet transform coding of this type is illustrated in Figure 9.26, where bandsplitting is carried out alternately in the horizontal and vertical directions. In the figure, L and H represent the low pass and high pass filters with a 2:1 down-sampling, respectively.

Figure 9.27 shows all seven sub-images generated by the encoder of Figure 9.26 for a single frame of the "Flower garden" test sequence, with a 5-tap low and 3-tap high pass analysis filter pairs, (5,3), with the filter coefficients of {−1, 2, 6, 2, −1} and {1,2,1}, as discussed.

The original image (not shown) dimensions were 352 pixels by 240 lines. Bands 1–4, at two levels of subdivision, are 88 by 60, while bands 5–7 are 176 by 120 pixels. All bands but band-1 (LL) have been amplified by a factor of 4 and an offset of +128 to enhance visibility of the low level details they contain. The scope for bandwidth compression arises mainly from the low energy levels that appear in the high pass sub-images.

The number of decomposition levels of the luminance is defined by the encoder in the input bit-stream. The chrominance components are decomposed to one level less than the luminance components. Also, in MPEG-4 the wavelet decomposition is performed using a Daubechies (9,3) tap biorthogonal filter pair

[18], which have been shown to have good compression efficiency. The filter coefficients (rounded to 3 decimal points) are:

Low pass ={0.033, –0.066, –0.177, 0.420, 0.994, 0.420, –0.177, –0.066, 0.033}
High pass ={–0.354, 0.071, –0.354}

(9.16)

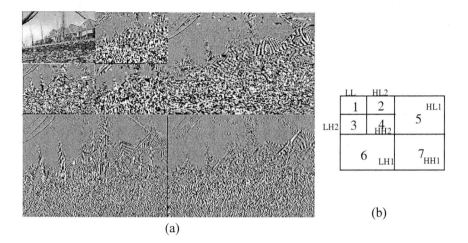

(a)

(b)

Figure 9.27(a) The seven sub-images generated by the encoder of Figure 9.26 and (b) layout of individual bands

Since at image borders all the input pixels are not available, a symmetric extension of the input texture is performed before applying the wavelet transform at each level [3]. To satisfy the perfect reconstruction conditions with the Daubechies (9,3) tap analysis filter pairs, two types of symmetric extensions are used.

Type-A is only used at the synthesis stage. It is used at the trailing edge of low pass filtering and the leading edge of high pass filtering stages. If the pixels at the boundary of the objects are represented by **abcde**, then the type-A extension becomes edcba|**abcde**, where the letters in bold type are the original pixels and those in plain are the extended pixels. Note that for a (9,3) analysis filter pair of equation 9.16, the synthesis filter pair will be (3,9) with $G_0(z) = H_1(-z)$ and $G_1(z) = -H_0(-z)$.

Type-B extension is used for both leading and trailing edges of the low and high pass analysis filters. For the synthesis filters, it is used at the leading edge of the low pass, but at the trailing edge of the high pass. With this type of extension, the extended pixels at the leading and trailing edges become edcb|**abcde** and **abcde**|dcba, respectively.

9.7.3   Coding of the lowest band

The wavelet coefficients of the lowest band are coded independently from the other bands. These coefficients are DPCM coded with a uniform quantiser. The prediction for coding a wavelet coefficient w_x is taken from its neighbouring coefficients w_A or w_C, according to

$$w_{prd} = w_C, \text{ if } |w_A - w_B| < |w_A - w_C|, \text{ otherwise } w_{prd} = w_A \qquad (9.17)$$

The difference between the actual wavelet coefficient w_x and its predicted value w_{prd} is coded. The positions of the neighbouring pixels are shown in Figure 9.28.

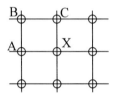

Figure 9.28 Prediction for coding the lowest band coefficients

The coefficients after DPCM coding are encoded with an adaptive arithmetic coder. First the minimum value of the coefficient in the band is found. This value, known as *band_offset*, is subtracted from all the coefficients to limit their lower bound to zero. The maximum value of the coefficients as *band_max_value* is also calculated. These two values are included in the bit-stream.

For adaptive arithmetic coding [19], the arithmetic coder model is initialised at the start of coding with a uniform distribution in the range of 0 to *band_max_value*. Each quantised and DPCM coded coefficient after arithmetic coding is added to the distribution. Hence, as the encoding progresses, the distribution of the model adapts itself to the distribution of the coded coefficients (adaptive arithmetic coding).

9.7.4   Zero-tree coding of higher bands

For efficient compression of higher bands as well as for a wide range of scalability, the higher order wavelet coefficients are coded with the *Embedded Zero-tree Wavelet* (EZW) algorithm first introduced by Shapiro [15]. The method is based on two concepts of quantisation by *successive approximation*, and exploitation of the similarities of the bands of the same orientation.

9.7.4.1 Quantisation by successive approximation

Quantisation by successive approximation is the representation of a wavelet coefficient value in terms of progressively smaller quantisation step sizes. The number of passes of the approximation depends on the desired quantisation distortions. To see how successive approximation can lead to quantisation, consider Figure 9.29, where a coefficient of length L is successively refined to its final quantised value of $\hat{L}$.

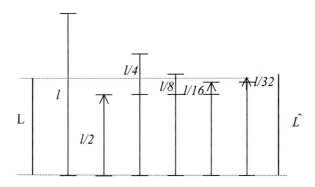

Figure 9.29 Principles of successive approximation

The process begins by choosing an initial yardstick length l. The value of l is set to half the largest coefficient in the image. If the coefficient is larger than the yardstick, it is represented with the yardstick value, otherwise its value is set to zero. After each pass the yardstick length is halved and the error magnitude, which is the difference between the original value of the coefficient and its reconstructed value, is compared with the new yardstick. The process is continued, such that the final error is acceptable. Hence increasing the number of passes, the error in the representation of L by $\hat{L}$ can be made arbitrarily small.

With regard to Figure 9.29, the quantised length L can be expressed as

$$\hat{L} = 0 \times l + 1 \times \frac{l}{2} + 0 \times \frac{l}{4} + 0 \times \frac{l}{8} + 1 \times \frac{l}{16} + 1 \times \frac{l}{32} \cdots = \frac{l}{2} + \frac{l}{16} + \frac{l}{32} \qquad (9.18)$$

where only yardstick lengths smaller than quantisation error are considered. Therefore, given an initial yardstick l, a length L can be represented as a string of "1" and "0" symbols. As each symbol "1" or "0" is added, the precision in the representation of L increases, and thus the distortion level decreases. This process is in fact equivalent to the binary representation of real numbers, called bit-plane representation, where each number is represented by a string of "0s" and "1s". By increasing the number of digits, the error in the representation can be made arbitrarily small.

9.7.4.2 Similarities among the bands

A two-stage wavelet transform (seven bands) of the "Flower garden" image sequence with the position of the bands was shown in Figure 9.27. It can be seen that the vertical bands look like scaled versions of each other, as do the horizontal and diagonal bands. Of particular interest in these sub-images is that the non-significant coefficients from bands of the same orientation tend to be in the same corresponding locations. Also, the edges are approximately at the same corresponding positions. Considering that sub-images of lower bands (higher stages of decomposition) have quarter dimensions of their higher bands, then one can make a quad-tree representation of the bands of the same orientation, as shown in Figure 9.30 for a 10-band (three stage wavelet transform).

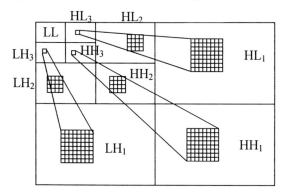

Figure 9.30 Quad-tree representation of the bands of the same orientation

In this figure a coefficient in the lowest vertical band, LH_3, corresponds to four coefficients of its immediately higher band LH_2, which relates to 16 coefficients in LH_1. Thus, if a coefficient in LH_3 is zero, it is likely that its children in the higher bands of LH_2 and LH_1 are zero. The same is true for the other horizontal and diagonal bands. This tree of zeros, called *zero-tree*, is an efficient way of representing a large group of zeros of the wavelet coefficients. Here, the root of the zero tree is required to be identified and then the descendent children in the higher bands can be ignored.

9.7.4.3 Embedded zero-tree wavelet (EZW) algorithm

The combination of the zero-tree roots with successive approximation has opened up a very interesting coding tool for not only efficient compression of wavelet coefficients, but also as a means for spatial and SNR scalability [15, 20].

The encoding algorithm with slight modification on the successive approximation, for efficient coding, according to [15] is described as follows:

1. The image mean is computed and extracted from the image. This depends on how the lowest band LL is coded. If it is coded independently of other bands, such as with DPCM in MPEG-4, then this stage can be ignored.

2. An R stage (3R+1 band) wavelet transform is applied to the (zero mean) image.

3. The initial yardstick length l is set to half of the maximum absolute value of the wavelet coefficients.

4. A list of the co-ordinates of the coefficients, called the *dominant list*, is generated. This list determines the order in which the coefficients are scanned. It must be such that coefficients from a lower frequency band (higher scale) are always scanned before the ones from a higher frequency band. Two empty lists of coefficient co-ordinates, called the *subordinate list* and the *temporary list*, are also created.

5. The wavelet transform of the image is scanned, and if a wavelet coefficient is smaller than the current yardstick length l, it is reconstructed to zero. Otherwise, it is reconstructed as $\pm 3l / 2$, according to its sign.

6. *Dominant pass:* The reconstructed coefficients are scanned again, according to the order in the dominant list, generating a string of symbols as follows: if a reconstructed coefficient is positive or negative, a "+" or a "−" is added to the string, and the co-ordinates of this coefficient are appended to the subordinate list. If a reconstructed coefficient is zero, its co-ordinates are appended to the temporary list. In the case of a zero valued reconstructed coefficient, two different symbols can be appended to the string; if all its corresponding coefficients in bands of the same orientation and higher frequencies are zero, a *zero-tree root* (ZT) is added to the string, and its corresponding coefficients are removed from the dominant list and added to the temporary list (since they are already known to be zero, they do not need to be scanned again). Otherwise, an *isolated zero* (Z) is added to the string. The strings generated from the 4-symbol alphabet of "+", "−", "ZT" and "Z" are encoded with an adaptive arithmetic encoder [19], whose model is updated to four symbols at the beginning of this pass. However, during the scanning of the highest horizontal, vertical and diagonal frequency bands (HL$_1$, LH$_1$ and HH$_1$ of Figure 9.30), no zero-tree roots can be generated. Therefore, just before the scanning of the first coefficient of these bands, the model of the arithmetic coder is updated to three symbols of "+", "−" and "Z".

7. The yardstick length l is halved.

8. *Subordinate pass:* The coefficients which previously have not been reconstructed as zero are scanned again to the order in the subordinate list,

and each one has added either +l/2 or –l/2 to it in order to minimise the magnitude of its reconstruction error. If l/2 is added, a "+" is appended to the string, and if l/2 is subtracted, a "–" is appended. At the end of the subordinate pass the subordinate list is reordered so that the coefficients whose reconstructed values have higher magnitudes come first. The "+" and "–" symbols of this pass are encoded with the arithmetic coder, which had its model updated to two symbols ("+" and "–") at the beginning of this pass.

9. The dominant list is replaced by the temporary list, and the temporary list is emptied.

10. The whole process is repeated from step 5. It stops at any point when the size of the bit-stream exceeds the desired bit rate budget.

An observation has to be made on the dominant pass (step 6). In this pass, only the reconstructed values of the coefficients that are still in the dominant list can be affected. Therefore, in order to increase the number of zero-tree roots, the coefficients not in the dominant list can be considered zero for determining if a zero-valued coefficient is either a zero-tree root or an isolated zero.

The bit-stream includes a header with extra information to the decoder. The header contains the number of wavelet transform stages, the image dimensions, the initial value of the yardstick length and the image mean. Both the encoder and decoder initially have identical dominant lists. As the bit-stream is decoded, the decoder updates the reconstructed image, as well as its subordinate and temporary lists. In this way, it can exactly track the stages of the encoder, and can therefore properly decode the bit-stream. It is important to observe that the ordering of the subordinate list in step 8 is carried out based only on the reconstructed coefficient values, which are available to the decoder. If it was not so, the decoder would not be able to track the encoder, and thus the bit-stream would not be properly decoded.

Analysis of the algorithm
The above algorithm has many interesting features, which make it especially significant to note. Among them one can say:

(a) The use of zero-trees, which exploits similarities among the bands of the same orientation and reduces the number of symbols to be coded.

(b) The use of a very small alphabet to represent an image (maximum number of four symbols) makes adaptive arithmetic coding very efficient, because it adapts itself very quickly to any changes in the statistics of the symbols.

(c) Since the maximum distortion level of a coefficient at any stage is bounded by the current yardstick length, the average distortion level in each pass is also given by the current yardstick, being the same for all bands.

(d) At any given pass, only the coefficients with magnitudes larger than the current yardstick length are encoded non-zero. Therefore, the coefficients with higher magnitudes tend to be encoded before the ones with smaller magnitudes. This implies that the EZW algorithm tends to give priority to the most important information in the encoding process. This is aided by the ordering of the subordinate in step 8. Thus for the given bit rate, the bits are spent where they are needed most.

(e) Since the EZW algorithm employs a successive approximation process, the addition of a new symbol ("+", "−", "ZT" and "Z") to the string just further refines the reconstructed image. Furthermore, while each symbol is being added to the string it is encoded into the bit-stream; hence the encoding and decoding can stop at any point, and an image with a level of refinement corresponding to the symbols encoded/decoded so far can be recovered. Therefore, the encoding and decoding of an image can stop when the bit rate budget is exhausted, which makes possible an extremely precise bit rate control. In addition, due to the prioritisation of the more important information mentioned in item (d), no matter where in the bit-stream the decoding is stopped, the best possible image quality for that bit rate is achieved.

(f) *Spatial/SNR scalability*: In order to achieve both spatial and SNR scalabilities, two different scanning methods are employed in this scheme. For spatial scalability, the wavelet coefficients are scanned in the sub-band-by-sub-band fashion, from the lowest to the highest frequency sub-bands. For SNR scalability, the wavelet coefficients are scanned in each tree from the top to the bottom. The scanning method is defined in the bit-stream.

9.7.5 Shape adaptive wavelet transform

Shape adaptive wavelet (SA-wavelet) coding is used for compression of arbitrary shaped textures. SA-wavelet coding is different from the regular wavelet coding mainly in its treatment of the boundaries of arbitrary shaped texture. The coding ensures that the number of wavelet coefficients to be coded is exactly the same as the number of pixels in the arbitrary shaped region, and coding efficiency at the object boundaries is the same as for the middle of the region. When the object boundary is rectangular, SA-wavelet coding becomes the same as the regular wavelet coding.

The shape information of an arbitrary shaped region is used in performing the SA-wavelet transform in the following manner. Within each region, the first row of pixels belonging to that region and the first segment of the consecutive pixels in the row are identified. Depending on whether the starting point in the region has odd or even co-ordinates, and the number of pixels in the row of the segment is odd or even, the proper arrangements for 2:1 down-sampling and use of symmetric extensions are made [3].

Coding of the SA-wavelet coefficients is the same as coding of regular wavelet coefficients, except that a modification is needed to handle partial wavelet trees that have wavelet coefficients corresponding to pixels outside the shape boundary. Such wavelet coefficients are called *out-nodes* of the wavelet trees. Coding of the lowest band is the same as that of the regular wavelet, but the out-nodes are not coded. For the higher bands, for any wavelet trees without out-nodes, the regular zero-tree is applied. For a partial tree, a minor modification to the regular zero-tree coding is needed to deal with the out-nodes. That is, if the entire branch of a partial tree has out-nodes only, no coding is needed for this branch, because the shape information is available to the decoder to indicate this case. If a parent node is not an out-node, all the children out-nodes are set to zero, so that the out-nodes do not affect the status of the parent node as the zero-tree root or isolated zero. At the decoder, the shape information is used to identify such zero values as out-nodes. If the parent node is an out-node and not all of its children are out-nodes, there are two possible cases. The first case is that some of its children are not out-nodes, but they are all zeros. This case is treated as a zero-tree root and there is no need to go down the tree. The shape information indicates which children are zeros and which are out-nodes. The second case is that some of its children are not out-nodes and at least one of such nodes is non-zero. In this case, the out-node parent is set to zero and the shape information helps the decoder to know that this is an out-node, and coding continues further down the tree. There is no need to use a separate symbol for any out-nodes.

9.8 Video coding with the wavelet transform

The success of the zero-tree in efficient coding of wavelet transform coefficients has encouraged researchers to use it for video coding. Although wavelet-based video coding is not part of the standard, here we show how the embedded zero-tree wavelet (EZW) can be employed in video coding.

Figure 9.31 shows a block diagram of a video codec based on the wavelet transform. Each frame of the input video is transformed into n-band wavelet sub-bands. The lowest LL band is fed into a DCT-based video encoder, such as MPEG-1. The other bands undergo a hierarchical motion compensation. First, the three high frequency bands of the last stage are motion compensated using the motion vectors from MPEG-1. The reconstructed picture from these four bands (LL, LH, HL and HH), which is the next-level LL band, only requires a ± 1 pixel refinement [21]. The other three bands at this stage are also motion compensated by the same amount. This process is continued for all the bands. Hence at the end all the bands are motion compensated. Now, these motion compensated bands are coded with the EZW method.

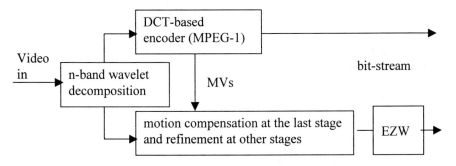

Figure 9.31 A hybrid MPEG/wavelet video coding scheme

9.8.1 Virtual zero-tree (VZT) algorithm

When the EZW is used for video coding, with the lowest band to be coded with a standard codec, it meets some problems. First, the sub-band decomposition stops when the top-level LL band reaches a size of SIF/QSIF or sub-QSIF. At these levels there will be too many clustered zero-tree roots. This is very common for either static parts of the pictures or when motion compensation is very efficient. Even for still images or I-pictures, a large part of the picture may contain only low spatial frequency information. As a result, at the early stages of the quantisation by successive approximation, where the yardstick is large, a vast majority of the wavelet coefficients fall below the yardstick. Secondly, even if the subband decomposition is taken to more stages, such that the top stage LL is a small picture of 16×16 pixels, then it is unlikely that many zero-trees can be generated. Hence the efficiency of EZW is greatly reduced.

To improve the efficiency of EZW, we have devised a version of it called *virtual zero-tree* (VZT) [22]. The idea is to build trees outside the image boundary, hence the word *virtual*, as an extension to the existing trees that have roots in the top-stage, so that the significant map can be represented in a more efficient way. It can be imagined as replacing the top-level LL band with zero-value coefficients. These coefficients represent the roots of wavelet trees of several virtual sub-images in normal EZW coding, although no decomposition and decimation actually takes place, as demonstrated in Figure 9.32. In this figure, virtual trees, or a virtual map, are built in the virtual sub-bands on the high frequency bands of the highest stage. Several wavelet coefficients of the highest stage form a virtual node at the bottom level of the virtual map. Then in the virtual map, four nodes of a lower level are represented by one node of a higher level in the same way a zero-tree is formed in EZW coding. The virtual map has only two symbols: *VZT root* or *non-VZT root*. If four nodes of a 2×2 block on any level of a virtual tree are all VZT roots, the corresponding node on the higher level will also be a VZT root. Otherwise this one node of the higher level will be a non-VZT node. This effectively constructs a long rooted tree of clustered *real* zero-trees. One node on the bottom level of the virtual map is a VZT root only when the four luminance coefficients of a 2×2 block and their two corresponding chrominance coefficients on the top-stage wavelet band are all zero-tree roots. Chrominance pictures are also wavelet decomposed and, for a 4:2:0 image format, four zero-tree roots of the luminance and one from each chrominance can be made a composite zero-tree root [22].

It appears at first that, by creating virtual nodes, we have increased the number of symbols to be coded, and hence the bit rate tends to increase rather than to decrease. However, these virtual roots will cluster the zero-tree roots into a bigger zero-tree root, such that instead of coding these roots one by one, at the expense of a large overhead by a simple EZW, we can code the whole cluster by a single VZT with only a few bits. VZT is more powerful at the early stages of encoding, where the vast majority of top-stage coefficients are zero-tree roots. This can be seen from Table 9.2, where a complete breakdown of the total bit rate required to code a P-picture of the "Park sequence" by both methods is given. The sequence has a super high definition (SHD) quality (2048×2048 pixels at 60 Hz, courtesy of NHK Japan [21]).

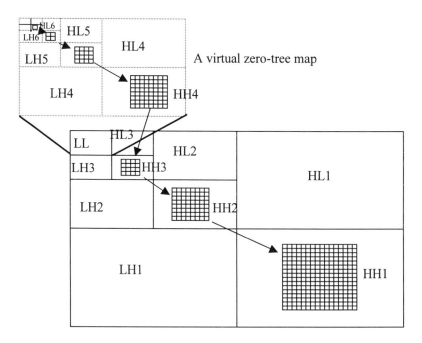

Figure 9.32 A virtual zero-tree

The SHD images after three-stage sub-band decomposition result in 10 bands. The LL band, with picture resolutions of 256×256 pixels, is MPEG-1 coded; the remaining nine bands are VZT and EZW coded in two separate experiments. The first row of the table shows that 171 kbits are used to code the LL band by MPEG-1. The second row shows that 15 kbits is used for the additional ± 1 pixel refinement in all bands. For the higher bands the image is scanned in five passes, where the bits used in the dominant and subordinate passes of VZT and EZW are shown. In VZT the dominant pass is made up of two parts: one used in coding of the virtual nodes and the other parts for real data in the actual nine bands. Note that although some bits are used to code the virtual nodes (do not exit in EZW), the total bits of the dominant pass in VZT are much less than for EZW. The number of bits in the subordinate passes, which code the real subordinate data, is the same for both methods. In the table the *Grand total* is the total number of bits used to code the P-frame under the two coding schemes. It can be seen that VZT requires two-thirds of the bit rate required by EZW.

We have also compared VZT against EZW in coding of high definition television pictures, using the test sequence "Gaynor". For this image sequence, a two-stage (7-band) wavelet transform is used and the LL band of the SIF size was MPEG-1 coded. Motion compensated higher bands were coded with VZT and EZW. Our results show that, while a good quality video at 18 Mbit/s can be achieved under EZW, the VZT only needs 11 Mbit/s [22].

Table 9.2 Breakdown bit rate in coding of a P-picture with VZT and EZW

	VZT [kbits]					EZW [kbits]		
	Virtual pass	Real pass	Domin. pass	Subord. pass	**SUM**	Domin. pass	Subord. pass	**SUM**
MPEG	-	-	-	-	171	-	-	171
MV	-	-	-	-	15	-	-	15
Pass-1	1.5	3.2	4.4	0.16	4.9	25	0.16	25
Pass-2	7.7	31	39	1.7	41	153	1.7	156
Pass-3	18	146	164	11	175	465	11	476
Pass-4	29	371	400	41	441	835	41	896
Pass-5	42	880	992	128	1050	1397	128	1326
Grand total					**1898**			**3265**

9.8.2   Set partitioning in hierarchical trees (SPIHT)

The compression efficiency of EZW as well as VZT is to some extent due to the use of arithmetic coding. Said and Pearlman have introduced a variant of coding of wavelet coefficients by successive approximation, that even without arithmetic coding outperforms EZW [20]. They call it set partitioning in hierarchical trees (SPIHT). The crucial parts of their coding process is the way the subsets of the wavelet coefficients are partitioned and the significant information is conveyed.

One of the main features of this scheme in transmitting the ordering data is that it is based on the fact that the execution path of any algorithm is defined by the results of the comparisons of its branching points. So, if the encoder and decoder have the same sorting algorithm, then the decoder can duplicate the encoder's execution path if it receives the results of the magnitude comparisons, and the ordering information can be recovered from the execution path.

The sorting algorithm divides the set of wavelet coefficients, $\{C_{i,j}\}$, into partitioning subsets T_m and performs the magnitude test:

$$\max_{\substack{(i,j) \\ (i,j) \in T_m}} \{|C_{i,j}|\} \geq 2^n \ ? \qquad (9.19)$$

If the decoder receives a "no" to that answer (the subset is insignificant), then it knows that all coefficients in T_m are insignificant. If the answer is "yes" (the subset is significant), then a certain rule shared by the encoder and decoder is used to partition T_m into new subset $T_{m,1}$ and the significant test is then applied to the new subsets. This set division process continues until the magnitude test is done to all single co-ordinate significant subsets in order to identify each significant coefficient.

To reduce the number of magnitude comparisons (message bits) a set partitioning rule that uses an expected ordering in the hierarchy defined by the subband pyramid is defined (similar to Figure 9.30, used in zero-tree coding). In Sec 9.7.4.2 we saw how the similarities among the sub-images of the same orientation can be exploited to create a special orientation tree. The objective is to create new partitions such that subsets expected to be insignificant contain a huge number of elements and subsets expected to be significant contain only one element.

To make clear the relationship between magnitude comparisons and message bits; the following function is used:

$$S_n(T) = 1, \ if \ \max_{\substack{(i,j) \\ (i,j) \in T}} \{|C_{i,j}|\} \geq 2^n \qquad (9.20)$$
$$= 0, \ otherwise$$

to indicate the significance of a set of co-ordinates T. To simplify the notation of single pixel sets, $S_n(\{(i,j)\})$ is represented by $S_n(i,j)$.

To see how SPHIT can be implemented, let us assume O(i,j) to represent a set of coordinates of all offspring of node (i,j). For instance, except the highest and lowest pyramid levels, O(i,j) is defined in terms of its offsprings as:

$$O(i,j) = \{(2i, 2j), (2i, 2j+1), (2i+1), 2j), (2i+1, 2j+1)\} \qquad (9.21)$$

We also define D(i,j) as a set of coordinates of all descendants of the node (i, j), and H, a set of coordinates of all spatial orientation tree roots (nodes in the highest pyramid level). Finally, L(i,j) is defined as

$$L(i, j) = D(i, j) - O(i, j) \tag{9.22}$$

With the use of parts of the spatial orientation trees as the partitioning subsets in the sorting algorithm, the set partitioning rules are defined as follows:

1) The initial partition is formed with the sets $\{(i, j)\}$ and $D(i, j)$, for all $(i, j) \in H$.

2) If $D(i, j)$ is significant, then it is partitioned into $L(i, j)$ plus the four single-element sets with $(k, l) \in O(i, j)$.

3) If $L(i, j)$ is significant, then it is partitioned into the four sets $D(k, l)$, with $(k, l) \in O(i, j)$.

4) Each of the four sets now has the format of the original set and the same partitioning can be used recursively.

Coding algorithm

Since the order in which the subsets are tested for significance is important, in a practical implementation the significance information is stored in three ordered lists, called the *list of insignificant sets* (LIS), *list of insignificant pixels* (LIP) and *list of significant pixels* (LSP). In all lists each entry is identified by a coordinate (i, j), which in the LIP and LSP represents individual pixels, and in the LSP represents either the set $D(i, j)$ or $L(i, j)$. To differentiate between them, it is said that a LIS entry is of type A if it represents $D(i, j)$, and of type B if it represents $L(i, j)$ [20].

During the sorting pass, the pixels in the LIP, which were insignificant in the previous pass, are tested, and those that become significant are moved to the LIP. Similarly, sets are sequentially evaluated following the LIS order, and when a set is found to be significant it is removed from the list and partitioned. The new subsets with more than one element are added back to the LIP while the single-coordinate sets are added to the end of the LIP or the LSP depending whether they are insignificant or significant, respectively. The LSP contains the coordinates of the pixels that are visited in the refinement pass.

Thus the algorithm can be summarized as:

1. **Initialisation**: let the initial yardstick, n, be $n = \lfloor \log_2 (\max_{(i,j)} \{|C_{i,j}|\}) \rfloor$. Set the LSP as an empty set list, and add the coordinates $(i, j) \in H$ to the LIP, and only those with descendants also to the LIS, as the type A entries.

2. **Sorting Pass**:

   2.1. for each entry (i, j) in the LIP do:

       2.1.1. output $S_n(i, j)$;

       2.1.2. if $S_n(i, j) = 1$ then move (i, j) to the LSP and output the sign of $C_{i,j}$;

2.2. for each entry (i, j) in the LIS do:

    2.2.1.   if the entry is of type A then

        2.2.1.1.   output $S_n(D(i, j))$;

        2.2.1.2.   if $S_n(D(i, j)) = 1$ then

            2.2.1.2.1.   for each $(k, l) \in O(i, j)$ do:

                2.2.1.2.1.1.   output $S_n((k, l)$;

                2.2.1.2.1.2.   if $S_n(k, l) = 1$, then add (k, l) to the LSP and output the sign of $C_{k,l}$;

                2.2.1.2.1.3.   if $S_n(k, l) = 0$ then add (k, l) to the end of the LIP;

            2.2.1.2.2.   if $L(i, j) \neq 0$ then move (i, j) to the end of the LIS, as an entry of type B, and go to step 2.2.2; otherwise, remove entry (i, j) from the LIS;

    2.2.2.   if the entry is of type B then

        2.2.2.1.   output $S_n(L(i, j))$;

        2.2.2.2.   if $S_n(L(i, j)) = 1$ then

            2.2.2.2.1.   add each $(k, l) \in O((i, j)$ to the end of the LIS as an entry of type A;

            2.2.2.2.2.   remove (i, j) from the LIS.

3. **Refinement Pass**: for each entry (i, j) in the LSP, except those included in the last sorting pass (i.e. with same n), output the nth most significant bit of $|C_{i,j}|$;

4. **Quantisation-step update**: decrement n by 1 and go to Step 2.

One important characteristics of the algorithm is that the entries added to the end of the LIS in Step 2.2 are evaluated before the same sorting pass ends. So, when it is said "for each entry in the LIS", it is meant those that are being added to its end. Also similar to EZW, the rate can be precisely controlled because the transmitted information is formed of single bits. The encoder can estimate the progressive distortion reduction and stop at a desired distortion value.

Note that in this algorithm, the encoder outputs all branching conditions based on the outcome of the wavelet coefficients. Thus, to obtain the desired decoder's algorithm, which duplicates the encoder's execution path as it sorts, the significant coefficients, we simply replace the words *output* with *input*. The ordering information is recovered when the co-ordinate of the significant coefficients is added to the end of the LSP. But note that whenever the decoder inputs data, its three control lists (LIS, LIP and LSP) are identical to the ones used by the encoder at the moment it outputs that data, which means that the decoder indeed recovers the ordering from the execution path.

An additional task done by the decoder is to update the reconstructed image. For the value of n when a co-ordinate is moved to the LSP, it is known that $2^n \le |C_{i,j}| < 2^{n+1}$. So, the decoder uses that information in the LSP, to set the reconstructed coefficients $\hat{C}_{i,j} = \pm 1.5 \times 2^n$. Similarly, during the refinement pass, the decoder adds or subtracts 2^{n-1} to $\hat{C}_{i,j}$ when it inputs the bits of the binary representation of $|C_{i,j}|$. In this manner, the distortion gradually decreases during both the sorting and refinement passes.

In coding of "Lena" test image, Said and Pearlman have shown that this method outperforms EZW in the entire bit rate range by almost 0.4 dB. When this method is combined with arithmetic coding, the compression efficiency is further improved by almost another 0.4 dB [20].

9.9 MPEG-7: Multimedia content description interface

As more and more audio-visual information becomes available in digital form, there is increasing pressure to make use of it. Before one can use any information, however, it has to be located first. Unfortunately the increasing availability of interesting material makes this search extremely difficult.

For textual information, currently many *text-based* search engines are available on the World Wide Web (www), and they are among the most visited sites. This is an indication of real demand for searching information on the public domain. However, identifying information for audiovisual content is not so trivial, and no generally recognised description of these material exists. In the mean time, there is no efficient way of searching the www for, say, a picture of a "lady with a red hat waiting for a taxi". However, in specific cases, solutions do exist. Multimedia databases on the market today allow searching for pictures using characteristics like colour, texture and information about the shape of objects in the picture. One could envisage a similar example for audio, in which a melody could be whistled to find a song.

The question of finding contents is not restricted to database retrieval applications. For example, in television news studios, there is an increasing demand to locate a video clip of a certain event. Another example is the selection of the program of interest from a vast number of available satellite television channels.

In October 1996, MPEG started a new program to provide a solution to these questions. This new member of the MPEG family is called *multimedia content description interface*, or for short MPEG-7 [23]. There have been several views as to why the number "7" has been chosen. Perhaps the most plausible one is that, since the multimedia content could be in one of MPEG-1, 2 or 4 forms, and the one which covers all of them should be MPEG(1+2+4=7).

The main goal of MPEG-7 is to specify a standard set of descriptors that can be used to describe various types of multimedia information coded with the standard codecs, as well as other data bases and even analogue audio-visual information. This will be in the form of defining descriptor schemes or structures and the relationship between various descriptors. The combination of the descriptors and description schemes will be associated with the content itself to allow a fast and efficient searching method for the material of user's interest. The audiovisual material that has MPEG-7 data associated with it can be indexed and searched for. This material may include still pictures, graphics, three-dimensional models, audio, speech, video, and information about how these elements are combined in a multimedia presentation.

Figure 9.33 shows a highly abstract block diagram of the MPEG-7 mission. In this figure object features are extracted and they are described in a manner that are meaningful to the search engine. As usual, MPEG-7 does not specify how features should be extracted, nor how they should be searched for, but only specifies the order in which features should be described.

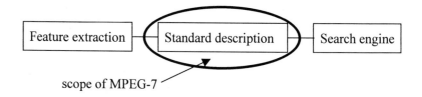

Figure 9.33 Scope of MPEG-7

Since the description features must be meaningful in the context of the application, they may be defined in different ways for different applications. Hence a specific audiovisual event might be described with different sets of features, if their applications are different. To describe visual events, they are first described by their lower abstraction level, such as shape, size, texture, colour, movement and their positions inside the picture frame. At this level, the audio material may be defined as key, mood, tempo, tempo changes and position in the sound space.

The high level of the abstraction is then a description of the semantic relation between the above lower level abstractions. For the earlier example of "lady with a red hat waiting for a taxi", the lower level of abstraction for the picture would be: human body, colour and shape of the hat, shape of the taxi, etc. For the audio, this level of abstraction could be the sound of passing cars in the background. All these descriptions are of course coded in a way to be searched as efficiently as possible.

The level of abstraction is related to the way the required features are extracted. Many low-level features can be extracted in a fully automatic manner. High level features, however, need more human interactions, to define the semantic relations between the lower level features.

In addition to the description of contents, it may also be required to include other types of information about the multimedia data. For example:

- *The form*: an example of the form is the coding scheme used (e.g. JPEG, MPEG-2), or the overall data size.
- *Conditions for accessing material:* This would include copyright information, price, etc.
- *Classification*: This could include parental rating, and content classification into a number of predefined categories.
- *Links to other relevant material*: This information will help the users to speed up the search operation.
- *The context*: For some recorded events, it is very important to know the occasion of recording (e.g. World Cup 1998, final between Brazil and France).

In many cases addition of textual information to the descriptors may be useful. Care must be taken such that the usefulness of the descriptors is as independent as possible from the language. An example of this is giving names of authors, films, places. However, providing text-only documents will not be among the goals of MPEG-7.

The MPEG group have also defined a laboratory reference model for MPEG-7. This time it is called eXperimental Model (XM), which has the same role of RM, TM and VM in the H.261, MPEG-2 and MPEG-4 respectively.

The current status of research at this very early stage of MPEG-7 development is concentrated into two interrelated areas, *indexing* and *query*. In the former, significant events of video shots are indexed, and in the latter, given a description of an event, the video shot for that event is searched for. Figure 9.34 shows how the indices for a video clip can be generated.

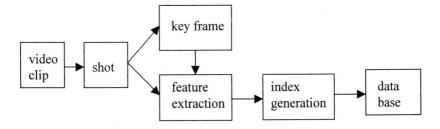

Figure 9.34 Index generation for a video clip

In this figure a video program (normally 30–90 min), is temporally segmented into video *shots*. A shot is a piece of video clip, where the picture content from one frame to the other does not change significantly, and in general there is no scene cut within a shot. Therefore a single frame in a shot has a high correlation to all the pictures within the shot. One of these frames is chosen as the *key-frame*. Selection of the key frame is an interesting research issue. An ideal key frame is the one that has maximum similarity with all the pictures within its own shot, but minimum similarity with those of the other shots.

The key frame is then spatially segmented into objects with meaningful features. These may include colour, shape, texture, where a semantic relation between these individual features defines an object of interest. As mentioned, depending on the type of application, the same features might be described in a different order. Also, in extracting the features, other information like motion of the objects, background sound or sometimes text might be useful. Here features are then indexed, and the indexed data along with the key frames are stored in the data base, sometimes called *metadata*.

The query process is the opposite of indexing. In this process, the database is searched for a specific visual content. Depending on how the query is defined to the search engine, the process can be very complex. For instance in our earlier example of "lady with a red hat waiting for a taxi", the simplest form of the query is that a single frame (picture) of this event is available. This picture is then matched against all the key frames in the database. If such a picture is found, then due to its index relation with the actual shot and video clip, that piece of video is located. Matching of the query picture with the key frames is under active research, since this is very different from the conventional pixel-to-pixel matching of the pictures. For example, due to motion, obstruction of the objects, shading, shearing, etc. the physical dimensions of the objects of interest might change, such that pixel-to-pixel matching does not necessarily find the right object. For instance, with the pixel-to-pixel matching, a circle can be more similar to a hexagon of almost the same number of pixels and intensity than to a smaller or larger circle, which is not a desired match.

The extreme complexity in the query is when the event is defined verbally or in a text, like the text of "lady with a red hat waiting for a taxi". Here, these data have to be converted into visual objects, to be matched with the key frames. There is no doubt that most of the future MPEG-7 activity will be focused in this extremely complex image processing task.

References

[1]   Koenen R., Pereira F. and Chiariglione L. 'MPEG-4: Context and objectives', *Image Communication Journal*, **9:4**, (1997).
[2]   MPEG-4: 'Testing and evaluation procedures document', ISO/IEC JTC1/SC29/WG11, N999, (July 1995).

[3] MPEG-4 video verification model version-11, ISO/IEC JTC1/SC29/WG11, N2171, Tokyo, (March 1998).

[4] Special issue on segmentation, *IEEE Transactions on Circuits and Systems for Video Technology*, **8:5**, (September 1998).

[5] Image processing in C, Dwayne Phillips, Prentice Hall, (1994).

[6] Sezan M.I., 'A peak detection algorithm and its application to histogram-based image data reduction', *Computer Vision, Graphics, and Image Processing*, **49**, pp. 36-51, (1990).

[7] Izquierdo M.E. and Feng X. 'Image-based 3D modelling of arbitrary natural objects', in Proc. *Very Low bit rate video coding, VLBV98*, University of Illinois at Urbana-Champaign, USA, pp. 109-112, (October 8-9, 1998).

[8] MPEG-4: 'Video shape coding', ISO/IEC JTC1/SC29/WG11, N1584, (March 1997).

[9] Ghanbari M., 'Arithmetic coding with limited past history', *Electronics Letters*, **27:13**, pp. 1157-1159, (June 1991).

[10] Pearson D.E., 'Developments in model-based video coding', *Proc. of the IEEE*, **83:6**, pp. 892-906, (June 1995).

[11] Wolberg G., 'Digital image warping', *IEEE Computer Society Press*, Los Alamitos, California, (1990).

[12] Seferidis V. and Ghanbari M., 'General approach to block matching motion estimation', *Journal of Optical Engineering*, **37:7**, pp. 1464-1474, (July 1993).

[13] Ghanbari M., de Faria S., Goh I.J. and Tan K.T., 'Motion compensation for very low bit-rate video', *Signal Processing, Image Communication*, Special issue on very low bit-rate video, **7:(4-6)**, pp. 567-580, (November 1995).

[14] JPEG-2000: 'Coding of still pictures, requirements and profiles version 4.0', ISO/IEC JTC1/SC29/WG1, (ITU-T SG8), N1105R, (November 1998).

[15] Shapiro J.M., 'Embedded image coding using zero-trees of wavelet coefficients', *IEEE Transactions on Signal Processing*, **4:12**, pp. 3445-3462, (December 1993).

[16] Crochiere R.E., Weber S.A. and Flanagan J.L. 'Digital coding of speech in sub-bands', *Bell System Technical Journal*, **55**, pp. 1069-1085, (1967).

[17] Le Gall D. and Tabatabai A. 'Subband coding of images using symmetric short kernel filters and arithmetic coding techniques', in *IEEE International Conference on Acoustics, Speech and Signal Processing*, ICASSP'98, pp. 761-764, (1988).

[18] Daubechies I. 'Orthonormal bases of compactly supported wavelets', *Communications on Pure and Applied Mathematics*, XLI, pp. 909-996, (1988).

[19] Witten I.H., Neal R.M. and Cleary J.G. 'Arithmetic coding for data compression', *Communications of ACM*, **30:6**, pp. 520-540, (June 1987).

[20] Said A. and Pearlman W.A. 'A new, fast and efficient image codec based on set partitioning in hierarchical trees', *IEEE Transactions on Circuits and Systems for Video Technology*, **6:3**, pp. 243-250, (March 1996).

[21] Wang Q. and Ghanbari M. 'Motion-compensation for super high definition video', in Proc of *IS&T/SPIE Symposium, Electronic Imaging, Science and Technology, Very High Resolution and Quality Imaging*, San Jose, CA, (Jan. 27-Feb. 2, 1996).

[22] Wang Q. and Ghanbari M. 'Scalable coding of very high resolution video using the virtual zero-tree', *IEEE Transactions on Circuits and Systems for Video Technology*, Special Issue on Multimedia, **7:5**, pp. 719-729, (October 1997).

[23] MPEG-7: ISO/IEC JTC1/SC29/WG211, N2207, Context and objectives, (March 1998).

Appendix A: A 'C'-program for the fast discrete cosine transform

```c
/*ffdct.c*/
/*fast forward discrete cosine transform in the current frame */

#include "config.h"
#include "global.h"

#define W1 2841          /* sqrt(2)cos(π/16)<<11 */
#define W2 2676          /* sqrt(2)cos(2π/16)<<11 */
#define W3 2408          /* sqrt(2)cos(3π/16)<<11 */
#define W5 1609          /* sqrt(2)cos(5π/16)<<11 */
#define W6 1108          /* sqrt(2)cos(6π/16)<<11 */
#define W7 565           /* sqrt(2)cos(7π/16)<<11 */
#define W10 2276         /* W1 - W7 */
#define W11 3406         /* W1 + W7 */
#define W12 4017         /* W3 + W5 */
#define W13 799          /* W3 - W5 */
#define W14 1568         /* W2 - W6 */
#define W15 3784         /* W2 + W6 */

/* global declarations */
void ffdct _ANSI_ARGS_((int *block));

void ffdct(block)
int *block;
{
int s[10],t[10],r[10];
int *p;
int j, temp;

/*forward transformation in "H" direction*/
p = block;
for(j=0; j<64; j +=8 )
    {
    /* first stage transformation */
    s[0]= (*(p)  + *(p+7));
    s[1]= (*(p+1) + *(p+6));
    s[2]= (*(p+2) + *(p+5));
    s[3]= (*(p+3) + *(p+4));
    s[4]= (*(p+3) - *(p+4));
    s[5]= (*(p+2) - *(p+5));
```

```
s[6]= (*(p+1) - *(p+6));
s[7]= (*(p)   - *(p+7));

/* second stage transformation */
t[0]= s[0] + s[3];
t[1]= s[1] + s[2];
t[2]= s[1] - s[2];
t[3]= s[0] - s[3];
t[5]= ((s[6] - s[5]) * 181) >> 8;
t[6]= ((s[6] + s[5]) * 181) >> 8;

/* third stage transformation */
r[4]= s[4] + t[5];
r[5]= s[4] - t[5];
r[6]= s[7] - t[6];
r[7]= s[7] + t[6];

/* fourth stage transformation */
block[0+j]= (t[0] + t[1]);
block[4+j]= (t[0] - t[1]);
temp = (r[4] + r[7]) * W1;
block[1+j]= (temp - r[4] * W10) >> 11;
block[7+j]= (r[7] * W11 - temp) >> 11;
temp = ( r[5] + r[6]) * W3;
block[3+j]= (temp - r[5] * W12) >> 11;
block[5+j]= (temp - r[6] * W13) >> 11;
temp = (t[2] + t[3]) * W6;
block[2+j]= (temp + t[3] * W14) >> 11;
block[6+j]= (temp - t[2] * W15) >> 11;
p += 8;
}

/* forward transformation in 'V' direction */
for(j=0; j<8; j++)
{
/* first stage transformation */
s[0] = block[j ] + block[j+ 56];
s[1] = block[j+8] + block[j+ 48];
s[2] = block[j+16] + block[j+ 40];
s[3] = block[j+24] + block[j+ 32];
s[4] = block[j+24] - block[j+ 32];
s[5] = block[j+16] - block[j+ 40];
s[6] = block[j+8] - block[j+ 48];
s[7] = block[j ] - block[j+ 56];

/* second stage transformation */
t[0] = s[0] + s[3];
t[1] = s[1] + s[2];
t[2] = s[1] - s[2];
t[3] = s[0] - s[3];
t[5] = ((s[6] - s[5]) * 181) >> 8;
t[6] = ((s[6] + s[5]) * 181) >> 8;

/* third stage transformation */
r[4] = s[4] + t[5];
r[5] = s[4] - t[5];
```

```
r[6] = s[7] - t[6];
r[7] = s[7] + t[6];

/* fourth stage transformation */
/* transform coefficients */
/* coefficients are divided by 8 and rounded */
block[0+j]= ((t[0] + t[1]) + 4 ) >> 3;
block[32+j]= ((t[0] - t[1]) + 4 ) >> 3;
temp = ( r[4] + r[7] ) * W1;
block[8+j]= ((temp - r[4] * W10) + 8192) >> 14;
block[56+j]= (((r[7] * W11) - temp) + 8192) >> 14;
temp = ( r[5] + r[6] ) * W3;
block[24+j]= ((temp - r[5] * W12) + 8192) >> 14;
block[40+j]= ((temp - r[6] * W13) + 8192) >> 14;
temp = ( t[2] + t[3] ) * W6;
block[16+j]= ((temp + t[3] * W14) + 8192) >> 14;
block[48+j]= ((temp - t[2] * W15) + 8192) >> 14;
}
```

Appendix B: Huffman tables for the DC and AC coefficients of the JPEG base-line encoder

Table B1: DC Huffman coefficients of luminance

Category (CAT)	Code-word
0	00
1	010
2	011
3	100
4	101
5	110
6	1110
7	11110
8	111110
9	1111110
10	11111110
11	111111110

Table B2: AC Huffman coefficients of luminance

(RUN,CAT)	Code-word	(RUN.CAT)	Code-word
0,0 (**EOB**)	1010		
0,1	00	4,1	111011
0,2	01	4,2	1111111000
0,3	100	4,3	1111111110010110
0,4	1011	4,4	1111111110010111
0,5	11010	4,5	1111111110011000
0,6	1111000	4,6	1111111110011001
0,7	11111000	4,7	1111111110011010
0,8	1111110110	4,8	1111111110011011
0,9	1111111110000010	4.9	1111111110011100
0,10	1111111110000011	4,10	1111111110011101
1,1	1100	5,1	1111010
1,2	11011	5,2	11111110111
1,3	1111001	5,3	1111111110011110
1,4	111110110	5,4	1111111110011111
1,5	11111110110	5,5	1111111110100000
1,6	1111111110000100	5,6	1111111110100001
1,7	1111111110000101	5,7	1111111110100010
1,8	1111111110000110	5,8	1111111110100011
1,9	1111111110000111	5,9	1111111110100100
1,10	1111111110001000	5,10	1111111110100101
2,1	11100	6,1	1111011
2,2	11111001	6,2	111111110110
2,3	1111110111	6,3	1111111110100110
2,4	111111110100	6,4	1111111110100111
2,5	1111111110001001	6,5	1111111110101000
2,6	1111111110001010	6,6	1111111110101001
2,7	1111111110001011	6,7	1111111110101010
2,8	1111111110001100	6,8	1111111110101011
2,9	1111111110001101	6,9	1111111110101100
2,10	1111111110001110	6,10	1111111110101101
3,1	111010	7,1	11111010
3,2	111110111	7,2	111111110111
3,3	111111110101	7,3	1111111110101110
3,4	1111111110001111	7,4	1111111110101111
3,5	1111111110010000	7,5	1111111110110000
3,6	1111111110010001	7,6	1111111110110001
3,7	1111111110010010	7,7	1111111110110010
3,8	1111111110010011	7,8	1111111110110011
3,9	1111111110010100	7,9	1111111110110100
3,10	1111111110010101	7,10	1111111110110101

(RUN,CAT)	Code-word	(RUN,CAT)	Code-word
8,1	111111000	12,1	1111111010
8,2	111111111000000	12,2	1111111111011001
8,3	1111111110110110	12,3	1111111111011010
8,4	1111111110110111	12,4	1111111111011011
8,5	1111111110111000	12,5	1111111111011100
8,6	1111111110111001	12,6	1111111111011101
8,7	1111111110111010	12,7	1111111111011110
8,8	1111111110111011	12,8	1111111111011111
8,9	1111111110111100	12,9	1111111111100000
8,10	1111111110111101	12,10	1111111111100001
9,1	111111001	13,1	11111111000
9,2	1111111110111110	13,2	1111111111100010
9,3	1111111110111111	13,3	1111111111100011
9,4	1111111111000000	13,4	1111111111100100
9,5	1111111111000001	13,5	1111111111100101
9,6	1111111111000010	13,6	1111111111100110
9,7	1111111111000011	13,7	1111111111100111
9,8	1111111111000100	13,8	1111111111101000
9,9	1111111111000101	13,9	1111111111101001
9,10	1111111111000110	13,10	1111111111101010
10,1	111111010	14,1	1111111111101011
10,2	1111111111000111	14,2	1111111111101100
10,3	1111111111001000	14,3	1111111111101101
10,4	1111111111001001	14,4	1111111111101110
10,5	1111111111001010	14,5	1111111111101111
10,6	1111111111001011	14,6	1111111111110000
10,7	1111111111001100	14,7	1111111111110001
10,8	1111111111001101	14,8	1111111111110010
10,9	1111111111001110	14,9	1111111111110011
10,10	1111111111001111	14,10	1111111111110100
11,1	1111111001	15,1	1111111111110101
11,2	1111111111010000	15,2	1111111111110110
11,3	1111111111010001	15,3	1111111111110111
11,4	1111111111010010	15,4	1111111111111000
11,5	1111111111010011	15,5	1111111111111001
11,6	1111111111010100	15,6	1111111111111010
11,7	1111111111010101	15,7	1111111111111011
11,8	1111111111010110	15,8	1111111111111100
11,9	1111111111010111	15,9	1111111111111101
11,10	1111111111011000	15,10	1111111111111110
The special symbol representing 16 "zero"		15,0 (**ZRL**)	11111111001

Appendix C: Huffman tables for quad-tree shape coding

Huffman tables for quad-tree shape coding. table_012.dat is used at levels 0,1 and 2 and table_3.dat is used at level 3.

table_012.dat

Index	Code	Index	Code
0	-	41	11110011
1	10011	42	11111111010
2	11110101	43	11110010
3	101101	44	0101
4	0010	45	1110011
5	1110110	46	1101111
6	111111011	47	11110111
7	1100110	48	111111111100
8	01110	49	11101111
9	101111	50	101110
10	10010	51	111111111111101
11	11110100	52	111111111001
12	1111111111100	53	110001
13	11110000	54	11110001
14	1110100	55	1111111111101
15	1111111111111111	56	111111111111110
16	111111111010	57	110000
17	1101110	58	1111111001
18	11111011	59	1111111111110
19	11111000	60	0100
20	110010	61	1101010
21	111111111111100	62	11111010
22	1111111000	63	10000
23	11111001	64	1111111011
24	1111111111111110	65	111111111000
25	11111111001	66	1101000
26	111111010	67	11110000
27	10001	68	11111111011

28	1111111010	69	11101110
29	111111111101	70	01101
30	01111	71	101100
31	1110101	72	0000
32	11111111000	73	1100111
33	1101011	74	1101101
34	1110010	75	1101001
35	11111100	76	0011
36	0001	77	10100
37	1110001	78	1101100
38	111111111011	79	01100
39	11110110	80	-
40	10101		

table_3.dat

Index	Code
0	-
2	1101
6	1111110
8	1011
18	11101
20	100
24	11111111
26	111110
54	1100
56	11111110
60	01
62	11110
72	00
74	1010
78	11100
80	-

Appendix D: Frequency tables for the CAE encoding of binary shapes

Frequency tables for Intra and Inter blocks, used in the context-based arithmetic encoding (CAE) method of binary shapes.

Intra_prob[1024] = {
65267,16468,65003,17912,64573,8556,64252,5653,40174,3932,29789,277,45152,1140,32768,2043,
4499,80,6554,1144,21065,465,32768,799,5482,183,7282,264,5336,99,6554,563,
54784,30201,58254,9879,54613,3069,32768,58495,32768,32768,32768,2849,58982,54613,32768,12892,
31006,1332,49152,3287,60075,350,32768,712,39322,760,32768,354,52659,432,61854,150,
64999,28362,65323,42521,63572,32768,63677,18319,4910,32768,64238,434,53248,32768,61865,13590,
16384,32768,13107,333,32768,32768,32768,32768,32768,32768,1074,780,25058,5461,6697,233,
62949,30247,63702,24638,59578,32768,32768,42257,32768,32768,49152,546,62557,32768,54613,19258,
62405,32569,64600,865,60495,10923,32768,898,34193,24576,64111,341,47492,5231,55474,591,
65114,60075,64080,5334,65448,61882,64543,13209,54906,16384,35289,4933,48645,9614,55351,7318,
49807,54613,32768,32768,50972,32768,32768,32768,15159,1928,2048,171,3093,8,6096,74,
32768,60855,32768,32768,32768,32768,32768,32768,32768,32768,32768,32768,32768,55454,32768,57672,
32768,16384,32768,21845,32768,32768,32768,32768,32768,32768,32768,5041,28440,91,32768,45,
65124,10923,64874,5041,65429,57344,63435,48060,61440,32768,63488,24887,59688,3277,63918,14021,
32768,32768,32768,32768,32768,32768,32768,32768,690,32768,32768,1456,32768,32768,8192,728,
32768,32768,58982,17944,65237,54613,32768,2242,32768,32768,32768,42130,49152,57344,58254,16740,
32768,10923,54613,182,32768,32768,32768,7282,49152,32768,32768,5041,63295,1394,55188,77,
63672,6554,54613,49152,64558,32768,32768,5461,64142,32768,32768,32768,62415,32768,32768,16384,
1481,438,19661,840,33654,3121,64425,6554,4178,2048,32768,2260,5226,1680,32768,565,
60075,32768,32768,32768,32768,32768,32768,32768,32768,32768,32768,32768,32768,32768,32768,32768,
16384,261,32768,412,16384,636,32768,4369,23406,4328,32768,524,15604,560,32768,676,
49152,32768,49152,32768,32768,32768,64572,32768,32768,32768,54613,32768,32768,32768,32768,32768,
4681,32768,5617,851,32768,32768,59578,32768,32768,32768,3121,3121,49152,32768,6554,10923,
32768,32768,54613,14043,32768,32768,32768,3449,32768,32768,32768,32768,32768,32768,32768,32768,
57344,32768,57344,3449,32768,32768,32768,3855,58982,10923,32768,239,62259,32768,49152,85,
58778,23831,62888,20922,64311,8192,60075,575,59714,32768,57344,40960,62107,4096,61943,3921,

```
39862,15338,32768,1524,45123,5958,32768,58982,6669,930,1170,1043,7385,44,8813,5011,
59578,29789,54613,32768,32768,32768,32768,32768,32768,32768,32768,32768,58254,56174,32768,32768,
64080,25891,49152,22528,32768,2731,32768,10923,10923,3283,32768,1748,17827,77,32768,108,
62805,32768,62013,42612,32768,32768,61681,16384,58982,60075,62313,58982,65279,58982,62694,62174,
32768,32768,10923,950,32768,32768,32768,32768,5958,32768,38551,1092,11012,39322,13705,2072,
54613,32768,32768,11398,32768,32768,32768,145,32768,32768,32768,29789,60855,32768,61681,54792,
32768,32768,32768,17348,32768,32768,32768,8192,57344,16384,32768,3582,52581,580,24030,303,
62673,37266,65374,6197,62017,32768,49152,299,54613,32768,32768,32768,35234,119,32768,3855,
31949,32768,32768,49152,16384,32768,32768,32768,24576,32768,49152,32768,17476,32768,32768,57445,
51200,50864,54613,27949,60075,20480,32768,57344,32768,32768,32768,32768,32768,45875,32768,32768,
11498,3244,24576,482,16384,1150,32768,16384,7992,215,32768,1150,23593,927,32768,993,
65353,32768,65465,46741,41870,32768,64596,59578,62087,32768,12619,23406,11833,32768,47720,17476,
32768,32768,2621,6554,32768,32768,32768,32768,32768,32768,5041,32768,16384,32768,4096,2731,
63212,43526,65442,47124,65410,35747,60304,55858,60855,58982,60075,19859,35747,63015,64470,25432,
58689,1118,64717,1339,24576,32768,32768,1257,53297,1928,32768,33,52067,3511,62861,453,
64613,32768,32768,32768,64558,32768,32768,2731,49152,32768,32768,32768,61534,32768,32768,35747,
32768,32768,32768,32768,13107,32768,32768,32768,32768,32768,32768,32768,20480,32768,32768,32768,
32768,32768,32768,54613,40960,5041,32768,32768,32768,32768,32768,3277,64263,57592,32768,3121,
32768,32768,32768,32768,32768,10923,32768,32768,32768,8192,32768,32768,5461,6899,32768,1725,
63351,3855,63608,29127,62415,7282,64626,60855,32768,32768,60075,5958,44961,32768,61866,53718,
32768,32768,32768,32768,32768,32768,6554,32768,32768,32768,32768,32768,2521,978,32768,1489,
58254,32768,58982,61745,21845,32768,54613,58655,60075,32768,49152,16274,50412,64344,61643,43987,
32768,32768,32768,1638,32768,32768,32768,24966,54613,32768,32768,2427,46951,32768,17970,654,
65385,27307,60075,26472,64479,32768,32768,4681,61895,32768,32768,16384,58254,32768,32768,6554,
37630,3277,54613,6554,4965,5958,4681,32768,42765,16384,32768,21845,22827,16384,32768,6554,
65297,64769,60855,12743,63195,16384,32768,37942,32768,32768,32768,32768,60075,32768,62087,54613,
41764,2161,21845,1836,17284,5424,10923,1680,11019,555,32768,431,39819,907,32768,171,
65480,32768,64435,33803,2595,32768,57041,32768,61167,32768,32768,32768,32768,32768,32768,1796,
60855,32768,17246,978,32768,32768,8192,32768,32768,32768,14043,2849,32768,2979,6554,6554,
65507,62415,65384,61891,65273,58982,65461,55097,32768,32768,32768,55606,32768,2979,3745,16913,
61885,13827,60893,12196,60855,53248,51493,11243,56656,783,55563,143,63432,7106,52429,445,
65485,1031,65020,1380,65180,57344,65162,36536,61154,6554,26569,2341,63593,3449,65102,533,
47827,2913,57344,3449,35688,1337,32768,22938,25012,910,7944,1008,29319,607,64466,4202,
64549,57301,49152,20025,63351,61167,32768,45542,58982,14564,32768,9362,61895,44840,32768,26385,
59664,17135,60855,13291,40050,12252,32768,7816,25798,1850,60495,2662,18707,122,52538,231,
65332,32768,65210,21693,65113,6554,65141,39667,62259,32768,22258,1337,63636,32768,64255,52429,
60362,32768,6780,819,16384,32768,16384,4681,49152,32768,8985,2521,24410,683,21535,16585,
65416,46091,65292,58328,64626,32768,65016,39897,62687,47332,62805,28948,64284,53620,52870,49567,
65032,31174,63022,28312,64299,46811,48009,31453,61207,7077,50299,1514,60047,2634,46488,235
};
```

Inter_prob[512] = {

65532,62970,65148,54613,62470,8192,62577,8937,65480,64335,65195,53248,65322,62518,62891,38312,

65075,53405,63980,58982,32768,32768,54613,32768,65238,60009,60075,32768,59294,19661,61203,13107,

63000,9830,62566,58982,11565,32768,25215,3277,53620,50972,63109,43691,54613,32768,39671,17129,

59788,6068,43336,27913,6554,32768,12178,1771,56174,49152,60075,43691,58254,16384,49152,9930,

23130,7282,40960,32768,10923,32768,32768,32768,27307,32768,32768,32768,32768,32768,32768,32768,

36285,12511,10923,32768,45875,16384,32768,32768,16384,23831,4369,32768,8192,10923,32768,32768,

10175,2979,18978,10923,54613,32768,6242,6554,1820,10923,32768,32768,32768,32768,32768,5461,

28459,593,11886,2030,3121,4681,1292,112,42130,23831,49152,29127,32768,6554,5461,2048,

65331,64600,63811,63314,42130,19661,49152,32768,65417,64609,62415,64617,64276,44256,61068,36713,

64887,57525,53620,61375,32768,8192,57344,6554,63608,49809,49152,62623,32768,15851,58982,34162,

55454,51739,64406,64047,32768,32768,7282,32768,49152,58756,62805,64990,32768,14895,16384,19418,

57929,24966,58689,31832,32768,16384,10923,6554,54613,42882,57344,64238,58982,10082,20165,20339,

62687,15061,32768,10923,32768,10923,32768,16384,59578,34427,32768,16384,32768,7825,32768,7282,

58052,23400,32768,5041,32768,2849,32768,32768,47663,15073,57344,4096,32768,1176,32768,1320,

24858,410,24576,923,32768,16384,16384,5461,16384,1365,32768,5461,32768,5699,8192,13107,

46884,2361,23559,424,19661,712,655,182,58637,2094,49152,9362,8192,85,32768,1228,

65486,49152,65186,49152,61320,32768,57088,25206,65352,63047,62623,49152,64641,62165,58986,18304,

64171,16384,60855,54613,42130,32768,61335,32768,58254,58982,49152,32768,60985,35289,64520,31554,

51067,32768,64074,32768,40330,32768,34526,4096,60855,32768,63109,58254,57672,16384,31009,2567,

23406,32768,44620,10923,32768,32768,32099,10923,49152,49152,54613,60075,63422,54613,46388,39719,

58982,32768,54613,32768,14247,32768,22938,5041,32768,49152,32768,32768,25321,6144,29127,10999,

41263,32768,46811,32768,267,4096,426,16384,32768,19275,49152,32768,1008,1437,5767,11275,

5595,5461,37493,6554,4681,32768,6147,1560,38229,10923,32768,40960,35747,2521,5999,312,

17052,2521,18808,3641,213,2427,574,32,51493,42130,42130,53053,11155,312,2069,106,

64406,45197,58982,32768,32768,16384,40960,36864,65336,64244,60075,61681,65269,50748,60340,20515,

58982,23406,57344,32768,6554,16384,19661,61564,60855,47480,32768,54613,46811,21701,54909,37826,

32768,58982,60855,60855,32768,32768,39322,49152,57344,45875,60855,55706,32768,24576,62313,25038,

54613,8192,49152,10923,32768,32768,32768,32768,32768,19661,16384,51493,32768,14043,40050,44651,

59578,5174,32768,6554,32768,5461,23593,5461,63608,51825,32768,23831,58887,24032,57170,3298,

39322,12971,16384,49152,1872,618,13107,2114,58982,25705,32768,60075,28913,949,18312,1815,

48188,114,51493,1542,5461,3855,11360,1163,58982,7215,54613,21487,49152,4590,48430,1421,

28944,1319,6868,324,1456,232,820,7,61681,1864,60855,9922,4369,315,6589,14

};

Index